PRAISE FOR *DEEP PURPOSE*

"Purpose isn't a 'nice-to-have' in the business world anymore. It's a 'must-have.' Purpose-driven organizations will lead the future, and Ranjay Gulati's *Deep Purpose* is essential reading for anyone who wants to be at the head of the pack. This comprehensive guide breaks down why cultivating purpose isn't just the right thing for businesses to do—it's the smart thing, too."

—Carmine Di Sibio, Global Chairman and CEO, EY

"*Deep Purpose* points to the conversations we must have right now about how to redefine the role of business in society, restore trust, and enhance our license to operate. As Gulati rightly argues, the winning formula is moral leadership and a multistakeholder model with purpose at its core. It entails both leadership *and* systems transformation. Highly recommended."

—Paul Polman, former CEO, Unilever

"Pursuing a purpose as a company means arriving at a clear understanding of what you were put on this planet to do. It helps you steer in the right direction, navigate tradeoffs, and, when connected to a social or personal purpose, it can inspire remarkable performance. *Deep Purpose* peels back the layers to unveil what it truly takes to cultivate a purpose-driven culture, one that enables both the company and its employees to experience its power and benefit from the growth it can generate."

—Corie Barry, CEO, Best Buy

"Brilliant and thought-provoking as ever, Ranjay Gulati applies scholarly rigor to the important topic of purpose. This book is a must-read for all leaders who wish to embark on or continue a journey toward a vibrant, high-performance business."

—Kasper Rorsted, CEO, Adidas

"Many leaders today strive to align purpose with financial success, but only a few succeed. Gulati analyzes the tough challenges that leaders everywhere must address if they are to save the planet while also delivering strong profits. He provides a compelling account of what it means to be purpose-driven—a crucial objective for us as well as other organizations in the social innovation space."

—Toshiaki Higashihara, Executive Chairman & CEO, Hitachi, Ltd.

"Leaders often invoke the rhetoric of corporate purpose to elevate their or their company's image. But for the people who work in these companies, the search for purpose is a real and defining part of their professional life. Gulati's book illustrates how the best leaders help employees discover a tangible link between the organization's stated purpose and what they do on the job. It's when people 'come alive' with a sense of purpose in their work that their motivation, energy, and creativity blossom."

—Kenneth Frazier, former CEO, Merck

"Many leaders give lip service to purpose, but few know how to create a compelling one. Ranjay Gulati is a preeminent scholar of organizational strategy, and in this book he shows what it takes to walk the talk on purpose. It's an insightful, practical, and timely read on building a mission that serves employees, customers, and communities along with shareholders."

—Adam Grant, #1 New York Times *bestselling author of* Think Again *and host of the TED podcast* WorkLife

"In this provocative and richly researched book, Ranjay Gulati argues that the pursuit of profits *without purpose* is no longer a sustainable business model. As he shows, the road to high performance, for both individuals and companies, depends on deepening our connection to enduring and essential human values. If you want to be inspired to build more sustainable organizations, *Deep Purpose* should be your next read."

—Arianna Huffington, Founder & CEO, Thrive Global

DEEP PURPOSE

THE **HEART AND SOUL** OF
HIGH-PERFORMANCE COMPANIES

RANJAY GULATI

With a Foreword by Larry Fink,
CEO of BlackRock

HARPER
BUSINESS
An Imprint of HarperCollinsPublishers

FIRST EDITION

Library of Congress Cataloging-in-Publication Data:
Names: Gulati, Ranjay, author.
Title: Deep purpose : the heart and soul of high-performance companies / Ranjay Gulati ; with a foreword by Larry Fink, CEO of BlackRock.
Description: New York : Harper Business, 2022. | Includes bibliographical references and index.
Identifiers: LCCN 2021045321 (print) | LCCN 2021045322 (ebook) | ISBN 9780063088917 (hardcover) | ISBN 9780063088931 (ebook)
Subjects: LCSH: Management by objectives. | Business planning. | Employee motivation. | Organizational effectiveness. | Leadership.
Classification: LCC HD30.65 .G85 2022 (print) | LCC HD30.65 (ebook) | DDC 658.4/012--dc23/eng/20211015
LC record available at https://lccn.loc.gov/2021045321
LC ebook record available at https://lccn.loc.gov/2021045322

22 23 24 25 26 LSC 10 9 8 7 6 5 4 3 2 1

To my wife, Anuradha, and my late mother, Sushma.
You are two of the most inspiring,
purpose-driven leaders I know.

It is not enough to be industrious; so are the ants. What are you industrious about?

—Henry David Thoreau

CONTENTS

FOREWORD

Larry Fink, Founder, Chairman, and CEO of BlackRock

I was deeply honored when my friend Ranjay asked me to write the foreword to this book. Discovering the power of corporate purpose, learning how to pursue it, and working to evolve purpose over time has been one of the most challenging—and fulfilling—elements of my career. While we know a sense of purpose is often the driving force behind high-performance companies, it's a very difficult concept to pin down. There's no doubt it shows up in long-term financial results, but corporate purpose can't be captured in the P&L, stock price, or market cap. With this book Ranjay has done the hard work of describing what purpose is and, almost more crucially, what it isn't. His distinctions, case studies, and tools for how to drive change will be invaluable to any business leader working to drive purpose as well as profit.

My own journey to understand corporate purpose has been a long one. In 1988, a group of seven others and I founded BlackRock to use technology and data analytics more deeply to manage money for people who are saving for retirement or other long-term concerns. Our purpose is to help more and more people experience financial well-being. But toward the end of the last decade, I realized that as a fiduciary to our clients and an investor it was important to speak more openly about the crucial role purpose plays in driving long-term success.

"Without a sense of purpose, no company, either public or private can achieve its full potential." That's what I wrote in a letter in 2018 to CEOs of companies in which our firm's clients were invested. I started writing letters to CEOs on behalf of our clients after becoming fed up with the obsession I saw day after day from the financial media and Wall Street about the market's daily ups and downs. I wanted to encourage more CEOs to take a longer-term view (as the best leaders already did) in order to create greater long-term value for our clients. Many people were

surprised when I, the leader of a global investment firm, wrote in that same annual letter about the need for every company to focus not just on profit but also on purpose. Some people thought I was losing my edge and becoming a little "new-agey." In fact, I was reflecting back what I had seen from years of talking to leaders of the best, most successful companies around the world. I was hardly the first person to observe the important role that purpose plays in building a company. Great business leaders as far back as Henry Ford built companies around compelling visions for what the company could contribute to all of its stakeholders, including shareholders. But in recent years, as society has raised its expectations for business, the importance of corporate purpose has grown dramatically.

During the 1980s and 1990s, many thought that a company's purpose was simply to turn a profit, sometimes without regard for the impact on the communities where it operated or even its own employees. In recent years, however, great companies—those that create significant value over an extended period of time—increasingly are guided by something much deeper, a purpose that extends beyond profit. Purpose creates a unifying vision for all of a company's stakeholders, including its employees, customers, partners, and shareholders. It drives ethical behavior and creates an essential check on actions that go against the best interests of stakeholders. Finally, it's a powerful driver of culture, providing a framework for consistent decision-making throughout an organization, which ultimately helps sustain long-term financial returns for the company's shareholders.

Some believe that there is an inherent tension between purpose and profit, that they are located at opposing ends of a spectrum. But as I wrote in my letter, "Purpose is not the sole pursuit of profits but the animating force for achieving them." I see this vividly when it comes to attracting and retaining the best talent and building relationships with partners and customers. Increasingly, employees and clients require a clear expression of purpose, and they want to see that purpose align with their values. This is clearest among younger people. We see in our own firm that the most talented young data scientists and software engineers want to work at a company whose purpose motivates and inspires them. In this book, Ranjay challenges the notion that purpose somehow exists in opposition to profit, or that it somehow entails building long-term value at the expense of short-term results.

Everything we do—whether it's designing a new product or pursuing an acquisition—aids our purpose of helping more and more people experience financial well-being. Our work over many years on retirement and making investing easier and more accessible, and, more recently, advancing sustainable investing, all deliver on our purpose.

People deserve financial security across their lifetimes. We act as a fiduciary, investing on behalf of doctors, nurses, and firefighters so that they can experience financial well-being in retirement. Having a secure retirement is not a foregone conclusion, especially here in the US. To save adequately for retirement, individuals and fiduciaries like Black-Rock that manage their assets need to think over a thirty- or forty-year time horizon. In short, preparing for retirement requires long-term planning, which is core to our purpose. Similarly, we've spent years working to make investing easier and more affordable by offering low-cost ways to invest, because we believe this is so fundamental to helping more people experience financial well-being.

Finally, our focus on advancing sustainable investing is deeply rooted in our conviction that it delivers better outcomes for investors. The climate crisis is having very real effects on the planet, generating increasingly severe weather events, flooding, and wildfires, and over time that will drive shifts in asset valuations. It is also creating opportunities as governments, investors, and consumers look for new technology that will power affordable, renewable energy sources. If we fail to take these realities into account, we will fail our investors, our clients, and our communities.

Articulating a clear purpose is the easy part. It's the *how* that's always the most challenging element for CEOs and other business leaders. Creating durable value for multiple stakeholders while also delivering for shareholders and clients is often a Herculean task. You need a framework for making difficult tradeoffs and the ability to mobilize people both inside and outside your company. All too often, well-intentioned leaders make short-term tradeoffs at the expense of embedding purpose deeply in the organization.

When I articulated the connection between sustainability and our purpose with my colleagues, a team from across the firm came together and said, "We want to do this, and we need to move even faster." It was one of the proudest moments of my career. My colleagues mobilized our talent in a way that went far beyond my expectations. They created a clear strategy for how to deliver value for all of our stakeholders, including our shareholders, our clients, our employees, our communities, and the planet. *Climate risk is investment risk* has become something of a mantra at BlackRock, and our leaders are generating greater value—and reducing risk—for our clients as a result. They're building new models to help our clients and investors quantify the changes happening to asset valuations, they're working with company boards on their long-term strategy to transition to a low-carbon economy, and they're creating new funds to bring private capital into emerging markets to finance sustainable infrastructure. They are living our purpose.

My appreciation for those who dedicate themselves to a purpose and take a long-term view has only deepened over time. Clearly articulating our purpose has given BlackRock a voice in the world and helped to drive our success through the decades. That's why I find this book so interesting. It communicates in a tangible way what has always been a guiding principle for how great leaders have run businesses.

As I wrote in my most recent annual letter, "The more your company can show its purpose in delivering value to its customers, its employees, and its communities, the better able you will be to compete and deliver long-term, durable profits for shareholders." As the evidence increasingly shows, a purpose encompassing multiple stakeholders yields stronger financial performance. Ranjay argues that leaders can and must orient themselves toward delivering long-term value. The best paradigm available for doing so is that of purpose.

But delivering on one's purpose for multiple stakeholders means reshaping a business's core operations. To realize purpose's promise and to create long-term value, Ranjay argues, companies must go deeper than "convenient purpose." It's not enough to articulate a purpose, you need to do the hard work of delivering on it, too, which is of course the major challenge for any leader. As Ranjay observes, the problem isn't one of wrong intentions on the part of business leaders. Rather, they find it an overwhelming task because they don't understand what a deeper pursuit of purpose is and how to execute it.

If this is a challenge you're facing, you will find this book extremely valuable. *Deep Purpose* is at once inspirational and pragmatic. Cutting through the miasma of writings about purpose, Ranjay offers us a powerful new way of thinking. It starts with a deeper understanding of what purpose is and the tradeoffs entailed in bringing it to life. Analyzing companies across many industries and geographies in search of best practices, Ranjay has arrived at a number of profound insights on how to discover your purpose, embed it into your organization, and sustain it over time.

Ultimately, Ranjay argues that leaders must make quite a big leap if they are to go from talking about purpose to truly absorbing and actualizing it. Deep purpose is an ongoing *process* to which leaders must commit with all of their heart and soul. It must serve as an operating system for the entire organization as well as a strategic compass for decision-making. A tall order, for sure, but the benefits for stakeholders, for leaders themselves, and for society are enormous.

PREFACE

I was once skeptical about purpose, dismissing it as one of those inspiring but trivial topics that leaders raise in company speeches or annual reports. On the question of companies yielding social benefits, I bought into the classic liberal argument that companies operating in free markets will naturally serve the public interest. The market's invisible hand would of course make everyone better off. If I simply focused on helping businesses succeed financially, I thought, I'd put them in a position to do good for society.

These attitudes came under strain in 2013, when extremists bombed the Boston Marathon, killing three and injuring hundreds. My students at Harvard, high-potential senior executives hailing from countries around the world, were devastated and organized a fundraising drive for the survivors. That felt good, but the students weren't satisfied. They wondered why businesses and leaders only behaved benevolently in times of crisis. Why couldn't leaders give back as part of their daily work? And what could my colleagues and I teach them about how to do business differently—how to build thriving, purpose-driven companies that at once served shareholders and society? Why, ultimately, did their companies exist? Surely it wasn't just to fill investors' pockets.

My students' questions prompted me to look inward and reexamine some of my earliest experiences of business. In 1972, my mother lost her job teaching at the American School in New Delhi, and my parents divorced. Uncertain how to support herself, she did something risky. Instead of immediately seeking a new job, she spent her entire savings on a flight to Paris. There, she showed up unannounced at the offices of major French fashion brands with a suitcase full of samples and tried to interest them in her handmade Indian garments.

My mother had long admired Indian fashion, wearing traditional garments along with Western styles to signal pride for her heritage.

While pursuing a master's degree in anthropology, she took summer trips to Greece, where other students inquired about her Indian clothing and expressed interest in purchasing it. Indian law forbade her from taking more than the equivalent of $50 out of the country, so to help support herself on these trips, she took along handmade garments with village designs and sold them. But it was one thing to impress a few classmates. Would trend-makers in the global fashion capital snap up my mother's garments? They did, and a thriving business was born. Within a few years, my mother's company directly or indirectly employed over one thousand people.

Although my mother didn't articulate it in these terms, she grew her company not just to earn a living but to realize a social purpose. Outsiders tended to disparage rural people as primitive, but she knew they possessed a strong, vibrant culture, a keen and sophisticated aesthetic sense, and an enviable proximity to nature. Her company's implicit purpose was to connect Western consumers with rural Indian village handicrafts in a way that enriched both communities.

Western consumers benefitted by gaining a deeper awareness of humanity and its diversity. Indian villagers benefitted because my mother sourced her products locally, loaning money to impoverished villagers to set up manufacturing facilities, which in turn provided jobs and created wealth. If you asked my mother if she was running a business, she would respond that of course she was, but she would also always allude to her broader purpose. That, I gathered, was her deepest motivation. It was the hidden operating principle informing her business and driving her success.

Remembering my mother and her business in the wake of the Boston Marathon bombing, I began to wonder if the concept of purpose—defined as a mission or reason for being that potentially has some kind of social dimension to it—could serve leaders as a general approach for operating a business that was at once profitable, high performance, and impactful. At the time I was collaborating on a book about how companies implement sustainability programs, and I was surprised to learn that corporate initiatives in this area often delivered handsome profits. Observing that certain purpose-driven firms had pursued such initiatives even in situations when the economics didn't look terribly compelling at first, I began to wonder whether firms in general could successfully pursue both commercial and social goals at once. If anything, perhaps a more ambitious focus would even enhance financial performance.

Investigating this hypothesis, I found that scholars had been hovering around this topic for years, trying to understand how purpose affected performance. Although scholars didn't know exactly how to measure purpose or how to distinguish its impact from those of other factors, the research findings were suggestive. As far back as the early 2000s, a review of ninety-five studies revealed that a majority "point to a positive relationship between corporate social performance [which some might take as a proxy for purpose] and financial performance."[1] Since then, a steady stream of academics and consultants have studied purpose's impact using surveys and other archival measures. One study of fifty companies in three sectors found that those scoring high on a measure of purpose tended to rank higher in total shareholder returns (TSR).[2] Another study of almost five hundred executives found that organizations that prioritized purpose were more likely to see revenue growth of more than 10 percent over three years.[3]

Again, these studies were suggestive—none of them claimed to have shown *definitively* that purpose drives financial performance. But my own direct observations pointed to such a conclusion. Looking at small, fast-growth entrepreneurial ventures, I noticed that regardless of their industry a number of them were intensely purposeful enterprises. The founder embodied the purpose, defining it either implicitly or explicitly. Everyone understood it, and employees and customers were attracted to and animated by it. Conversely, as I observed large, successful companies falling into decline, I noticed that their demise seemed to occur because they lost a sense of purpose, to the point where work became a grind and employees viewed their jobs dispassionately and transactionally.

Eager to unpack the intriguing connections between purpose and performance, I undertook a painstaking study of companies across industries and geographies that have gone unusually deep with purpose (for details, see appendix). As I found, these firms treated purpose as an existential intention that informed every decision, practice, and process.

They adopted purpose as their operating system, perceiving it as a vital animating force with near-spiritual power. As a result, they navigated the tumultuous terrain of multi-stakeholder capitalism far more adeptly than most, increasing value for all stakeholders, including investors, over the long-term. The passionate embrace of purpose unleashed a range of benefits, including better strategy-making, a highly engaged and passionate workforce, and tremendous loyalty from customers, suppliers, and other external partners.

My interviews with well over two hundred executives across eighteen firms revealed the secrets of these companies—not the usual facile frameworks, but new ways of thinking about business that allow leaders and companies to operate with heightened passion, urgency, and clarity. By learning to practice the discipline I call "deep purpose," you can empower your business to thrive financially and organizationally while unleashing its full potential as a force for good. Your company can come to represent humanity's best hope, leaving a lasting legacy for future generations. You can create a business that possesses not just physical assets or people, but the missing element behind both exceptional performance *and* social impact: a perceptible, energizing soul.

I've written this book because I believe that purpose provides new answers to companies and leaders struggling to achieve superior performance amid unforeseen crises and disruptions. At a time when many of the world's largest investors (pension funds, insurance companies, sovereign wealth funds, and so on) increasingly look for performance spanning decades not quarters, I want to show you how to resist the siren's song of a short-term, performance-at-all-costs mentality and instead create an upward spiral of performance *inspired by* purpose. As BlackRock's CEO Larry Fink has observed, "The more your company can show its purpose in delivering value to its customers, its employees, and its communities, the better able you will be to compete and deliver long-term, durable profits for shareholders."[4]

This book shows you how to deliver those durable profits by truly embracing deep purpose. It demonstrates, in fact, that long-term value and short-term performance need not be as oppositional as leaders often presume. Short-term performance obviously matters, but not to the exclusion of a firm's long-term interests. Contemplating long-term value broadens your perspective, naturally prompting you to consider the interests of multiple stakeholders. Purpose, which as we'll see is rooted in a multi-stakeholder view of business, can thus serve as the foundation of long-term strategic thinking. As Carmine Di Sibio, global chairman and CEO of the global professional services organization EY (formerly Ernst & Young), told me, "To really have a long-term strategy, you have to have a purpose. It's all interconnected and you can't have one without the other. Strategy is based on clients, on people, on society. A purpose incorporates these stakeholders."[5]

By facilitating a long-term focus, purpose has broader implications for the future of capitalism. In recent decades, our system's traditional moral center has been hollowed out. Influenced by thinkers like Milton Friedman, leaders have turned firms into arid, unfeeling places fueled by the narrow pursuit of profit. Externally, the profit imperative has exacted a heavy toll on planet and people. But times are changing. Following the example of earlier generations of purpose pioneers such as Paul Polman at Unilever and Yvon Chouinard at Patagonia, enlightened voices have embraced the concept of stakeholder capitalism and sought to develop common metrics to make it a reality (consider, for instance, the efforts of the International Business Council at the World Economic Forum, chaired by Bank of America CEO Brian Moynihan). We're at a "reset moment," it appears, when new opportunities have opened to remake capitalism's operating norms globally. We're also at a sobering, do-or-die moment: if we don't make profound changes now, humanity risks suffering through violent upheaval and even extinction because of economic, environmental, and political crises of its own making.

Although purpose receives airplay in conversations about reimagining capitalism, we still haven't taken enough time to understand what a serious pursuit of purpose really entails and how it might enhance businesses commercially and socially. I hardly wish to minimize government's crucial role in reforming capitalism as regulators of markets. But I do hope that this book will inspire companies to take more responsibility for our collective welfare, embracing a noble purpose as an organizing principle. Deep purpose companies have pioneered a way to reinject passion, meaning, identity, and an abiding sense of community into the enterprise. They've enlivened themselves by re-moralizing their operations, imbuing them with a renewed sense of social responsibility that in turn magnifies the social *and* financial value they create.

This book is a guide for every leader who has wondered about how to make their company more purpose-driven. Based on my field research, each chapter describes several conceptual discoveries I made about purpose, offering lessons from deep purpose leaders that you can use to better orient your business around a reason for being. The first three chapters examine powerful ways that deep purpose leaders think about purpose, while chapters 4 through 7 explore key actions leaders take to define and embed a reason for being so that it truly drives performance. These actions include linking purpose to the company's history, communicating purpose more effectively, connecting personal and organizational purpose, and supporting purpose by injecting more autonomy and collaboration into the organization. Chapter 8 describes several traps that cause purpose to erode over time, presenting techniques deep purpose leaders deploy to keep their companies on the right track.

Let these leaders inspire you, as they have me. Learn from them about how to organize with more urgency and meaning. Your company can rethink purpose, developing it as a new foundation for galvanizing people around a set of goals. Your company can cultivate an existential awareness that unifies and guides the enterprise, energizing stakeholders and enlivening all areas of the business, including culture, strategy, brand, and operations. Most fundamentally, your company can dedicate itself to perpetually asking and answering Thoreau's question: "What are you industrious about?"

DEEP PURPOSE

CHAPTER 1

WHAT IS PURPOSE *REALLY?*

> Most leaders think of purpose functionally or instrumentally, regarding it as a tool they can wield. Deep purpose leaders think of it as something more fundamental: an existential statement that expresses the firm's very reason for being. Rather than simply pursuing a purpose, these leaders project it faithfully out onto the world. In their hands, purpose serves as an organizing principle that shapes decision-making and binds stakeholders to one another.

If you've got a sweet tooth, you might be a fan of the legendary entrepreneur Forrest Mars Sr., mastermind of products like the Mars bar, M&M's chocolate candies, and Twix bars. The company Mars's father founded and that his descendants now own, Mars, Inc., is one of the largest privately held firms in the United States, with 2019 revenues of $37 billion and consumer brands in a number of categories, including chewing gum (Wrigley), ice cream (Dove bars), pet food (Whiskas), and pet hospitals (Banfield).

Mars apparently was a tough-minded businessman who sought to squeeze out every last bit of profit from his business. "He was legendary for his extreme temper, and his fanatical behavior," one journalist remarked.[1] At some point, and for reasons that remain murky, Mars's perspective seems to have shifted and he became, dare I say, a man of purpose.

In 1947 Mars wrote an internal communication stating that the company existed "to promote a mutuality of services and benefits" among diverse stakeholders, ranging from consumers to employees, suppliers, and shareholders.[2] Mars clarified that "this expresses the total purpose for which the Company exists—nothing less" and stated his expectation that managers, the board, and employees "will be motivated by this basic objective, and will keep it constantly in mind as the guiding principle in all their work for the company." Although Mars's statement doesn't reference communities or the planet as stakeholders, it remains an early and powerful expression of multi-stakeholder-oriented business.

In reflecting on Mars's memo, you might wonder what an organizational purpose is precisely. The most compelling purpose statements among the hundreds I've reviewed have two basic and interrelated features. First, they *delineate an ambitious, longer-term goal for the company*. Second, they *give this goal an idealistic cast*, committing the firm to fulfillment of broader social duties.[3] Transcending the selfish pursuit of profit or commercial advantage, the best purpose statements call upon organizations to render service to society or humanity in some way. Throughout this book, I'll refer to purpose in the deepest sense as embodying these two dimensions—a goal that not just animates but elevates via the call to a higher, socially oriented duty.[4] We can interpret Mars's statement of mutuality as such a purpose, for it calls upon the company to deliver benefits for multiple players in its ecosystem, not just shareholders.

It's unclear how far this memo galvanized Mars's employees and leaders to extend a "mutuality of services and benefits" to stakeholders. We do know that in 1983 Forrest Mars's children promulgated five principles that, as the present-day Mars website says, "form the foundation of how we do business today and every day."[5] The most recent version of this document, which one observer called a "bible of corporate rectitude,"[6] includes one principle that seems to reference Mars's original memo, reading, "We base decisions on mutuality of benefit to our stakeholders."[7] Other principles evoke the company's intention to behave responsibly, deliver high quality, operate efficiently, and maintain financial independence, all with the goal of helping to "build a better world for generations to come."

In recent years, Mars has become increasingly transparent and vocal about its purpose. During the 2000s and 2010s, reportedly under the influence of Mars family members and company chairman Stephen Badger, Mars sought to breathe new life into the concept of "mutuality," developing it into a business philosophy that companies everywhere could embrace.[8] The company took steps to make the five principles part of the culture at the company, posting them on the walls of its facilities and disseminating a booklet about the principles to every employee.[9]

Mars also adopted a formal purpose statement that emphasizes social good as a core part of doing business: "The world we want tomorrow starts with the business we build today."[10] The company reconfigured its brand around its purpose, creating the new role of global corporate brand and purpose director. But does Mars actually deliver on its purpose of creating a "better world"?

The answer is "yes, but . . ." Over the past decade, Mars took many steps to provide value for multiple stakeholders, in many cases emerging as an industry leader. The company's "What's Inside" labeling program voluntarily disclosed information about its products' nutritional features, including fat, sugar, and calories. Mars became a leader in sustainability, adopting in 2008 its "Sustainable in a Generation" plan. In 2014, the company announced plans to build a wind farm that would provide enough power to run all of Mars's US operations.[11] In 2017, Mars devoted $1 billion to its sustainability initiatives.[12] The company also embarked on a plan to slash two-thirds of its emissions across its entire value chain by 2050.[13] Other initiatives included an "Economics of Mutuality" research program funded by the company's think tank and an accelerator to help nurture new, socially minded food companies.[14]

Mars hasn't just pursued its purpose peripherally—it has embedded it into its organization and reimagined its core operations to help create "the world we want tomorrow." Still, the company's transformation into a purpose-driven business is far from complete for a simple reason: the company still derives a great deal of revenue from selling unhealthy foods.

Defenders of Mars might contend that candy bars have social value because they satisfy people's need for fun and pleasure. Be that as it may, many people would have trouble squaring the provision of treats with Mars's lofty goal of making the world a better place. If Mars were really considering "every business decision through the lens of whether it is helping establish the tomorrow we want to create," it would be making one decision above all, weaning itself off its reliance on confectionary sales and replacing these businesses with healthier ones.

Is it hard for a company to abandon successful products? Absolutely. But until Mars infuses its purpose more deeply into its strategy and shifts its portfolio of products accordingly, its commitment to a higher cause will seem less authentic and meaningful than it otherwise might.

Convenient Purpose

In truth, any number of firms adopt idealistic purpose statements, take a range of actions to serve society, and yet continue to sell products and services that cause serious harm to stakeholders. Depending on your moral perspective, firms that sell fossil fuels, tobacco, alcohol, junk food, weapons, and some social media services all fall into this category. These companies practice what I call "convenient purpose." They articulate a core reason for being (usually framed as either a purpose or a mission statement) that extends beyond the pursuit of profits. Like Mars, the best of them take strong action to enhance communities, improve the lives of customers and employees, or benefit the planet. But their commitment isn't sufficiently strong or broadly conceived to lead them to part with socially questionable, "cash cow" businesses.

We can discern other varieties of convenient purpose companies. Unlike Mars, some companies exploit a high-minded reason for being (as well as similarly high-minded mission, vision, and values statements) as cover to pursue egregiously selfish goals or even criminal activity. We can think of this as *purpose-as-disguise*. Elizabeth Holmes, the disgraced founder of the diagnostics firm Theranos, proudly proclaimed her belief that "you can build a business that does well by doing good,"[15] while

Theranos itself articulated a lofty-sounding mission: "to facilitate the early detection and prevention of disease and to empower people everywhere to live their best lives."[16] That didn't stop Holmes from perpetrating a multibillion-dollar fraud that as of 2021 had her facing criminal charges. Other scandal-plagued companies like Purdue Pharma, Turing Pharmaceuticals, and Enron have also pulled from the purpose-as-disguise playbook, using lofty language to mask questionable, if not nefarious, conduct.

The vast majority of firms that *don't* sell arguably harmful products or *aren't* criminal enterprises likewise practice convenient purpose. Some practice what I call "purpose-on-the-periphery": they adopt a purpose statement and take steps to deliver on it, only to treat these efforts as secondary to their core businesses.[17] They divide their efforts into "doing good" through purpose-driven corporate social responsibility (CSR) and "doing well" through their core businesses, perceiving these as separate. They give themselves a pass on reimagining their businesses to serve a higher purpose, thinking it's enough that they return some social value in the form of charity on the side. They fail to transform their operations to become more purpose-driven—more sustainable, more beneficial to local communities, more valuable to employees, and so on. Many convenient purpose companies practicing purpose-on-the-periphery also fail to engineer creative new products or services that serve a higher purpose while also generating profit. These companies take maximizing shareholder value as their primary measure of success, giving back just enough to maintain a veneer of respectability.[18]

In addition to firms that practice convenient purpose by treating their reason for being as peripheral, others fall short in a less obvious way. Some leading-edge firms aspire to re-engineer their core businesses to deliver value for both shareholders and society, what they describe as "win-win" solutions. In a seminal 2011 article, Michael E. Porter and coauthor Mark R. Kramer introduced the concept of "shared value," which begins by recognizing that "societal needs, not just conventional economic needs, define markets, and social harms can create internal costs for firms."[19] Instead of writing off social harms as externalities for government to handle and regarding social imperatives as constraints or taxes on the business, the notion of shared value holds that companies' policies and practices must contribute to both social and economic objectives at once.

Firms in many cases have misconstrued these powerful ideas, aiming *only* for the sweet spot where social and economic value intersect. In a practice I dub "purpose-as-win-win-only," they focus exclusively on seeking creative solutions that overcome seeming dilemmas—desirable, win-win solutions that maximize both profit and social good. This application of shared value has an inherent appeal: you need not make tough tradeoffs when you operate in a world where you can simultaneously discover both social and economic value. This extreme view of win-win regards business as a magical place where you can always be your best self *and* satisfy shareholders. John Mackey and Raj Sisodia seem to articulate such a position with their notion of "conscious capitalism." Conceiving of the various stakeholders as composing a single, broader system, they suggest that businesses must fuse "doing good" with "doing well," arriving at integrative solutions that expand the overall pie and benefit all stakeholders simultaneously.[20]

Leaders of firms that pursue purpose-as-win-win-only are far ahead of their peers, pushing purpose into the core of what their companies do. But as we'll see in the next chapter, they still don't do it as fully as they might. Companies exclusively pursuing win-win solutions tend to deliver on their purposes only to the extent that a perceived win-win is possible—which it often isn't. Forced to choose between financial performance and social good, leaders at these firms usually wind up operating the enterprise for shareholders' primary benefit. Although these leaders strive to serve society, they tend to perceive shareholder value as a performance baseline or nonnegotiable, and social value and purpose as (sometimes) negotiable. They limit their pursuit of social value projects to those where the economic payoffs are also clear. To this extent, we can describe these firms' commitment to purpose as "convenient."

As my analysis suggests, practitioners of convenient purpose are not morally equivalent. We can and should rank these companies relative to one another. On the bottom level we can place the Theranoses of this world, companies that exploit social purpose for clearly nefarious ends. Next, we can place companies that relegate purpose to the periphery of their operations, whether because they sell inherently harmful products (depending on your moral viewpoint) or because they follow a conventional approach separating CSR from their core operations.

At the highest level of convenient purpose, we find companies that practice purpose-as-win-win-only. Committed to transforming capitalism, these companies embrace a multi-stakeholder approach, consciously seeking to go beyond CSR. They energetically pursue business opportunities that deliver value for society *and* shareholders. But despite their ardent commitment, they often can't innovate perfect win-win solutions. In these instances, the financial performance of the company or its ability to deliver for customers trumps a focus on other stakeholders. Rather than prioritizing social value, these companies revert to business as usual, reasoning that as businesses they must operate for the primary benefit of shareholders. They often adopt a portfolio mindset, aligning only a small portion of their business with their purpose—the parts that lend themselves to win-win opportunities. They strive to grow this portion, but only when the opportunities to do so become obvious. In this way, they pursue convenient purpose, despite their best intentions and enlightened mindset.

THREE LEVELS OF CONVENIENT PURPOSE

**Purpose
as Win-Win**

**Purpose on
the Periphery**

**Purpose
as Disguise**

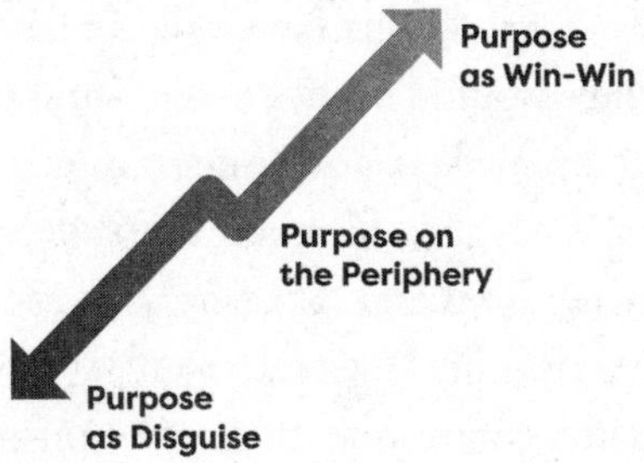

Figure I: Three Levels of Convenient Purpose

The prevalence of convenient purpose in all its forms has spawned cynicism not just about purpose, but about capitalism's broader ability to reform itself and tackle existential problems like climate change, inequality, and racial justice.[21] I'll spare you the usual statistics about the decline of public trust in business, particularly among young people. We all know that capitalism and individual companies have an image problem, and that public professions of purpose often appear as little more than public relations exercises. One witty observer likened purpose-talk to high-minded "yoga babble"—"as if my yoga instructor went into investor relations."[22] What we don't acknowledge openly enough is that companies and leaders bear responsibility for such cynicism by treating their commitment to purpose and by implication social value as a matter of convenience.

In August 2019, the Business Roundtable, a highly influential group comprising CEOs of the largest, most powerful companies in the United States, issued a "Statement on the Purpose of a Corporation" that committed signatories to serve not just shareholders, but an array of stakeholders, including customers, employees, suppliers, and communities. "Each of our stakeholders is essential," the statement read. "We commit to deliver value to all of them, for the future success of our companies, our communities and our country."[23]

You might think that corporate leaders, alert to the importance of purpose and determined to deliver on it, rushed to revolutionize their companies' operations. Not exactly. As one journalist sourly observed on the first anniversary of the Roundtable's statement, "There have been few signs that major corporations have taken real steps to serve non-shareholders that they wouldn't have taken without outside pressure, whether from public opinion or government regulation."[24] Some companies raised minimum wages for their employees, but only to meet current government requirements or as an attempt to head off future mandates. Despite the Roundtable's statement, some companies continued to mobilize against environmental regulations, just as they always had. To some observers, the Roundtable's statement was ultimately a publicity move instead of "the harbinger of a major change."[25]

An Alternate Paradigm of Purpose

For capitalism's critics, the prevalence of convenient purpose is hardly surprising. In their view, executives, shareholders, and other insiders might advocate for the reform of capitalism, but they remain bound to an inherently exploitative system in which they retain privileged positions. These insiders will reform capitalism superficially, but they will always decline to make changes that diminish their own financial fortunes and alter society's balance of power. If change is to come, government must regulate companies, exercising a check on capitalism's excesses and ensuring that companies really do serve the public good.[26]

I strongly favor government regulation to curb capitalism's excesses. I don't believe we must conduct a broad-based, sweeping reform of the entire system, as some have suggested.[27] But I do think we should embrace purpose as part of a larger agenda that includes some institutional reform of capital markets and corporate legal frameworks. CEOs don't operate in a vacuum, and many won't just take socially beneficial actions on their own. They require external incentives and constraints to keep them on that path in sufficient numbers to benefit all stakeholders in the long run. At the same time, regulatory reform won't solve every problem. To achieve maximal change, we must also call upon companies to reform themselves and give them powerful conceptual tools to operate for the benefit of a full range of stakeholders. In addition, we must wield regulation as an option if businesses fail to take action on their own. Ultimately, we stand to obtain the best results for society if we couple the "hard power" of regulation with the "soft power" of internal, purpose-driven change.

Companies can deliver exceptional value to stakeholders *and* elevate themselves beyond a merely commercial logic by energetically and *inconveniently* pursuing a reason for being. It's essential to pursue shared value, but companies can deliver it more completely by going further and starting with purpose as the foundation. Rather than dismissing capitalism's ability to reform itself, the most responsible and productive course, it seems to me, is to convert the mass of partially engaged companies, helping them transform into true devotees of purpose.

When I talk to leaders, I find that most of them *want* to be converted. They like how it feels at moments of crisis when they or their companies step up and help people. Why, they ask, can't we do this *all* the time? But they don't understand how to get purpose right—how to deliver on it so that it's more than some nice-sounding words on a web page. It's no surprise that a 2019 McKinsey study of employees found that 82 percent agreed that company purpose was important, but only 42 percent felt that "their organizations' purpose statements drive impact."[28]

My study of deep purpose companies, undertaken primarily between 2019 and 2021, revealed that these firms adopted purpose more fully than their peers because they understood better how to embed and activate it. What distinguished these companies weren't just executional tactics or even broader strategies. These companies had a *qualitatively different way of understanding and approaching purpose.* Self-consciously or not, leaders at deep purpose companies regarded purpose more expansively and, frankly, in a more elevated way than other executives.

Most leaders think of purpose as, in essence, a tool they can wield. Some focus on the world outside the enterprise, thinking of purpose as a means of building brands and enhancing reputations. Others are more internally focused, regarding purpose as a means of shaping culture and engaging employees. This instrumental notion of purpose is so ingrained that leaders, companies, and consultants often incorporate it into their very definitions of purpose. They further retain an instrumental mindset when considering how to embed purpose into an organization, inventing yet another set of tools, frameworks, or formulas that leaders can use. The logic goes like this: "Want to build a high-performing, beloved organization? Embrace purpose. Want to embrace a purpose? Do A, B, C, and D."

There is nothing wrong with treating purpose as a tool. As we'll see in chapter 3, purpose is immensely useful as an instrument of value-generation. And deep purpose leaders understand purpose's instrumental value more fully than most leaders, reaping performance gains from purpose more fully as well. But deep purpose leaders ultimately don't conceive of purpose as a mere tool. To them, it's something more fundamental: an existential statement that defines the firm's very reason for being.

Starting with that simplest of questions—what's a business for?[29]—deep purpose leaders frame this statement as the ultimate basis for understanding the enterprise, its identity, and its activities. As the psychologist William Damon writes, "Purpose is a stable and generalized *intention* to accomplish something that is at the same time meaningful to the self and consequential for the world beyond the self."[30] Similarly, deep purpose leaders orient their organizations existentially around the "North Star" of purpose, articulating a *conscious intent* to conduct their business in a more elevated way. Purpose in their minds is a *unifying statement of the commercial and social problems a business intends to profitably solve for its stakeholders.*

A DEEPER WAY TO THINK ABOUT PURPOSE

Purpose is a unifying statement of the commercial and social problems a business intends to profitably solve for its stakeholders. This statement encompasses both goals and duties, and it succinctly communicates what a business is all about and who it's intended to benefit.

The concept of intent seems simple enough. When we act with intent, we don't behave indiscriminately, but rather deliberately, even mindfully. Look a bit deeper, though, and you realize that intent is actually quite a profound concept related to self-knowledge and higher awareness. When we act with intent, we behave with urgency, commitment, energy, and focus, basing our behavior on a keen and often hard-won sense of who and what we are.

Most major religions think of intent this way. In rabbinic Judaism, the word *kavvanah* roughly translates as "directed intention," what one authority has described as "a state of mental concentration and devotion."[31] In Eastern philosophies, the Sanskrit word *dharma* translates as "pillar," but it also signifies purpose. In this regard, one observer connects it with intention: "Following our dharma in the deepest sense means that all of our thoughts, intentions, words and actions support our highest purpose. We're not merely acting out of a sense of duty or obeying the laws set down by society but are behaving in integrity with our spiritual purpose."[32]

For the deep purpose leaders I studied, purpose was a deeply felt intention that defined how they conducted business. These leaders had a sense, sometimes articulated and sometimes not, that their purpose originated inside them. These leaders knew some truth or had some vision they wanted to realize, and they approached business as the vehicle for accomplishing that. They didn't simply pursue purpose but rather felt, understood, and committed to their purpose and then *projected* it faithfully out onto the world. They radiated their purpose very much like prophets or artistic geniuses beaming divine revelation.

At many younger, fast-growth companies, business intent is so ingrained and faithfully radiated that leaders need not articulate it formally. Everyone understands the purpose, takes it for granted, and acts on it. This was the case at one firm I studied, Gotham Greens. If you shop at Whole Foods Market, you probably know the company's products: fresh, high-quality, pesticide-free produce grown in urban greenhouses using advanced hydroponic farming techniques. In 2020, a little over a decade after its founding, Gotham Greens ran 500,000 square feet of greenhouses, with facilities in New York City, Chicago, Denver, Baltimore, and Providence, distributing fresh lettuces, herbs, and value-added foods like sauces and dressings to over forty US states.[33] One of the company's Chicago facilities occupied a former steel mill; in Providence, Gotham Greens remediated a brownfield to build its greenhouse on a site that had once been a General Electric light bulb component factory; and its initial facility was located on the rooftop of a Brooklyn building that had formerly housed a bowling alley.[34] The company's facilities recirculate water, using 95 percent less of it than conventional farms, while also using 97 percent less land. Impressively, the company delivers this social value while succeeding commercially. It turned a profit during its very first year and has since grown rapidly, with plans to expand nationally. As of 2020, it attracted $130 million in investment and won awards including a mention on Business Insider's "50 Coolest New Businesses in America" list.[35]

On its website, Gotham Greens describes its area of focus as creating "new ways to farm, produce local food, revitalize communities and innovate for a sustainable future."[36] The website doesn't identify these words as a purpose, but they conform to the company's reason for being as Viraj Puri, Gotham Greens' cofounder and CEO, described it to me. And yet, the company doesn't promote this purpose methodically throughout the company. Adherence to a purpose or a mission arises naturally as leaders and teams operate the business. In company communications, Puri says, "Just by default we're talking about some of the positive impacts that we're making. So when we talk about how much produce we've grown and sold, we also typically talk about how much land and water we've also saved using our production methods." The purpose is universally understood within the company, naturally permeating the organization's "entire DNA," and it isn't "something we have to write on every wall and remind our team of every minute."[37]

Gotham Greens could radiate its intention to serve society *and* function profitably in part because its founding team framed this intention at the outset. As Puri told me, he and his two partners, cofounder and CFO Eric Haley and Chief Greenhouse Officer Jenn Frymark, all firmly aligned around the idea of building a viable business dedicated to sustainability and urban agriculture. This intention ran especially deep for Puri, overlapping with his own lifelong personal purpose. Describing his connection to the business, he revealed that from a young age he had "always been drawn to sustainability and held a deep appreciation for natural resources and what the earth provides." This moral imperative to protect the planet became solidified during a year he spent volunteering with an NGO in India near the border with Tibet.

Today, this existential awareness radiates outward into the company and its operations. "I say this with no hubris, but, at our core, Gotham Greens is a visionary company," Puri said. "So part of our DNA is to think about what's possible and see if we can do it," taking into account of course the need to turn a profit for investors (a tension we'll explore in the next chapter). Although Puri acknowledged the difficulty of measuring it objectively, he described the company's purpose as "a sense and a spirit that sort of permeates the organization."

As the example of Gotham Greens suggests, treating purpose as an inner intent projected faithfully onto the world has implications for the specific ambitions that companies embrace as their reason for being. It's hard to feel burning intent or commitment if your goal is only marginally ambitious or beneficial to others. As I found, the fiery commitment that deep purpose companies had toward their purpose usually tied back to a reason for being that was clearly noble, elevated, and far-reaching. While companies that pursued purpose conveniently often embraced commercial goals (as ambitious as those might be) as their reason for being, deep purpose companies devoted themselves existentially to goals that clearly embraced but also transcended a commercial logic and spoke to deep-seated moral values.

Connecting with a Company's Soul

The intentional pursuit of a higher ambition had profound implications for organizing at deep purpose companies. Instead of overlaying purpose superficially over the organization, including onto parts of the business incompatible with the purpose, leaders and companies naturally infused it into all facets of the enterprise, including its strategies, core products and processes, and relationships with stakeholders. Purpose served as a fountainhead for meaning, the basis for what the organizational theorist Karl Weick described as "sense-making." It was the prism through which you understood your place in the world, and that in turn shaped your actions and priorities. Purpose also gave rise to a field of meaning inside the enterprise, influencing how people saw and spoke about decisions, products, processes, initiatives, structures—everything. This field of meaning served as a context for action, including as it did a shared set of rules, conditions, assumptions, and emotions. Ultimately, the presence of a purpose caused an otherwise colorless panorama of commercial activity to burst out into brilliant hues, suddenly familiar, comprehensible, and, indeed, inviting to the beholder.

We might say that purpose served as an "organizing principle" for the business. Leaders often perceive strategy as the origin of all action, including the creation of structures and processes, but since purpose influences meaning creation in an organization, it precedes even strategy.[38] In this sense, deep purpose leaders perceive purpose as perhaps the most enduring element inside their organizations. As Microsoft's CEO Satya Nadella told me, he thought of purpose as an "anchor" that sustains organizations. "In our context, technologies will come and go. Strategies will come and go. But how you invent and anchor yourself—you need this strap [holding you in place] which is a sense of purpose."[39]

An organizing principle is the logic by which work is coordinated and information is gathered, disseminated, and processed within and between organizations. The notion of intentional purpose as an organizing principle for companies and individuals is hardly novel. Since the first half of the twentieth century, the discipline of organizational behavior has explored how companies might help people work harmoniously toward common goals. Economists such as Ronald Coase conceived of the enterprise as a dry, rational thing—a "nexus of contracts" between individuals, not a field of meaning derived from a single, common intent. According to this view, financial incentives motived people to take concerted action, but little else. Organizations moved according to strict market mechanisms as individuals pursued their economic self-interest, with leaders manipulating incentives to the organization's advantage.[40]

Alongside notions of companies as purely economic organizations, an alternate picture of the enterprise took shape, that of a more human place redolent with moral values, spiritual energy, warmth, and fellow feeling. Following the Supreme Court decision *Santa Clara County v. Southern Pacific Railroad,* an 1886 ruling which conceptualized companies as individual "persons," debate broke out as to whether companies had that central attribute of human beings, a soul.[41] Critics said no, but companies asserted that they did. To evoke a sense of soulfulness, firms like the Colorado Fuel and Iron Company and the National Cash Register Company instituted welfare capitalism, building kindergartens, offering cultural activities, and providing health care. They also sought to imbue their organizations with palpable "personalities," for instance by publicly associating the firm with its founder or with distinctive images of its factory facilities. They further humanized themselves in the eyes of the public with advertising that portrayed individual employees as heroes rendering service. As an executive at AT&T remarked in 1937, the company had once seemed "soulless" but now had become soulful by adopting "the radiant raiment of a . . . service ideology."[42]

A number of thinkers also took issue with economic models of organizing, arguing that economic relationships alone weren't enough to galvanize people around a common cause. Writing during the late 1950s, the sociologist Philip Selznick argued that organizations could serve as carriers of meaning, emotion, and moral values rather than operating as strictly economic entities. Instead of mere organizations, companies could become true institutions that are "infused with value as they come to symbolize the community's aspirations, its sense of identity."[43] Other thinkers, noting that economic incentives alone wouldn't impel employees to take action to adapt to threatening external conditions, argued that employees had to "internalize a common purpose and perceive the connection between their actions and the organization's ability to fulfill this common purpose."[44]

The notion that the pursuit of economic self-interest alone cannot sufficiently motivate people to act collectively gained adherents over the years. Scholars across a number of fields recognized that humans possess inherent needs for meaning, community, and purpose. These intrinsic motivations compel us to act, not just extrinsic incentives. Drawing on the seminal writings of holocaust survivor Viktor Frankl on the importance of meaning, management scholar Colin Mayer argues that meaning, purpose, and morality are precisely what drive people to give themselves over to organizational goals. "We derive well-being from a sense of purpose, achievement, and contribution not just profit, income, and consumption. We seek to fulfill larger goals and the importance of the corporation is in its ability to assist us in this. We once constructed temples, pyramids, and shrines to satisfy the gods, but we now make washing machines, cell phones, and movies."[45] Other thinkers have called for an "economics of higher purpose" and the transformation of the enterprise from a nexus of contracts into one of covenants.[46]

The deep purpose companies I studied embraced their function as carriers of meaning and morality, and they did so despite institutional pressures to deliver short-term results. These companies weren't simply aiming to "win" in conventional terms. They were on a sacred mission and had a sizzling energy about them, one that transcended mundane description and was grounded in both a sense of their interconnection with the wider world and a vision of a better future they sought to realize. Deep purpose leaders reached for religious or spiritual language to describe this energy, associating the purpose with words like "soul," "soulfulness," and "spirit."

In his book *Hit Refresh*, Microsoft's CEO Satya Nadella described the company's reorientation around a new purpose—"To empower every person and every organization on the planet to achieve more"—as not merely a refreshment or renewal of the company, but a rediscovery of the company's soul. He recounted equating the purpose with the company's soul when communicating with employees: "We must rediscover our soul—our unique core," he said in an all-company email. "We must all understand and embrace what only Microsoft can contribute to the world and how we can once again change the world."[47]

The notion that a company can have a "soul" isn't as exotic as it might sound. In my past fieldwork with fast-growth start-ups, I found that founders and early employees often detect the presence of an intangible *something* that they conceive as the "soul." They perceive this energy as the company's very essence, its beating heart and the secret behind its initial success. This soul functions much like a purpose, giving meaning to the company's work. Often, founders speak of the soul and the purpose in the same breath. But as I also found, this soul was fragile and seemed to weaken or vanish entirely as the company grew and a stifling bureaucracy took hold. Leaders needed to focus on sustaining their company's initial soul or spirit even as they worked on establishing the systems and processes essential for operating at scale.[48]

Deep purpose companies solve this dilemma by developing the reason for being as an operating principle. At these firms, purpose infuses systems and processes with meaning and moral value. Instead of feeling impersonal and alienating, the operational guts of the company support emotional engagement and a sense of community. It's no secret that corporate leaders as diverse as Starbucks' Howard Schultz and Microsoft's Nadella have framed a renewed commitment to purpose as a means of reconnecting with their companies' previously neglected "souls."

	Deep purpose firms	Convenient purpose firms
Conception of purpose	Existential	Functional
Scope/orientation	Commercial and social	Commercial
Intensity	Organizing Principle	Tactically applied

Figure 2: Comparing Deep and Convenient Purpose Firms

Lessons for Leaders

Business books often speak of a "knowing-doing gap" to explain performance failures: leaders understand which strategies to implement, but they can't seem to execute them well. With purpose, most leaders don't even know what it means to pursue a purpose fully, much less how. Influenced by experts who extoll purpose's benefits for the enterprise, they're stuck seeing purpose instrumentally, as a means to an end. They have a harder time understanding it as an existential intent that companies project from the inside out. The first step to a deeper engagement with purpose is to pause and reflect more seriously on purpose, conceiving of it as not just another management tool, but as a foundational principle for organizing that reflects your company's very sense of self.

Rethinking the nature of purpose should prompt you in turn to reimagine your role as a leader. Yes, you're charged with creating economic value. But your primary job is to define a reason for being and in turn infuse the enterprise with meaning. How attuned to purpose are you really? Do your communications internally and externally orient the company around a desire to do good for multiple stakeholders via core businesses in addition to creating value for shareholders? Are you injecting purpose methodically into strategy, your oversight of working conditions, and your company's relationships with stakeholders?

More broadly, you can initiate your company's movement toward a deeper engagement with purpose by assessing its current state of commitment. If your company currently pursues a reason for being, its commitment might be limited or convenient. Think about the pyramid presented earlier and where your company might reside. Are your core offerings inherently harmful? Is purpose a side hustle, relegated to CSR initiatives? If you're actively pursuing win-win solutions, do you find yourself reluctant to make decisions commensurate with your purpose that hurt shareholders but create value for other stakeholders? If so, you might be practicing convenient purpose and hence have more opportunity than you think to go deeper in projecting your company's purpose.

Think about your purpose statement itself. Does it evoke higher ambitions that transcend purely commercial concerns? Who precisely are you there to serve, and what kind of moral stand are you taking? A strong purpose statement alone won't make for a deep purpose company, but it does matter. If your purpose statement doesn't clearly state an intention to do good for a variety of stakeholders, it probably isn't functioning as an intention that is compelling and emotionally resonant.

In staking out moral ground, your purpose statement should express an implicit or explicit critique of the world, even at the risk of polarizing members of the public. Leaders sometimes become uneasy at mention of morality, but we should remember that morality and markets have never been as diametrically opposed as they might seem. Before Adam Smith wrote *The Wealth of Nations*, he penned *The Theory of Moral Sentiments*, arguing that humans aren't merely selfish but also inherently sympathetic toward others and driven to help them without hope of personal benefit. In contriving to bypass morality and avoid taking principled stands in the course of doing business, we risk conducting commerce in ways that contravene our very humanity.

Moreover, societal expectations have changed, and in our polarized times moral neutrality is no longer an option. Companies and leaders must take stands, wading into political debates whether they like it or not. Leaders at companies such as CVS, Dick's Sporting Goods, Delta Air Lines, Salesforce, Patagonia, and many others do precisely that, increasingly taking on roles as "CEO activists."[49] They contribute to a remoralization of our society, reinforcing notions of shared values that might in turn help to stabilize and sustain our democracy.

Companies like Gotham Greens understand this reality and lean into their moral sensibilities. Most of them aren't out there in the media at every opportunity wielding their pitchforks. Their approach is more targeted, strategic, and closely aligned with their corporate purpose. In pushing to realize an existential intent such as a healthier population, a more equitable society, or a cleaner environment, they implicitly evoke both an image of the good society and critique the present state of society in their area of interest. They indicate their willingness to become activists dedicated to a cause—not all causes necessarily, but certainly this one.

This observation brings me to a final point: think more deeply about your own, personal purpose and its alignment with the company's reason for being. As the examples in this chapter suggest, leaders ultimately are the source of intent within deep purpose companies. If you can't channel the corporate intention with every fiber of your being, taking on the role of an activist personally,[50] you won't lead your company toward a deep purpose.

As John Maynard Keynes is reputed to have said, "Capitalism is the astounding belief that the most wickedest of men will do the most wickedest of things for the greatest good of everyone."[51] These days, a belief in the wickedness of capitalism's practitioners and practices persists, alongside skepticism that our economic system can produce the greatest good. Still, some companies really do take purpose deeper than the rest, earning profits while addressing some of the greatest problems plaguing humanity. By shifting their approach to purpose, convenient purpose companies can join them, paving the way for a more widespread reform of capitalism.

Companies and leaders must understand purpose in an existential sense rather than instrumentally, embracing their role as moral guides and creators of purpose. But they must also commit themselves to the hard work of imbuing business dealings with meaning and moral sense. As we'll see in the next chapter, they must approach the pursuit of purpose as an ongoing and often frustrating process, that of reaching for the ideal in an imperfect world.

CHAPTER 2

WALKING ON THE RAZOR'S EDGE

*The sharp edge of a razor is difficult to pass over; thus
the wise say the path to Salvation is hard.*

—The Katha Upanishad, as paraphrased in
W. Somerset Maugham's *The Razor's Edge*

Acknowledging the challenges inherent in pursuing a purpose, deep purpose leaders dedicate themselves to the navigation of tradeoffs between stakeholders and between commercial and social logics. Inspired and empowered by the purpose, they negotiate stakeholder interests to arrive at sometimes painful decisions that stakeholders may or may not find "good enough" in the short term but that pay off for everyone eventually. These leaders are uniquely willing to linger in a space of discomfort, ambiguity, and contradiction, staying as true as possible to their animating intent.

In June 2017, Josh Silverman, the newly arrived CEO of ecommerce crafts marketplace Etsy, had one of the most delicate conversations of his career. It wasn't with his board. It wasn't with an angry investor. It wasn't with employees. It was with his thirteen-year-old daughter. Inviting her to join him on a walk, he told her she needed to prepare herself for some unpleasant encounters she might have at school. "We're making difficult decisions at the company," he said. "Many people aren't going to like them. And some of them are going to say mean things about me in the media. If kids at school say anything to you about it, I want you to know that as hard and unpleasant as these decisions are, I think what we're doing is right, and that they will ultimately help people. Sometimes doing the right thing can cause stress for people, and they lash out."[1]

The next day, Etsy announced plans to lay off 160 employees, on top of 80 who had been shown the door immediately before Silverman's installation—in all, about a quarter of the company's workforce. During the weeks that followed, the company made other moves to restructure, shutting down projects popular with employees, disbanding the company's existing sustainability group, announcing that Etsy would let its B Corp certification lapse, and modifying the company's mission statement.[2] The blowback was harsh. Dozens of employees signed a petition protesting the layoffs as well as Silverman's decision to shut down a number of "values-aligned" projects.[3] On Glassdoor, Etsy's ratings tanked, with many reviews lambasting the company and its new direction. Sellers and former employees publicly accused Silverman of gutting the company and everything that made it special. "Etsy had the potential to be one of the truly great ones," one of them told the *New York Times*, "But it looks like they are cutting anything that's not essential to the business. This is a cautionary tale of capitalism."[4]

Since its founding in 2005 by the craftsman Rob Kalin and three others, Etsy saw itself as a company defined by its social purpose and humanitarian mindset. It dedicated itself to serving small craftspeople, providing them with a venue and tools to market their wares and establish thriving small businesses. According to an early blog posting, the company's core mission was to "help artists and crafters make a living from what they make."[5] But Kalin, who served as the company's initial CEO, framed the company's purpose more broadly than this. The company, he suggested, sought to help legions of small businesses—a community of makers—compete in a destructive economy that favors big corporate players. "We believe that the world cannot keep consuming the way it does now, and that buying handmade is part of the solution," he said in 2008.[6] Etsy was a radical project built around empowering the "little guy" and bringing back an older, community- and relationship-based form of commerce. "This is what Etsy stands for: The little guy being able to organize a better marketplace."[7]

Etsy blossomed under Kalin, positioning itself as more purposeful and humane than behemoths like Amazon and Walmart. By 2011, when Kalin resigned as CEO (he had left in 2008 only to return the following year), some 400,000 craftspeople on Etsy sold over $500 million of cufflinks, knives, sweaters, and countless other handmade items.[8] Kalin's replacement, former CTO Chad Dickerson, sought to grow the company while remaining deeply committed to its founding purpose. He announced he would run Etsy to serve all stakeholders, not just investors: "I'm going to prioritize the needs of the Etsy community in the broadest sense—Etsy's sellers, how we work with each other within the company, our local communities, and everyone whose lives we touch."[9] Although Etsy angered some sellers by allowing the sale of factory-produced goods on the site, it adopted a new, more ambitious mission—"To reimagine commerce in ways that build a more fulfilling and lasting world"[10]—and in 2012 became a certified B Corporation, a step reflecting its conviction that "business has a higher social purpose beyond simply profit."[11]

Sticking close to purpose proved a powerful recipe for growth. By 2015, when Dickerson took Etsy public, some 1.4 million makers were selling $2 billion in merchandise each year. The company attracted top talent, including many employees lured by Etsy's purpose and correspondingly generous workplace policies.[12] What Etsy hadn't delivered was profits—it had lost money since 2012. No registered B Corporation of its size had ever gone public,[13] and in the runup to the IPO it wasn't clear whether a firm formally committed to serving multiple stakeholders could perform well enough to satisfy investors. In a blog posting celebrating the IPO, Dickerson affirmed the company's intent to thrive financially as a public company by delivering on its purpose: "Etsy's strength as a business and community comes from its uniqueness in the world and we intend to preserve it. We don't believe that people and profit are mutually exclusive. We believe that Etsy can be a model for other public companies by operating a values-driven and human-centered business while benefiting people."[14]

Would Etsy really manage to create a win-win situation that benefited both society and investors? In its first SEC filings, the company set a low bar for financial performance, advising potential investors that "We have a history of operating losses and we may not achieve or maintain profitability in the future."[15] That was good enough at first, allowing Etsy to raise almost $300 million at a valuation of more than $3.5 billion.[16] But Wall Street quickly lost patience. Growth slowed following the IPO even as costs were growing, and it seemed like employees and society were winning, while investors were losing. Nine months after its IPO, with profits still elusive, Etsy's stock price had plunged by 75 percent. Private equity firms swooped in, taking stakes in the company and arguing it should be taken private so its new owner could make much-needed reforms. In May 2017, Dickerson was gone, replaced by Silverman, who faced the question of what to do to bring costs in check and most importantly, make the company grow again.

Dickerson's ouster and Silverman's arrival triggered an outpouring of sadness and anger. At an emergency meeting, employees sobbed as Dickerson tearfully announced he'd been fired and eighty employees would lose their jobs. At a meeting the next day with Silverman and a high-profile investor, employees challenged the moves as, in the words of one of them, "impersonal, unempathetic, and decidedly un-Etsy."[17] Silverman himself felt qualms about the workforce reductions. He had never thought of himself as a leader who "did" layoffs, and he had avoided them in his previous roles as CEO of Skype, president of consumer products and services at American Express, and CEO of shopping.com. But Silverman believed that restructuring measures including layoffs were essential for Etsy's long-term viability. Not only would they help the company succeed financially; despite appearances, they would enable the company to realize its ideals more fully than it had in the past.

As Silverman related to me, he subscribes to the basic idea of shared value or multi-stakeholder capitalism, the notion that "you can be a great corporate citizen and a great business."[18] The problem, he suggested, was that the Etsy he inherited, although strong in many respects, wasn't focused enough on delivering for all its stakeholders, including not just investors and end users but sellers and the community at large. A lack of efficiency and agility born of organizational bloat likewise prevented the company from delivering. To remedy these issues, Silverman wasn't content to simply put shareholders first via layoffs and then address other stakeholders' needs. Rather, he sought to look comprehensively at the company and rethink how it could better operate to everyone's benefit, rebalancing between stakeholders and injecting more accountability into both the commercial and social dimensions.

In particular, decision-making at Etsy had long benefitted employees, but now the company needed to pay more attention to serving the sellers who were Etsy's direct "customers." Although critics accused Silverman of lacking empathy for employees, he countered that the company had to show empathy for *all* stakeholders, including makers who would benefit from his restructuring plans. As he remarked, "There's two million people, many of them working in far-flung places with very few opportunities who count on us. Who's having empathy for them?"

Silverman argues that sellers had been losing, since the company hadn't done enough to attract buyers to the site and significantly increase gross merchandise volume (GMV), the site's total value of goods sold. Searching on Etsy posed an especially big problem: some claimed they could more easily search on Google for products on Etsy than use Etsy's own search function.

For all the talk about purpose, the social impact the company delivered was also subpar. "It was really hard for me to find a measure in which Etsy's social impact was outsized to the positive," Silverman said. "Well, except one. I think employees were treated unusually well. So, if you were lucky enough to be one of the one thousand people on the payroll at Etsy, you had an unusually good gig." Silverman sought to fix Etsy's economic and operating model so that the company would not only remain profitable but drive growth by attracting more buyers to the site. That in turn would enable its sellers to increase their revenues, which would allow Etsy to become more profitable.

The implementation of reforms proved stressful during the first months of Silverman's tenure as masses of employees headed for the exits.

Silverman stuck it out, going on to focus spending on a few key areas that would have the greatest impact. Devoted to Etsy's social purpose, he also moved to refocus the company's social impact efforts on three key areas (empowering people, environmental responsibility, and diversity), publicly committing the company to quantitative goals in these areas by publishing an impact report in 2019 and an integrated report (on both social and financial performance) in 2020. As of this writing, Silverman's resolve appears to have paid off. Etsy's stock price has risen fifteenfold and its GMV by a factor of five under his leadership, and the company has made quantifiable progress on its social priorities (described below).

Companies and leaders have embraced the notion that purpose-driven companies can solve social and environmental problems while also generating wealth. As the thinking goes, companies can transcend traditional approaches to CSR and instill purpose into their core operations, generating powerful win-win decisions that benefit everyone, with little compromise if any required on any side. A manufacturing company might change wasteful processes, for instance, using less energy while also cutting back on costs. A bank might hire a more diverse workforce, benefitting the community while also getting closer to its customer base and spurring innovation. But idealized win-win solutions such as these are both difficult and relatively uncommon. Many purpose-driven companies chase an ideal of "responsible business without tradeoffs," but they revert to a quest for profits when win-win solutions prove more difficult than they imagined.[19]

Deep purpose leaders like Silverman take a more pragmatic approach. Acknowledging the challenges inherent in pursuing a purpose, *they dedicate themselves self-consciously to the ongoing and imperfect navigation of tradeoffs between stakeholders*. They recognize that so-called win-win solutions almost always involve intelligent tradeoffs as well as imperfect apportioning of the mutual benefits. Inspired and empowered by the purpose, they negotiate stakeholder interests to arrive at sometimes painful decisions that stakeholders may or may not find "good enough" in the short term but that pay off for everyone eventually. Decision-making at deep purpose companies becomes an exercise in "practical idealism," a discipline of honest and often messy problem-solving. Rather than try to be superhuman enterprises that magically get decision-making right for everyone every time, deep purpose companies prove themselves uniquely willing to linger in a space of discomfort, ambiguity, and contradiction, staying as true as possible to their animating intent.

The Lure of the "Simultaneous Solve"

The notion that companies should align profit with social purpose is an important one, undergirding hopes that we might reinvent capitalism to address global ills.[20] Such win-win thinking takes a number of guises. Like Forrest Mars in the previous chapter, some refer to it as achieving a "mutuality of benefits" between stakeholders.[21] Others follow Michael E. Porter and Mark R. Kramer in speaking of "shared value,"[22] or they argue that leaders should "grow the pie" of value for all stakeholders, investors included.[23] Still others advocate for "simultaneous solve[s]" that deliver both profits and social benefits,[24] or they envisage a "conscious capitalism" that delivers "exceptional financial performance over the long term" while creating "social, cultural, intellectual, physical, ecological, emotional, and spiritual value for all stakeholders."[25]

Such ideas represent state-of-the-art management thinking, a vast step forward over shareholder value maximization doctrines. Still, not all observers are convinced. Anand Giridharadas takes idealized win-win thinking to task for its "promise of painlessness," the idea that "what is good for me will be good for you" and that investors and other business elites need not sacrifice for the public good. As he observes, "there will always be situations in which people's preferences and needs do not overlap, and in fact conflict. And what happens to the losers then? Who is to protect their interests? What if the elite simply need to part with more of their money in order for every American to have, say, a semi-decent public school?"[26]

Other critics argue that getting firms to aim for more than profits will wind up *hurting* stakeholders by impeding the efficient movement of capital. Determined to save employee jobs, for instance, companies might hesitate to shut down obsolete business models, saddling customers with subpar products and inhibiting growth. The doctrine of win-win—or "collective capitalism," as the *Economist* has called it—also falters, these critics argue, because it turns business executives into moral arbiters, charging them with tuning in to society's needs and legislating tradeoffs among stakeholders. Recognizing the difficulties that arise when trying to balance between competing interests, these critics conclude it's both more efficient and more just to let executives stick to earning profits, relying on shareholders to exercise moral leadership.[27]

Walking on the Razor's Edge

Research suggests that idealized win-win solutions often prove elusive. Rosabeth Moss Kanter observes that business thinking oriented around the delivery of social benefits—what she describes as "social logic"—differs from the commercial or "financial logic" firms follow to maximize shareholder value. "Great companies," she says, "combine financial and social logic to build enduring success."[28] But precious few companies ever manage to achieve greatness by this definition. As Julie Battilana and her coauthors have pointed out, firms are "quick to abandon social goals in the quest for profitability."[29] To handle the challenges of merging the social and the economic, she argues, companies must transform core elements of their business models, including measurement, structure, hiring, and leadership, adopting an approach she calls "hybrid organizing." They must change their "DNA," which is set up for profit maximization, a frightfully challenging task. Even companies that do succeed can expect to confront serious tensions and tradeoffs on an ongoing basis.

The task of reconciling individual stakeholders' competing needs is inherently difficult. We can conceive of leaders and companies as "negotiating" with stakeholders about how much value to share with each of them. Sometimes this negotiation occurs via actual, face-to-face conversations between leaders and representatives from stakeholder groups. More often, it happens figuratively in leaders' minds. Either way, it's a struggle. In engineering solutions that are mutually beneficial overall, we must usually live with localized arrangements that involve tradeoffs. Each party will need to make smaller sacrifices to gain desired benefits, often bartering away something they care less about and that the other party cares more about. The challenge in these cases isn't to devise solutions that benefit all parties equally. Rather, it's to arrive at arrangements that afford *the greatest benefits possible* to all parties without any party losing, and that also balance the benefits acceptably. It's an emotionally demanding task, one that becomes even more complex when more than two parties sit down at the table.[30]

All of this is not to say that idealized win-win solutions that benefit all stakeholders equally—or put differently, that perfectly merge social and commercial logics—become impossible. Sometimes, leaders arrive at creative arrangements that do deliver significant value for everyone at once, dividing up that value in ways that everyone finds agreeable. Most of the time, though, companies navigating tradeoffs must satisfy themselves with *imperfect* decisions that require some parties to make partial or short-term sacrifices, but that deliver wins for all stakeholders over the long-term.[31]

For all their flaws, these long-term wins can still be quite extraordinary. As Josh Silverman told me, the company's restructuring allowed it to become five times more productive, judging from the number of weekly software releases its engineers churned out (the company's main productivity metric). By improving its support of its sellers (and in turn improving buyers' experience on the site), the company positioned itself to notch gains in gross merchandise sales and revenues in 2018 and 2019 and made a big leap forward in 2020.[32] As of 2019, some 2.5 million sellers marketed their wares on Etsy's marketplace, generating almost $5 billion in gross merchandise sales and over $800 million in fees and other revenue for Etsy.[33] Although the COVID-19 pandemic hit many businesses hard the following year, Etsy's fortunes boomed. Not only did the company sell about $850 million in masks in 2020; the company's non-mask sales roughly doubled as well. As of August 2020, the site's base of active sellers had risen to 3.1 million, with sales growth of 136 percent in the second quarter. Etsy's stock price, meanwhile, soared by 200 percent since the beginning of the year.[34]

Employees would ultimately benefit from such financial performance, because a stronger, more financially successful Etsy would be able to safeguard jobs and other employee benefits for years to come (indeed, as of 2021 the company had about 1,400 employees, roughly 200 more than at its peak before the layoffs). But Etsy also delivered more value for communities and the environment thanks to its focus and accountability around its social impact activities (an improvement that also benefitted employees, who cared about working for a purpose-driven company). By 2019, the company had contributed over $6 billion to the economy, up almost 15 percent from 2018; it had surpassed its goal of doubling the number of underrepresented minorities it hired; and it had achieved carbon-neutral status by becoming "the first major online shopping destination to offset 100 percent of emissions from shipping."[35] Although most public companies loaded their executive suites and boardrooms with men, Etsy boasted gender parity as well as a workforce that was majority female.[36] The company also publicly committed to goals around its three areas of social impact focus and began voluntarily reporting on its performance. As Silverman mused, Etsy had earnestly attempted to have social impact before, but the outside world hadn't held it to account. Thanks to restructuring, the company made measurable gains even as it improved its commercial performance.

Idealized win-win solutions (again, those that don't involve significant tradeoffs) are worth striving for, but we must not do so rigidly or dogmatically, assuming that *only* decisions that perfectly marry commercial and social imperatives or that benefit all stakeholders at once are worth obtaining. If we do, we'll frustrate ourselves and revert back to shareholder value maximization, providing more fodder for those who claim we can't trust companies to behave morally, and for others who argue companies shouldn't deign to try. We'll excuse ourselves from doing the hard work of attempting to reconcile stakeholder interests over the short and long terms, sacrificing real, albeit incomplete, progress in the name of perfection. Research shows it's possible to serve two masters at once—profit and social purpose. Companies that pursue social goals tend to improve their financial performance (we'll explore why in chapter 3, at least as far as purpose-driven firms are concerned).[37] But to achieve the best long-term results for all stakeholders, we simply must accept imperfection. We must roll up our sleeves and navigate vexing tradeoffs as best as we can, pushing meaningfully if incompletely toward win-win.

The Mindset of Practical Idealism

Deep purpose leaders such as Silverman don't simply accept tradeoffs—they *immerse* themselves in them, adopting a mindset we might call "practical idealism."[38] As a group, these leaders are unabashedly idealistic, driven by an existential awareness of their companies' reasons for being and determined to bring the purpose to life with every action or decision. At the same time, they understand that businesses can only do good if they're healthy, and that means playing and winning within the constraints of the commercial system. Rather than bemoaning the need to turn a profit or regarding it as a necessary evil, they laud commercial logic as a valuable constraint that forces companies to operate at a higher level. Driven by purpose, commercial activity becomes a valuable pathway to realizing social good.

To gain a clearer sense of practical idealism and its implications, consider the following chart visualizing individual business decisions:

TYPOLOGY OF BUSINESS DECISION-MAKING

Figure I: A typology of business decision-making

The x-axis reflects the intensity with which social considerations motivate leaders' decision-making. The y-axis reflects the intensity with which leaders decide based on commercial concerns. Note that while commercial logic generally translates into a direct concern for share-holders' and customers' interests (and an indirect concern for employees or suppliers), leaders following a social logic might show concern for local communities, the environment, employees, or customers, depend-ing on the business.[39]

Let's move onto the boxes. Box 2, what I'm calling "Purpose with Profit," represents win-win decisions that satisfy both commercial and social logics. These are moves we make hoping to deliver both financial results *and* benefits for other stakeholders. They include both idealized win-win solutions and those that on the whole convey both financial and social benefits, even if some tradeoffs come into play. At the other end of the spectrum (Box 1), we find poor, "Underachiever" decisions that do little good for anyone. Shareholders lose out, as does society.

Boxes 3 and 4, "Profit First" and "Good Samaritan," respectively, rep-resent situations in which companies choose with an eye toward ben-efitting either shareholders or society, but not both. Companies might land in these boxes for any number of reasons. Some convenient purpose companies might aspire to Purpose with Profit, but when you assess how they allocate resources, you find they spend most of their time in Profit First territory, aiming primarily for profits. These companies might take a portfolio approach, making some decisions or running some of their businesses according to a social logic and others according to a commer-cial one. Firms dedicated to a multi-stakeholder approach might make it more often to Purpose with Profit, but Profit First remains for them both a baseline and a fallback position if they can't engineer a perfect merging of social and commercial logics. These well-intentioned, shared value companies start in Profit First and strive to achieve escape veloc-ity, but gravity yanks them back down to Earth again and again. They want to do good, but they find they just can't without a hit to profitabil-ity, so they content themselves with making money.

What defines practical idealism isn't the deep purpose leader's abil-ity to stake out perpetual residence in the Purpose with Profit box (al-though my research suggests they do reach this box much more often than other companies). It's their *existential intent to do everything possible to reach Purpose with Profit from either Profit First or Good Samaritan, and especially from Good Samaritan.*

Deep purpose leaders follow three principles of practical idealism. First, they aim at all times for Purpose with Profit. Committed to purpose as an existential intent, they immerse themselves in difficult tradeoffs required to create value for everybody. Rather than simply seeking to do good, they challenge themselves to do the harder work of doing good *and* doing well. They sustain the tension that emerges between both commercial and social logics and between specific stakeholders embodying those logics.

Second, deep purpose leaders avoid Profit First decisions that only yield commercial gain with no prospect of social benefit. But if a decision or solution exists that is profitable and that might one day do social good, they might take it on and then go as far as possible to adapt that decision or solution to benefit a wider group of stakeholders, not simply investors.

And third, deep purpose leaders go bold. If they have a Good Samaritan business idea that they think might become profitable over time, they'll take a risk on it. They'll then do everything possible to ensure that the idea can work financially, understanding that a failure to do so would threaten the company's future.

THREE FOUNDATIONAL PRINCIPLES OF PRACTICAL IDEALISM

Principle #1: Go beyond Good Samaritan and obsess over Purpose with Profit.

Principle #2: Avoid Profit First solutions that don't deliver social value.

Principle #3: If you think you can transform a Good Samaritan solution into Purpose with Profit, go bold and take it on. Otherwise, drop it.

The Courageous Pursuit of Practical Idealism

Let's focus on Principle #3. Deep purpose leaders' willingness to start with an idealistic, purpose-based project and do what it takes to make it work is the crowning expression of practical idealism. In a world where most leaders and companies prioritize investors, it requires tremendous courage on leaders' part to start in the Good Samaritan box, as they must assuage investors and convince them to wait for eventual financial returns. Think of the leap of faith you would make in taking a project, product, or decision that will benefit society and rolling with it, believing (but not feeling certain) that you'll eventually achieve favorable economics. In addition to relying upon rigorous financials to make an investment decision, as most leaders do,[40] you also proceed out of an abiding sense of purpose and a desire to have social impact *and* remain profitable. Deep purpose leaders consistently put themselves in this position, inspired as they are by their existential awareness of their purpose. They feel startlingly confident that given a chance and some time, they will find a way to shift Good Samaritan into Purpose with Profit.

Recruit Holdings Co., a multibillion-dollar Japanese conglomerate with holdings in media, staffing, business support, and advertising, realized initial success after its founding in 1960 by publishing a magazine called "Invitation to Companies" that disseminated recruiting information, thus creating an employment marketplace for new graduates (formerly, only large companies could easily recruit top talent at Japanese universities). The company grew steadily, creating sector-specific magazines for an array of industries and job functions and entering new markets with the goal of addressing important social challenges. In 1988, a new, less pleasant chapter of Recruit's history opened when the company became embroiled in a massive scandal that shook Japan's political and business elite. Recruit's founder Hiromasa Ezoe gave prominent members of the elite Recruit's stock before the company went public.

The scandal sent shock waves through Japan and received massive, front-page coverage in the country's major newspapers. The entire Japanese cabinet was forced to resign, as were dozens of other individuals, and some faced criminal charges.[41] To make matters worse, a tough economy hit the company hard, leading to a 20 percent decline in revenues. Nevertheless, the company pulled through, going on to survive near bankruptcy during the mid-1990s (thanks to bad investments and competitive pressures related to the rise of the Internet) before returning to solid growth.

The scandal left an indelible impression on personnel who experienced it. "I thought the company was over, every one of us felt that way," recalls former Senior Managing Corporate Executive Officer, CHRO, and Board Director Shogo Ikeuchi.[42] With the company's future hanging in the balance, leaders scrambled to regain the trust of consumers, the companies that advertised in its magazines, and the Japanese public. Rather than dictate a solution, they beckoned employees to step up with suggestions. After much discussion, including a number of dramatic late-night sessions, leaders decided that they should first work on restoring the company's damaged credibility by creating a new Recruit more keenly attuned to its social roles and responsibilities as well as its duties to shareholders. The company adopted a "corporate philosophy" that affirmed its intention to "help establish a free, dynamic human community by creating new value through information and continuously working toward harmony with society."[43]

In keeping with this philosophy, the company adopted a new set of three management principles: "create new value," "respect each individual," and "contribute to society." These approximated principles the company had previously followed, with one big exception: "create new value" replaced a principle called "quest for commercial rationality," which explicitly referenced a commercial logic. As the company noted, it understood that "the quest for commercial rationality is vital to the existence of a company," but changed the principle "after examining why we are needed in society and how we can contribute to society." Recruit sought to emphasize its desire to be a "conscientious, sincere company that is embraced by and consistently moves hand in hand with society."[44] Over the decades since, the company has updated this basic management philosophy, most recently in 2019 when the three principles became, respectively, "wow the world," "bet on passion," and "prioritize social value."[45]

What does it mean to "prioritize social value"? Does the company pursue social value without concern for financial performance, or vice versa (putting itself in the Good Samaritan and Profit First boxes, respectively)? As Ikeuchi assured me, Recruit would "never, ever" fund a project that delivered only commercial value, since that would violate its purpose. But it also wouldn't fund projects that serve society but lack commercial potential. "In my experience working at Recruit for more than thirty years," Ikeuchi says, "I don't think we have ever made a decision with only social purpose in mind. Always, always we have borne in mind the balance between social value and economics." What Recruit *would* do is fund a project with clear social value but uncertain commercial prospects in hopes that the company might eventually make the project commercially viable. Recruit will courageously start in the Good Samaritan box, having faith that with smart thinking and hard work it can get to Purpose with Profit. That kind of pro-social risk-taking is what Recruit means by "prioritizing social value."

As of 2020, Recruit has funded one of its ventures, the online learning Study Sapuri, for *eight years* in hopes of making it profitable. Launched in 2012, Study Sapuri allowed low-income and rural students a fighting chance to excel at the standardized exams that determined students' admission to elite universities. Since these exams covered topics Japanese schools didn't teach, students had to attend test-prep classes in order to excel. If your family couldn't afford to pay for these classes, or you lived far from the urban centers where prep classes were taught, you were out of luck. Study Sapuri initially allowed students to take classes online for about $60 each, about a quarter of what a comparable in-person class cost. In 2013, Study Sapuri changed its offering, charging only around $10 for a subscription that allowed unlimited access to its online classes. The site also allowed students to access additional study materials such as past tests for free.

By 2018, almost a half-million members paid for Study Sapuri's services, which had grown to include a coaching service and offerings for younger students. Although the high school test preparation business turned a profit, the business overall continued to lose money.[46] That apparently remained true two years later, when the company moved to double its monthly fees for new subscribers.[47] "It's required a lot of patience," Ikeuchi notes. "It has taken more investment and funding than we had anticipated [to get the business off the ground and scaled]." In showing patience, leaders didn't simply sit by passively and wait for revenues to increase. "We asked ourselves, 'How can we possibly generate more revenue?' We had a heated debate, discussion on how we can grow this business."

Despite pushing hard on the commercial logic, Recruit has shown extraordinary care for Study Sapuri's social impact and an unusual ability to wait for the economic logic to materialize. It helped, Ikeuchi allows, that Recruit executive and Study Sapuri founder Fumihiro Yamaguchi felt so passionately about the business and its prospects, and that Recruit had a culture oriented around nurturing and harnessing the passion and entrepreneurial zeal of its employees. But ultimately Recruit bet on a business that was less profitable in the short term but potentially viable over the long term and that would deliver clear social value because of its unusually strong commitment to its purpose. As Ikeuchi notes, "We put the highest priority on social value. Having learned some lessons from the scandal in 1988, we continue to update our core value and ensure that our business embodies it."

The Art of the Tradeoff

If you buy Gotham Greens' fresh produce, you'll notice that it comes packaged in single-use plastic packaging, which is terrible for the environment. Why didn't a company so dedicated to reinventing agriculture to be more sustainable and less polluting use planet-friendly packaging? It wasn't an oversight. As founder Viraj Puri recalls, when the company was starting out, his team researched alternative options, eventually landing on highly attractive packaging made of compostable fiber. "We thought very highly of ourselves and patted ourselves on the back for doing such an amazing job and for the impact we were going to make."

As workers began harvesting lettuce and putting it into the eco-friendly packages, they ran tests to determine the product's shelf life so that they could print expiration dates on the packages. It turned out the greens lasted only a few days in fiber-based packaging as compared with two weeks or longer in plastic. The fiber acted as a desiccant, drying out the greens, causing them to wilt and wither. This put Puri and his team in a bind: Would they have to compromise on their social purpose and use plastic? Or could they come up with a different solution?

Team members had an idea: What if they sold their produce to supermarkets unpackaged, and supermarkets retailed it to consumers in loose bins? The team went to supermarket produce buyers and proposed this solution. The buyers agreed, but they indicated they would only want to purchase a small fraction of the order that they had originally placed with Gotham Greens since the demand wasn't there. As the produce buyers explained, consumers were gravitating away from unpackaged greens and toward locally-grown packaged greens, which are cleaner, retain their quality, and are safer to eat.

After extensive research, the team perceived the inherent tension between environmentally friendly packaging and food waste. According to Puri, "when you look at a complete life cycle analysis, food waste is a major factor,"[48] having tremendous harmful environmental impacts due to the unnecessary expenditure of natural resources to grow products that consumers don't actually use, plus the additional emissions related to disposing of a previously edible product. The team concluded that alternative packaging solutions weren't as green as they purported to be if they didn't perform well in their main function: storing and preserving the food they contained. Recognizing they would need to use plastic packaging if they were to market a commercially viable product, Puri and his team researched the types of plastic available to them, seeking options that did the least damage to the environment. Recyclable and recycled plastic intrigued them as a relatively sustainable solution, but the team worried that it was more costly than conventional plastic. At one point, compostable plastic seemed like a godsend: perhaps Gotham Greens could create packaging from plastic that degraded naturally and replenished the soil.

As team members learned more about this option, however, they concluded that compostable plastic wasn't as sustainable as it seemed. Suppliers used subsidized, genetically modified corn to manufacture it, and only consumers in locations with municipal composting facilities could compost this packaging. Most of the company's compostable plastic would wind up in landfills, or even worse, consumers would put it in their recycling bins and it would create operational inefficiencies in recycling facilities, which can't recycle compostable plastic.

After months of research and analysis, Puri and his team resolved to package their produce in #1 PET plastic, the type most universally accepted at recycling facilities. "As an ESG (Environmental, Social, and Governance) company rooted in natural resource conservation as part of our DNA, it was a really hard, emotional decision for us," Puri says, "but we're still using plastic boxes ten years later because there isn't an alternative available commercially on the market today" that delivers longer shelf life and gives consumers the product quality they expect.

Observing this decision from a distance and out of context, a skeptic might question Gotham Greens' commitment to its purpose, concluding it had chosen a commercial logic over a social one. With more information, a different picture emerges. Gotham Greens has an ongoing sustainable packaging team that stays abreast of new technologies as they emerge, continually searching for more sustainable options. Puri believes that a lack of suitable eco-packaging alternatives that perform well and are accessibly priced so that consumers can still afford groceries is the reason we see so much plastic in grocery aisles today. "Despite our best efforts, Gotham Greens is a small company with limited influence in the packaging sector. Changing the landscape requires the collective action of consumers demanding better, large companies making commitments that influence the supply chain, and governments creating proper incentives and market dynamics to fuel innovation and usher in improvements."

Puri and his team did indeed make the decision to use plastic despite its negative environmental impacts in order to create a viable business with sufficient consumer demand and investor interest. But they did so knowing that if the company could get its product right, grow its sales and geographical footprint, and succeed in its larger vision of reinventing agriculture, the social and environmental benefits would far outweigh the harms caused by plastic packaging. One day, they hope to be able to switch to a truly green alternative as packaging technology advances.

The world is a messy place. Gotham Greens' struggle with packaging illustrates how hard companies and leaders embracing practical idealism must work to arrive at meaningful Purpose with Profit solutions, and the imperfect nature of many of these arrangements. Even when a product offering or a strategy represents a clear Purpose with Profit solution overall, specific executional decisions might reside in either Profit First or Good Samaritan. In Gotham Greens' case, leaders couldn't arrive at a perfect solution given the needs of its stakeholders, because no such solution existed. But they could and did do their utmost to find a solution that was not quite as bad as other options and that would allow the company to stay in Purpose with Profit overall. In deciding to stick with recyclable plastic due to a lack of viable alternatives, the company did its best to negotiate the interests of investors, end consumers, supermarkets, and the environment. And judging from the company's overall social and commercial impact to date, these efforts were quite worthwhile.

This example leads us to an important theme: purpose's role in helping leaders navigate tradeoffs. During the months-long process of selecting packaging, Puri and his team looked toward the company's purpose for guidance at every turn. Clarity about the reason for being led in turn to clarity about priorities. As a business, the company had to see to a commercial logic that pleased customers and did so economically. But as a business with a purpose, its intent was clear: it had to ensure that even highly tactical decisions such as this one supported the company's ambitions and moral vision. The deeply felt, existential commitment enshrined in the purpose served as a set of guardrails for commercial activity, indicating options that just wouldn't work or that the company would avoid if it could. In my research, many deep purpose leaders described the purpose as a "North Star" that helped orient them and see them through the complexity of negotiating tradeoffs.

Purpose also plays a *motivational* role, inspiring leaders to push through difficult tradeoffs they might otherwise avoid or fail to undertake in the first place. As one scholar observes, leaders often become fatalistic when confronting tradeoffs, "declaring the problems irresolvable and simply the costs of doing business." Companies gain an edge if they can learn to "persevere until they reconcile those tensions."[49] Because deep purpose companies like Gotham Greens approach purpose as existential intent, they regard every operational decision, however small, as an opportunity to realize the company's reason for being and achieve Purpose with Profit. Another produce company might have used the same plastic packaging everyone else was using. Gotham Greens was *deliberate* about its decision, prepared to negotiate intensively to obtain the best, most purposeful result.

A convenient purpose company might have tried at first to use alternative packaging, reverting quickly back to the Profit First solution of plastic upon discovering that the alternative didn't work as well. But that's not what Gotham Greens did. Inspired by the company's reason for being, Puri and his team worked for months on this one operational detail, performing a comprehensive environmental life cycle analysis before finally reverting to plastic. To this day, he and his team are still searching for more environmentally friendly packaging and he is committed to making the transition once the technology catches up. All along, Puri relates, the team has listened to the "voices" of stakeholders. Describing his decision-making process in general, he says, "We look at consumers. Are we delivering a product they find useful? Are we delivering a product that retail chains and food service operators find useful? And we have to look at our investors"—all this, and the environmental impact besides.

You might question whether Puri and his team were wasting time researching packaging when in the end they did wind up using plastic. Is it worth it to strive so intently for Purpose with Profit with every last decision? It is, not least because the motivation to navigate tradeoffs in pursuit of win-win solutions can lead to unanticipated opportunities to deliver idealized Purpose with Profit solutions.

Etsy's Josh Silverman told me that when he first became CEO, the company already sought to make its offices carbon neutral. Determined to pursue sustainability as energetically as it could in service to the company's purpose, leaders realized they needed to consider the carbon footprint associated with shipping the products sold on the site to consumers. An analysis found that this was really the company's biggest source of carbon emissions. Silverman wanted to know whether the company could possibly pay to offset it. One idea was to pass the cost on to customers. That meant a tradeoff: less value for customers, more for the environment (overall, a Purpose with Profit solution). The company decided to run an experiment, asking consumers how much extra at checkout they would consider paying to help the company offset the carbon dioxide emitted during shipping.

Before they could run the test, they hired consultants to figure out how much the offsetting would cost per order. The answer shocked Silverman and his team: only a penny per package. Since offsetting the carbon was so inexpensive, Etsy opted to pay the cost itself rather than passing it on to consumers. What appeared at first to be a tradeoff between customers and the planet turned out to be an idealized Purpose with Profit solution. The increased cost to investors was marginal, and offsetting carbon dioxide would benefit them by enhancing Etsy's reputation with customers and employees. Thus it was that the company became "the first major online shopping destination to offset 100% of carbon emissions from shipping."[50] Between February 2019 and March 2020, the company offset more than 170,000 metric tons of carbon dioxide by investing in environmental projects and became an outspoken advocate for decarbonizing logistics and other business activity.[51]

The decision proved to be a smart one in commercial terms. Tests the company ran revealed that consumers bought more when the company informed them at checkout that it was offsetting carbon dioxide from shipping.[52] Leaders sometimes can spot true win-win opportunities, but only if they look hard enough and remain willing to make tough choices if need be.

A final way purpose helps leaders navigate difficult tradeoffs has to do with its considerable organizational benefits. As we've seen, individual stakeholders sometimes lose in the short term so that everyone can benefit over the long term. In negotiating imperfect solutions that ultimately deliver the greatest possible shared value, leaders must convince stakeholders facing short-term losses to stick with the company anyway. The shared field of meaning provided by the purpose forms a basis for trust, understanding, and collective resolve to take root (a phenomenon we'll explore in the next chapter). Purpose serves as what sociologists call a "superordinate goal," one that brings people together and creates a group identity.

Respect for Etsy's purpose prompted investors to stick with the company for the first year or so after it went public, even if their impatience soon grew. Once Silverman took over, his decision to lay off employees and other moves associated with restructuring triggered criticism both inside and outside the company. In the end, though, there was no mass exodus of either employees or buyers. Quite the contrary: in a 2019 engagement survey, 92 percent of employees rated it a "great place to work," as compared with a national average of 59 percent, and 96 percent agreed with the statement, "I'm proud to tell others I work here."[53] Employees understood and respected Etsy's purpose, and they also came to respect and understand the need for sacrifice to achieve it.

Lessons for Leaders

You can take purpose deeper at your company by parting with the notion that idealized win-win solutions are the only ones that count, and by reorienting yourself toward patiently negotiating tradeoffs to arrive at the best possible solutions. Make purpose meaningful by approaching every decision with the intention of benefitting every stakeholder. Carefully research, analyze, and test your options, thinking creatively about how you might act in ways that deliver as much benefit as possible to all stakeholders over varying time horizons. To sharpen your thinking, consult with stakeholders to learn what each of them needs and what decisions of yours might comprise deal breakers for them. Scholars have set forth potential frameworks for use in making tradeoffs.[54] However you make these decisions, bring your purpose to life by using it as the starting point for your deliberations, whether you're framing long-term strategy for your organization or addressing a small-scale tactical question.

As you forge tradeoffs, communicate them by explaining how they connect to and support the purpose. Being explicit builds cohesion by giving meaning to sacrifices stakeholders are making and by further reinforcing the field of meaning emanating from the purpose. To win over employees and build trust, Josh Silverman had to explain why his unpopular restructuring measures were necessary to save Etsy and its ability to function as a deep purpose company. "We were fighting for our life," he remembers, "and I don't think the team really fully understood it." He and fellow leaders explained that if the company couldn't improve its business performance, investors might buy the company for pennies on the dollar. In that case, the world would perceive Etsy as having failed, and it would have drawn from that failure the lesson that a company cannot do good and remain commercially viable. "What was riding on this was more than just the fate of Etsy, which I think is important to two million [sellers on the platform]. Even more than that, it's the concept that you can be a great citizen and be a great business, and in fact, that being a great citizen *makes* you a better business." As employees came to understand the stakes and how layoffs and other measures would help the company become healthier as a business, they rallied behind the changes.

When forming your strategies, assess where existing or prospective businesses fall on the business decision-making typology presented earlier. If a business of yours resides in the Good Samaritan box and you think you can make it profitable, give yourself a clear time horizon for doing so. Companies will vary in how much runway they can give managers—not all will feel comfortable allowing eight or more years for profitability, as Recruit did. Privately held firms and those with other, highly profitable businesses might allow managers more time to take a Good Samaritan business and push it into the Purpose with Profit category. Companies might also allow for more time if they feel that the eventual commercial opportunity stands to be great.

If you have a Profit First business and you wish to push it into the Purpose with Profit category, you have two basic options. First, you can try to graft purpose onto your existing product, for instance by making your operations more sustainable and socially responsible or by making your product safer or healthier. Second, you can take a portfolio approach, keeping your existing product but supplementing it with others that clearly operate as Purpose with Profit businesses. Companies with hugely successful existing Profit First businesses might wish to take this second approach as a transitional strategy, gradually down-shifting their reliance on the Profit First business and investing more heavily in Purpose with Profit segments of their portfolios. In this way, convenient purpose companies can transition over time to become more recognizably deep purpose enterprises. Companies like Mars and Pepsi-Co are both following these strategies and making important progress. Here again, your time horizon can't be open-ended. Set clear goals for moving toward Purpose with Profit and establish quantitative metrics for tracking your progress.

Leaders can also take purpose deeper by embracing "yes, and" think-ing. In his book *Winning Now, Winning Later*, former Honeywell CEO David M. Cote describes the importance of "accomplishing two seemingly conflicting things at the same time." As he notes, "Any ninny could improve a given metric—that didn't take much thought or cre-ativity. The best leaders acknowledge the tensions that pop up all the time in organizations, and they get better results by probing deeper to resolve them."[55] Cote goes on to explain how cultivating a discipline of accomplishing multiple conflicting goals at once enabled leaders at Honeywell to boost performance and turn the company around. Like-wise, deep purpose leaders don't just satisfy themselves with doing good, making excuses for their company's poor financial performance by portraying it as simply a cost of delivering social benefit. Nor do deep purpose leaders shrug their shoulders and take a "realist" stance, saying, "I wish we could save the world, but we've got a business to run." Deep purpose leaders challenge themselves to deliver both social benefits *and* exceptional financial results. It's excruciatingly difficult, much more so than simply aiming for one of these goals. And you won't get it perfectly right for everyone all the time. But you will get closer to the ideal of contributing to society while building a thriving business.

It's easy to look at capitalism's recent track record and dismiss talk of a higher purpose as naive, misguided, self-serving, or even exploitative—a foolish idealism. Charles Dickens wrote in *A Tale of Two Cities* of the "glorious vision of doing good, which is so often the sanguine mirage of so many good minds."[56] But we in business very much need more idealism in our midst, not less. Deep purpose leaders are the best kind of idealists, struggling endlessly to marry their dream-seeking with the realist's hard edge. This injection of "reality" doesn't pollute idealism, but rather enables people with lofty ideals to actually improve human existence. And here's the greatest paradox of them all: in bending idealism's arc to accommodate the messiness and imperfection of commerce, deep purpose leaders ultimately do generate more value for everyone. Understanding and pursuing such value-creation to the fullest can empower more leaders to do the hard, never-ending, but ultimately fulfilling work of bringing purpose to life.

CHAPTER 3

FOUR LEVERS FOR SUPERIOR PERFORMANCE

Many leaders pursue purpose superficially because they don't fully understand how devotion to a purpose enhances business performance. Deep purpose leaders grasp more acutely the mechanisms by which purpose galvanizes organizations and generates outsized performance. They point to four distinct categories of benefits: the ability of purpose to help focus strategy-making, foster relationships with customers, engage with external stakeholders, and inspire employees.

In a world riven by tribalism, hatred, mistrust, and misinformation, it's reassuring to know that at least one big company is working to spread more peace and harmony. In 2017, this firm rolled out a new purpose for itself that specifically referenced an intention to heal rifts between people. The company existed "to give people the power to build community and bring the world closer together."

Introducing this new purpose, the company's founder and CEO argued passionately that human beings needed to gain a keener sense of their common humanity if we are to solve global problems. "We have to build a world where we care about a person in India or China or Nigeria or Mexico as much as a person here. That's how we'll achieve our greatest opportunities and build the world we want for generations to come."[1] The founder promised that his firm would deliver on its purpose by providing tools customers could use to build safe, healthy communities of their own. As these communities took shape, the world would make progress on systemic problems like climate change and pandemics.[2]

Several years have passed since the launch of this new purpose. Has the company helped to bring people closer together? Not exactly. While it did take some steps to build community and reduce hatred, many of its policies and decisions served to *increase* tribalism, hatred, mistrust, and misinformation. To many observers, the company seemed to have become a malign presence in the world, fomenting the very social disintegration the company purported to address. In one survey conducted in late 2019, only 40 percent of respondents saw the company as having a positive impact on society, while 72 percent felt the company wielded an excessive amount of power in society.[3]

This company, of course, is Facebook, a poster child for convenient purpose.[4] Facebook's new reason for being appeared in the wake of public uproar about the proliferation of fake news on the platform during the 2016 US election. If that timing alone fuels suspicion of "purpose-washing," the company's own actions—or failures to act—don't help. In 2018, false rumors on Facebook's WhatsApp platform led to lynchings in India, prompting government outrage.[5] That same year, the United Nations accused the company of contributing to the genocide of Muslims in the country of Myanmar by failing to stop Buddhist nationalists from using Facebook to spread anti-Muslim hate speech. Following an independent review it commissioned, Facebook acknowledged that "we weren't doing enough to help prevent our platform from being used to foment division and incite offline violence."[6]

In 2019, activists accused Facebook of serving as a haven for terrorists, sex traffickers, drug dealers, and more.[7] A 2020 report found that Facebook was infested with white supremacist groups—this despite founder and CEO Mark Zuckerberg's vow in 2018 to ban these groups from the platform.[8] Also in 2020, employees publicly criticized Facebook and companies large and small pulled their advertising from the platform after Zuckerberg refused to ban controversial posts from then US president Donald Trump.[9]

Even when Facebook moved against hate and divisiveness, its efforts seemed to lack sincerity. In October 2020, Facebook announced it would ban materials on its site related to the denial of the Holocaust. As one former Facebook employee remarked, "The fact that Zuckerberg has finally, after years of advocacy from anti-hate groups like the [Anti-Defamation League] and others, accepted that Holocaust denial is a blatant anti-Semitic tactic is, of course, a good thing. The fact that it took him this long to accept that these organizations had more experience than him and knew what they were talking about is dangerous."[10] The same month as the announcement, the *New Yorker* magazine ran a long exposé detailing the company's lackluster efforts to cleanse itself of hate, questioning whether Facebook really wished to make progress.[11] Derrick Johnson, CEO of the NAACP, remarked, "We have not seen this level of deafness from a corporate entity who served society. We have had many conversations with Facebook, and they have refused to address basic issues of keeping people safe and protecting our democracy."[12]

Zuckerberg and Facebook have defended their refusal to take stronger action against harmful content by claiming to be a neutral platform and citing their determination to protect free speech.[13] At other moments, they've apologized for harmful content on the platform, promised to improve, argued they were making progress, and pointed to the billions they invested to fight hate speech and misinformation.[14] Those sympathetic to Facebook might allow that in making content-related decisions the company is under intense and conflicting pressures from stakeholders, that defining precisely what constitutes hate speech or disinformation can prove difficult, that it can prove logistically difficult to quickly find and remove every last objectionable posting, and that we have to let innovative companies like Facebook make their mistakes and learn from them. But for many critics of the company, such arguments are beside the point. Facebook continues to harm society with its core product for one simple reason: because it cares more about profits than purpose.

In a *USA Today* op-ed published in 2017, early Facebook investor Roger McNamee held that the platform's tendency to foment polarization "was the result of countless Facebook decisions, all made in pursuit of greater profits."[15] McNamee subsequently argued that the company's advertising-based business model was inherently flawed, producing profits to the detriment of the public good. The platform must keep users' attention to bring in advertising dollars, its primary source of revenue. The algorithms Facebook uses to determine which news items users see in their feeds aim to keep them as engaged and interested as possible. "One of the best ways to manipulate attention is to appeal to outrage and fear, emotions that increase engagement," McNamee said.[16] Another former Facebook leader in charge of monitoring political ads agreed, noting that the company needed to revamp its business model if it was to truly make strides against harmful speech. Facebook had it in its power to change its algorithms so those spewing disinformation and hate enjoyed less visibility. But that would mean adjusting the algorithms so they didn't optimize for user engagement—a move the company didn't seem inclined to make.[17]

If you think about it, Facebook's apparent resolve to sacrifice purpose at the altar of its highly profitable business model seems puzzling. Why would a company interested in delivering value for shareholders neglect its purpose? As mentioned earlier in this book, a growing body of research in recent years suggests that the pursuit of purpose can *boost* financial performance. One study of a cohort of public firms embracing a multi-stakeholder approach found that they performed better than the S&P 500 by a factor of eight over the course of a decade.[18] A report by EY and *Harvard Business Review* found that companies that had most fully pursued a purpose were more likely than other companies to report rapid growth over the previous three years.[19] Research by George Serafeim and his coauthors found that firms whose middle manager ranks emphasized purpose "have systematically higher accounting and stock market performance."[20]

And it's not like the compatibility of purpose and profits is a tightly guarded secret. In his widely read 2019 letter to CEOs, BlackRock

CEO Larry Fink argued that "purpose is not the sole pursuit of profits but the animating force for achieving them. Profits are in no way inconsistent with purpose—in fact, profits and purpose are inextricably linked."[21] Surveys of CEOs further suggest that such views are hardly radical or fringe but rather "something close to the conventional wisdom," as Rebecca Henderson observes.[22]

Why do Facebook and so many other convenient purpose companies chase profits and pay short shrift to purpose despite the apparent financial benefits? It's true, as the economist Alex Edmans notes, that while research generally supports a purpose-performance link, some evidence belies it. Further, this link might not apply evenly to all players everywhere at all times.[23] But based on my conversations with dozens of leaders, I believe a more basic dynamic is at play. Leaders pursue purpose superficially because for all their apparent enthusiasm, they don't fully understand *how* devotion to a purpose enhances business performance. As a result, they continue to perceive purpose as a tax on the business rather than as a performance booster. The ethic of shareholder value maximization is so firmly entrenched that leaders assume the traditional levers that yielded profits in the past are still the best ones for doing so. They can't imagine that another set of levers linked to purpose might generate not only strong profits, but exceptional ones.

As I studied deep purpose companies and leaders, I realized they understood more acutely the underlying mechanisms by which purpose galvanizes organizations and generates outsized performance. In explaining why their devotion to purpose made for good business, leaders tended to point to four distinct categories of benefits: directional, relational, reputational, and motivational. Understanding these benefits emboldened deep purpose leaders and helped them to channel their efforts. Unlike convenient purpose companies, deep purpose companies pushed hard to wring the maximum benefits from purpose in each of these four areas. Let's examine each of these "purpose levers," exploring how one deep purpose company, the Swiss plant equipment manufacturer Bühler Holding AG, pulls them to achieve sustained high performance and growth.[24]

Directional: Deep purpose serves as a "North Star" and helps you channel innovation.

Relational: Deep purpose helps you sustain credibility and trust with ecosystem partners and establish long-term relationships.

Reputational: Deep purpose helps you build affinity, loyalty, and trust with customers.

Motivational: Deep purpose elevates work, allowing you to motivate and inspire employees.

A "North Star" to Guide Your Growth (Purpose Lever #1: Directional)

What if Facebook *had* taken its purpose seriously? What would it have done? Clearly, it would have changed its algorithms and policies and more aggressively policed itself to minimize hate speech and disinformation, even if this disrupted its business model somewhat. But a Facebook deeply invested in its purpose would have gone much further. It would have become an *activist* on behalf of its purpose, leading the change it wanted to see in the world. It would have adopted its reason for being as the foundation for strategy and abandoned or altered strategies that flouted its purpose.

Recognizing that it alone couldn't solve the systemic problems of hate speech and disinformation online, Facebook also would have tried to spark a social movement, convening its entire ecosystem around the challenge of "giving people the power to build community and bring the world closer together." Facebook would have publicly set bold, even seemingly impossible goals for the reduction of hate speech and disinformation, appealing to customers and strategic partners to collaborate on innovative solutions. It would have funded and celebrated innovations and made its efforts to ensure safe, harmonious online communities the basis for all of its stakeholder conversations. Understanding the value of its purpose for its own business, it would have leaned hard into it *before* critics demanded it do so, confident that the company would come out ahead despite any required tradeoffs.

You might object that such extreme devotion to purpose is unrealistic for a large company like Facebook. Trying to lead a social movement is complicated, likely fruitless, and in any case, beyond the purview of companies. By expending so much effort on behalf of its purpose, Facebook would be taking its eye off its business, and its performance would suffer. Perhaps Facebook could be doing more on behalf of its purpose, but not *this* much.

Actually, one purpose-driven company has made such an expansive commitment to solving a big, complex social problem. And rather than compromising its performance and growth, this extreme commitment to purpose has *fueled* it. This company is the Swiss multinational food-processing equipment manufacturer Bühler, which over the past ten years has devoted itself to slashing the global food industry's massive carbon footprint.

If you haven't heard of Bühler, this family-owned company plays a key role in the global food supply chain, helping to feed some two billion people every day. From Lindt chocolate to Barilla pasta, Bühler machines produce it all in plants owned by some of the world's biggest food companies. All told, Bühler's machines process about 65 percent of the world's grain harvests, 40 percent of the world's pasta, and 30 percent of the global breakfast cereal supply.[25] Bühler grew its food business globally during the 2010s by pursuing a strategy of selling manufacturing-related services to customers rather than only machinery. Incorporating big data and analytics, Bühler's services help customers optimize production lines in their plants, improve food safety, and develop new food products.

From its inception in 1860, Bühler operated in enlightened ways that today we associate with deep purpose. But the company's celebration of its 150th anniversary in 2010 was an important turning point, prompting deep introspection on the part of leaders as to what the company was all about and how it could remain relevant and successful. After much deliberation, and with strong encouragement from Bühler family members, executives adopted "innovations for a better world" as the company's purpose. As generic as that phrase might sound, it was rich with meaning inside Bühler, capturing the organization's determination to reimagine food production globally to solve pressing humanitarian and environmental problems.

Leaders understood the tremendous social, environmental, and commercial value that reform of the global food supply chain could produce. As Dipak Mane, Bühler's former chief human resources officer, told me, one-third of the world's energy went into food production, a quarter of global carbon dioxide emissions came from agriculture, and one-third of all food was wasted via production and distribution. If Bühler engineered technologies that reduced waste and energy use across the entire food supply chain, it could help to address climate change, save its customers money, and continue to grow its business. Bühler had a unique opportunity to help transform food production at massive scale due to its central position in the food production value chain.

After clarifying its reason for being, Bühler moved boldly to realize it. In 2011, the company implemented sustainability reporting, noting that it would expand its reporting to cover not only its own facilities but those it had established on behalf of clients.[26] In 2012, Bühler adopted a public goal of slashing energy usage at its customers' plants by a quarter in eight years.[27] In 2016, the company went further, announcing its intention of lowering energy usage, waste, and water usage in its customers' production processes by 30 percent by 2025.[28] In 2019, spurred by the 2018 report of the United Nations Intergovernmental Panel on Climate Change (IPCC) as well as by an awareness of food production's heavy environmental impact, the company issued still more ambitious goals: a 50 percent reduction in these areas in its customers' production processes by 2025.[29]

For Bühler as for many of the deep purpose companies I researched, purpose served as a foundation for framing clear, cogent strategies to drive business growth.[30] As one study of purpose has suggested, purpose clarifies strategic decision-making, serving as a kind of litmus test: if a given strategy or a project or initiative associated with a strategy aligns with the purpose, leaders might wish to embrace it. If not, then they should jettison it.[31] As I've mentioned, many leaders I spoke with described purpose as a "North Star" that simplifies decision-making and helps them move their companies forward in complex, fast-changing, highly competitive markets.

Research by others bears out purpose's ability to strengthen strategy-making and execution generally. As one study found, of companies that most fully pursued a purpose, about half reported altering strategy on account of their purpose, with a third pointing to adjustments in their business models.[32] High purpose companies reported more success in a range of growth initiatives including mergers, entrance into new markets, launches of new products, and geographic expansion. We should note that investors increasingly recognize purpose's value in helping set a course for long-term success. One survey of investors found that almost all of them—93 percent—felt that companies needed purpose "to set a long-term business strategy that creates value."[33]

Purpose didn't simply serve Bühler as a "North Star." It enhanced strategy by helping the company channel innovation more powerfully.[34] Looking to the future, companies often struggle to select from among numerous potential business models or technologies they might pursue. By narrowing leaders' field of vision, purpose facilitates the allocation of innovation budgets. This focus in turn enables firms to think more broadly and holistically inside this narrower area, taking a systems approach to arrive at innovations they might never have thought to pursue. It's a paradox: by going narrower, you wind up going much *broader* and having more impact. In this respect, purpose helps companies to address complex or "wicked" problems that require collaborative solutions.[35]

In Bühler's case, "innovations for a better world" focused the company on developing solutions to make production more energy-efficient and sustainable as well as profitable. Within that focus, Bühler looked broadly across the food production value chain for new technologies and business models. Thus it was, for instance, that Bühler began researching the potential to harvest insects at scale to fill nutritional needs while minimizing the use of land, water, and other resources. Since insects feed on waste, their use as food for animals can support a circular and sustainable economy. In 2019, Bühler helped the insect protein manufacturer Protix open an industrial-scale plant dedicated to making protein for use in animal feed.[36] "The fact that we are now producing protein flour, lipids, and fertilizers based on insects, and doing so on an industrial scale, is something new," said the head of Bühler's insect technology business. "You can, perhaps, imagine the beginnings of modern mills 150 years ago occurring in a similar way."[37]

Examples abound of purpose-driven companies whose more focused pursuit of innovation led them to seek out opportunities in unforeseen spaces. Seeking to "enrich lives through technology," retailer Best Buy pioneered business models that used mobile technology to help seniors manage their health-care needs while living at home, acquiring the health technology firm GreatCall in 2018.[38] Inspired by its purpose of "advancing the world of health," the medical devices maker Becton Dickinson invested $20 million to develop a device called the Odon that could dramatically reduce deaths due to childbirth in developing countries.[39] As one study of twenty-eight high-growth companies found, purpose helped companies innovate and grow by "redefining the playing field," freeing them up, within the confines of the purpose, to "think about whole ecosystems, where connected interests and relationships among multiple stakeholders create more opportunities." It also allows them to respond to modify their value propositions in more cogent, focused, meaningful ways.[40]

A Tightly Bound Ecosystem
(Purpose Lever #2: Relational)

Stefan Scheiber, Bühler's CEO, remembers when it first occurred to him that his company should have a purpose. The year was 1986, and he was twenty-one years old, fresh out of college and working for Bühler in Nairobi, Kenya. Just being in Africa was mind-blowing after Scheiber's comfortable upbringing in Switzerland. One day, he visited a customer in a remote corner of the country. As he and his party drove through the savannah, they encountered a group of kids emerging from the bush. "I gave them a bit of food, all that I had left," Scheiber said, "and I remember this encounter so vividly. I said to myself, okay, here I am, a white man trying to contribute to somebody's life, purely coincidence. So, let's make that a mission. And that's where it started, thirty-three years ago."[41]

That moment continues to inform Scheiber's personal purpose as a leader, inspiring him to pursue social good in his decision-making and his relationships with stakeholders. It also energized him to help frame and execute an organizational purpose for Bühler. In 2010, Scheiber participated in the internal working group that devised the company's formal purpose statement, "Innovations for a better world." Afterward, under previous CEO Calvin Grieder, he helped drive the company's initial efforts to embed this purpose and stake out public sustainability goals. Upon becoming CEO himself in 2016, Scheiber deepened and evolved the company's commitment to its purpose, positioning Bühler as the leader of a social movement around sustainability. As he saw it, Bühler couldn't develop the pathbreaking new solutions required to reinvent the global food system by itself. The entire value chain was wasteful and inefficient, not just a single company, geography, or industry sector. If Bühler was to meet its newer, more ambitious goals and realize its purpose, it would have to collaborate with a range of partners, including industry leaders, academic experts, and start-ups, and even its competitors.

Scheiber and his team came up with the idea of developing a gathering that would serve as a "Davos" for the industry. In 2016, the company created a three-day conference and trade show called Networking Days that convened customers, suppliers, and start-ups to discuss sustainability. Leaders were unsure at first how the industry would react, or whether it would even show up. They needn't have worried. Networking Days generated an impressive turnout—the approximately 750 attendees hailed from companies that processed food for about half of the world's people.[42] Bühler unveiled some three dozen new products and services, but its presentation went beyond just a sales pitch. In his keynote address, Scheiber described the monumental challenges facing the food industry and made a moral call to participants. As Ian Roberts, Bühler's chief technology officer, reported, most customers loved what they heard. Customers had wanted someone to take leadership on these issues, and Bühler's central position in the food production value chain made it a logical choice. "Some customers wrote us letters," Roberts said, "CEOs of food companies, saying 'you have moved [our relationship] from transactional to transformational' . . . we have very strong buy-in from the customers."[43]

Bühler continued to wield its "convening power," as Scheiber put it, holding smaller Networking Days events over the next couple of years. In 2019, it held its second full-scale Networking Days event under the motto "creating tomorrow together." Showcasing an array of innovations by itself and other firms that incorporated artificial intelligence and digital technologies, the company called upon all of its industry partners to join together to find solutions at the individual, company, and industry levels. Once again, the response was positive. As an executive at the American food company Hershey's remarked, "There are so many industries represented at the event and so many different companies with different perspectives. It is very inspiring to hear all the ideas and to learn more about the solutions that we can jointly develop."[44]

As Bühler's experience suggests, purpose confers *relational benefits*, enabling close bonds to form between the organization and external stakeholders, including customers, suppliers, NGOs, and local communities. Purpose does this in two ways. First, it provides a logic for building an ecosystem of longer-term partnerships with suppliers, entrepreneurs, and others. Purpose lays the groundwork for these partnerships, whether in the form of formal events like Networking Days or more informal contacts between marketplace players that mature into formal business relationships. It facilitates collaboration by defining shared "superordinate" goals (larger goals that require collaboration to realize) that partners can agree on and behind which they can rally. It also allows companies to determine precisely which firms to count as partners. In the absence of purpose, it might be difficult to help potential partners understand precisely why and how they should collaborate with you.

But purpose does more than provide a grounding logic for partnership. It enhances the *quality* of relationships by fostering trust and comity. When firms pursue social purposes, they convey their intention to elevate business beyond a mere commercial logic in the pursuit of long-term goals. Potential partners feel confident that a purpose-driven company will take an elevated view of partnership in general, treating all stakeholders respectfully and helping to engineer solutions in which everyone wins. As some scholars have observed, companies that embrace social purpose are more inclined to operate in lockstep with their suppliers and other stakeholders, negotiating and collaborating closely to achieve the best results for everyone.[45] Purpose also fosters credibility by facilitating the hiring of people who care about social issues and are open to collaboration.[46]

The mere articulation of a purpose doesn't suffice to build trust. Companies must take action to live the purpose. To convey their purposes' authenticity, companies must "signal" it through actions such as adopting integrated reporting, aligning incentives with the purpose, or embracing external certifications such as becoming B Corporations.[47] Bühler took a wide variety of actions that signaled authenticity, including its ongoing investment in Innovation Days, its adoption of aggressive sustainability-related goals, and its adoption of integrated reporting.

A Stronger Reputation with Customers (Purpose Lever #3: Reputational)

If Mark Zuckerberg thought a superficial embrace of its purpose would allow Facebook to score points with its customers, he was mistaken. In 2020, an initiative called Stop Hate for Profit supported by prominent civil rights organizations urged businesses to suspend their advertising on Facebook for thirty days as a means of finally forcing change on the platform. Over one thousand brands quickly signed up, including large advertisers such as Coca-Cola, Ford, Microsoft, Starbucks, and Unilever.[48] Although the financial impact of the campaign appears to have been fairly insignificant,[49] Facebook's failure in recent years to live up to its purpose has caused a broader erosion of its brand reputation among customers (advertisers) and end users of the platform. According to one ranking of the 100 most visible US companies, Facebook's ranking dropped from #50 on the list to #94 between 2018 and 2019.[50]

In our age of social media, a superficial pursuit of purpose can sink a company's brand reputation. But the converse is also true: fidelity to purpose can deliver huge reputational gains. Customers today are more eager to make purchasing decisions based on a company's reason for being and the moral values it embodies than they were a decade or two ago. Younger customers in particular feel drawn to buy from companies that share their beliefs and that seek to do good in the world. Consumers also show more loyalty to companies they perceive as serving a social purpose. A wealth of opinion surveys and other research bears out these well-known points.[51]

Much of this research concerns consumer-facing brands, but as Bühler's experience suggests, purpose also enhances reputation with customers for business-to-business brands. Bühler features its purpose on its website, annual report, and in other corporate communications. More profoundly, the reason for being serves as the basis for forging new relationships and deepening existing ones with customers who possess similar intentions and values. Bühler's purpose creates a community based on shared values, as well as a positive dynamic between Bühler and its customers in which the idealism of each inspires the other to new heights while engaging commercially with one another. As Scheiber remarks, "What we do and what we talk about in terms of the Bühler story is a reflection of many of our customers' stories, and vice versa. What we do in many cases is a reflection of the values of these companies, which somehow get mirrored in what we do. And somehow it's like a wheel: they inspire us; we inspire them."

An example is the company's decades-long partnership with the Brazilian food manufacturer M. Dias Branco, one of that country's largest flour makers and a manufacturer of biscuits and other consumer foods. Like Bühler, M. Dias Branco seeks to benefit local communities and the environment in addition to performing well financially. "They have always done this on account of their own values," Scheiber notes, not because Bühler prodded them. Through strategic acquisitions, Bühler now manufactures equipment covering the entire biscuit-making process, enabling it to drive tremendous efficiencies and sustainability gains at M. Dias Branco. Bühler also conducts experiments at M. Dias Branco's plants to help it develop innovations that will drive more sustainable production.[52] Noting that M. Dias Branco and Bühler are both family-owned companies, Scheiber remarks that "We see our own values in that of this fantastic company, and I could tell you dozens and dozens of similar stories."

As leaders at another customer, the North American milling company Ardent Mills, told me, Bühler's purpose helped their two firms nurture a longstanding relationship built on trust. When I spoke with Dan Dye, Ardent Mills's CEO, he remarked that his firm sees tremendous value in working with Bühler based on the quality, service, and innovation it receives, but also on account of its "cultural fit" with Bühler. "I think what's emerged . . . has been leadership around this purpose part of things, around sustainability, making a difference in our planet, doing good with business as well as a passion for innovation. And I think those come together . . . we've aligned well."[53] Another customer, a pet food manufacturer, partnered with Bühler to reduce energy consumption significantly by innovating a key part of the production process. As an executive at this company told me, the company in decades past might have tried simply to sell a piece of equipment. More recently, Bühler's concern with energy efficiency led it to take a broader view of the overall efficiency of the customer's production line. Driven by its purpose, Bühler became a strategic manufacturing partner for the customer, helping it improve manifold aspects of production. The result was not merely a more sustainable production capacity, but a more cost-effective one as well.[54]

Just because purpose boosts reputation doesn't mean it attracts *all* customers. Pursuing a purpose will often make a company less appealing to some customers who don't share the company's values or who harbor concerns that they regard as competing. A few of Bühler's customers didn't like Networking Days, perceiving that the company had become overly moralistic and was "lecturing" them about how to run their businesses. These customers feared that by focusing on sustainability, Bühler risked becoming distracted from delivering business value.[55] More generally, customers in emerging markets tend to be more price-conscious, leading to skepticism about Bühler's emphasis on sustainability. To get them to the next level, Bühler has to deliver attractive economics on its machinery and service offerings.

In fact, this is Bühler's challenge with *all* customers, even those in developed markets. As an employee of one of their large customers told me, "No one is going to sit there and say, 'Oh, this is great. It's a perfectly sustainable company, so I'll just spend several percent more of my shareholders' money on that.' Sustainability alone is not enough."[56] Dipak Mane told me that for most customers, the decision to invest in a Bühler product or service is at its core a rational decision based on strict economics. To become a final contender in a bidding process, Bühler needed to deliver on "hard" dimensions such as quality, longevity, and price. But once Bühler was in the selection set, purpose helped to distinguish the company from competitors whose product or service specs seemed equally attractive. Purpose made a profound emotional impact on prospective customers, helping them justify their choice of Bühler.

Bühler's leaders acknowledge they haven't yet won over all of their customers to their purpose, although they hold out hope that they will make headway over time. They adamantly agree with the necessity of delivering solid economics in addition to social purpose. "What's the value?" Stefan Scheiber says. "If I cannot answer that even though it is sustainable, then it's not good. It's not a good product. Then our product management did not succeed. . . . So we always want to look at these sustainability aspects at the same time through a lens of economic sober assessment."[57] As Michael Beer and his colleagues at the Center for Higher Ambition Leadership have argued, purpose doesn't excuse a company from the need to excel in its conventional duties of delivering superior value to customers. On the contrary, leaders must nurture a "collective commitment to high performance" if their companies are to achieve the higher ambition expressed in their purpose.[58]

As with relational benefits, companies can't simply proclaim the purpose and assume that customers sharing similar values will line up to do business. As a Bühler customer told me, action speaks far louder than words: "When we talk of purpose, somebody who is simply making grand statements probably won't be credible. But somebody who sticks to values they have upheld over the course of a longstanding customer relationship likely will be. Often, this doesn't even need to be spelled out, or not in many words."[59] Likewise, when companies fail to back up purpose statements with actions, or when their actions seem to contradict their reason for being (as in Facebook's case), they can come across as inauthentic or, worse, as attempting to manipulate consumers by purpose-washing.[60]

Attract and Inspire Employees
(Purpose Lever #4: Motivational)

Facebook faces another challenge because of its superficial or convenient embrace of purpose: recruiting top talent and motivating them to perform. As media reports have noted, the company has taken a significant hit with prospective recruits on account of its recent bad press. "Surprisingly, a lot of my friends now are like, 'I don't really want to work for Facebook,'" one young computer science student remarked. Another said, "I just don't believe in the product, because like, Facebook, the baseline of everything they do is desire to show people more ads."[61] Facebook's struggles to deliver on its purpose also appear to be affecting morale and motivation within the company.[62] Leaders and employees have left the company in protest in recent years, with Facebook's cofounder Chris Hughes openly calling for a breakup of the company.[63]

Leaders and companies tend to understand purpose's usefulness in attracting and motivating employees, and also the negative effects that accrue when companies don't deliver on purpose. Still, given that most employees still report feeling disconnected from their company's purpose and disengaged in their jobs (a "crisis of purpose," as some experts have put it),[64] it's worth reviewing exactly why purpose matters so much when it comes to employees.

Companies can't motivate workers intrinsically—forging powerful, emotional connections between employees, their work, and their employers—merely by setting ambitious strategic goals.[65] They must also draw on our inherent human need to elevate ourselves by contributing to something bigger or transcendent. According to a psychological theory called the meaning maintenance model, we all seek meaning or purpose in our lives as human beings. We look to meaning to understand our relationship with others, we make meaning ourselves, and we quickly seek out new forms of meaning when our ways of seeing the world come under attack.[66]

Scholars have further observed that humans need purposeful work and the ability to integrate work with their personal reasons for being. Humans also must establish a *consistency* between how they think of themselves and what they do in their lives, including at work.[67] "Before one can bring the whole self to work," one scholar notes, "one has to first be aware of one's own values, beliefs and purpose in life. The sense of self also includes constantly striving to reach one's potential and believing in one's ability to reach that potential. And it includes an alignment between one's purpose in life and the purpose for the work."[68] As we'll also see, purpose yields a shared sense of identity, one rooted in belonging to a shared community. Identity in turn can fire up intrinsic motivation.[69]

A wealth of data suggests that employees today—particularly younger ones—seek more than a paycheck when they clock in to work. They aim for higher meaning, a chance to pursue work that connects with their own, personal reasons for being as well as their cherished values and beliefs.[70] Companies that pursue deep purpose deliver this meaning for employees, changing the nature of their relationship with their work and with the organization. Rather than a nexus of contracts, work becomes sacralized, transformed into a nexus of covenants.[71]

The business impacts of this shift are profound. Purpose becomes a major selling point for employer brands, as important as salary or even more so.[72] Further, purpose tends to motivate stronger teamwork and collaboration, serving as a "moral glue."[73] But as with customer reputation, the ability of companies to motivate employees via purpose depends on their ability to enact the purpose, not merely talk about it. One study found that employee engagement *falls* when companies talk about purpose. When they take meaningful actions, engagement soars.[74]

Leaders at deep purpose organizations affirmed to me the power of purpose to inspire not just engagement, but a desire on the part of employees to put out their best work. Since its founding in 2014, the consumer digital health provider Livongo has pursued the purpose of "empowering people with chronic conditions to live better and healthier lives." As leaders at the company told me, their intensive focus on purpose enabled them to compete with vastly larger Silicon Valley companies for the best digital talent. Once employees came on board, the vast majority were utterly transfixed and energized by the purpose, not least because they likely connected with the purpose on a personal level (in 2019, some two-thirds of employees had a family member with a chronic condition and a third had one themselves).

Excitement about the purpose in turn led to superior levels of commitment on the job. Founder Glen Tullman related that the work environment was intense, with many employees sacrificing other parts of their life to deliver on the purpose. "If you're growing a company and changing an industry and changing the world, [the relationship between various parts of your life] is not going to be perfectly balanced," he said.[75] Of course, not everyone sought that kind of work experience or bought into Livongo's purpose, but the impact of the purpose on employee dedication and drive was unmistakable.

Raghu Krishnamoorthy, former senior vice president of global human resources at General Electric, likened purpose to "a secret energy that makes you want to do, want to give."[76] A number of Bühler executives told me that the company's emphasis on purpose had galvanized employees, inspiring them to put out their best effort, to build long careers there, and to seek out the company as an employer. "People genuinely love to work in this company because they realize we care," Bühler Chief Human Resources Officer Irene Mark-Eisenring said. "We'll make something good. It's not quick money."[77] Although salary levels at the company are only about average for the industry, annual turnover at the company is extremely low, only about 6 percent annually—a direct benefit of the emphasis on purpose, leaders believe. The company has also moved up significantly in recent years in the "Best Places to Work" rankings.

Bühler doesn't sit back and wait for its purpose to positively impact employees and their motivation. The company *leans into* purpose, embedding it into its human resources communications and activities. To engage younger employees, Bühler created an initiative called Generation B that allows employees at all levels to have a voice in the company and pursue projects that excite them and serve the company's purpose. The company also gave local teams and businesses around the world guidance, tools, and encouragement to measure their own carbon footprints so that they could document it and join the effort to deliver on Bühler's purpose. Bühler incorporated discussion of the purpose into its recruiting efforts with internal candidates. And the company revamped its extensive training programs to make them more focused on the company's purpose and values.

Lessons for Leaders

Many leaders don't go deep on purpose because they don't see it as a pathway for generating new value. Despite all the talk about integrative solutions and shared value, they remain locked in a shareholder-value mindset and remain dubious that their firms can deliver value to diverse stakeholders *and* make money for shareholders. Leaders equate purpose with social responsibility and regard it as little more than a tax or a license to operate. But as we've seen in this chapter, purpose isn't just a new, more socially acceptable way of divvying up the existing economic value created by the firm. It's *generative*, increasing value for everyone, including external stakeholders and shareholders. The more you understand purpose's four main levers, and the more you actively work to pull those levers, the more effective and profitable your firm will be.

Although its pursuit of deep purpose remains ongoing, Bühler has seen impressive growth and performance gains. Between 2010 and 2019, revenues soared from 1.9 billion Swiss francs to 3.2 billion, while the size of the workforce has grown from 7,800 employees to 12,700.

Bühler's net profit rose from 158 million Swiss francs to 202 million, while its research and development spending increased from 79 million Swiss francs to 149 million.[78] The company has won a number of awards in recent years for excellence, including the Swiss Leading Employer Award (presented to the top 1 percent of companies in that country) and the Queen's Award for Enterprise. Scheiber is adamant that the diligent pursuit of purpose has propelled the company's performance. "If we compromised in certain areas [related to purpose] we might cut costs over the short term, but over the long term we'd lose our differentiation in the marketplace, and I'm sure that would translate into lower profits." In his mind, the company's impressive short-term results understate how well purpose has positioned Bühler for future success.

To deepen your engagement with purpose and your performance, look for underutilized levers and consider how you might pull them harder or more effectively. Most companies will find that they are concentrating more on some levers than on others, and that room exists for more purpose-related performance gains. The more levers you pull, the better, as they work synergistically with one another. A company enjoying a strong reputation with customers on account of its reason for being will find that this naturally yields a more motivated workforce, and vice versa, or that it enjoys enhanced relationships with its strategic partners and an enhanced ability to forge strategic partnerships. More broadly, performance gains realized through all of these levers make the tradeoffs described in chapter 2 easier to manage, creating more value for everyone and reducing the likelihood of win-lose situations. This in turn strengthens partnerships, improving performance even more.

Making the most of the purpose levers requires that you modify how you think about leadership, recognizing both your moral standing and your interdependence with stakeholders. The sociologist Émile Durkheim thought of religions as "moral communities" grounded in shared "beliefs and practices."[79] Similarly, your job isn't just to ensure that your company delivers economic value for customers and investors. As we saw in Bühler's case, that's just the price of entry. You must create a larger *moral community* around your purpose that encompasses the organization as well as its customers, employees, strategic partners, and other stakeholders. With social institutions such as religion, extended families, and civic organizations declining as sources of meaning and identity in people's lives, an opening has arisen for business to fill the gap.

The more you can bring stakeholders into a common field of meaning generated by the purpose, the more you'll enhance performance by elevating formerly transactional relationships into trusting partnerships. Purpose doesn't solve intractable problems you might have with stakeholders, but it does lay the groundwork for new, more productive conversations, and in turn, mutually beneficial value creation.

You can't forge a moral community unless you're willing to stake out a clear moral ground related to your company's purpose and also make difficult choices that confirm your moral stance. Deep purpose companies and leaders aren't out to offend anyone, but they do realize they can't create an integrated moral community and attain the full performance benefits from purpose if they don't articulate a clear vision of the world. Many customers, employees, and other stakeholders applauded Nike when it featured Colin Kaepernick in its advertising, but many didn't. By taking a stand, Nike brought its purpose to life, reinforcing its meaning and invigorating the moral community associated with the Nike brand while prompting a self-sorting on the part of customers. The long-term performance gains related to purpose likely outweighed any lost sales the company might have suffered over the short term.

To pull the four purpose levers most effectively, CEOs must become more comfortable speaking out as activists on key issues relating to the purpose. More executives have adopted activist postures in recent years, staking out positions on an array of social and environmental topics. Leaders must strengthen their activism so that it comes across as genuine and meaningful. It's one thing to write an occasional op-ed, stick a Black Lives Matter sticker onto your company website, or suspend advertising on Facebook for a few weeks. It's quite another to speak out consistently, to become personally involved in causes, and to put money behind cause-related initiatives.

Leaders have hesitated to deepen their activism, unsure when to take a stand and which causes to support. Here, purpose can serve as a valuable guardrail. Just as companies can use it to narrow the field for innovation so that they can go broader and deeper within that field, so leaders can use purpose to filter out the relatively few causes they *should* support deeply and broadly from the many other noble causes out there. Take powerful stands that matter given the purpose you and your company are pursuing. Be disciplined about avoiding the rest. That's how a strong moral community is built, one that yields profits while doing good.

Rather than turn up our noses at companies like Facebook, we must draw lessons from them. It's not too late to reimagine our roles in society. If you and your team have uncovered a purpose that resonates emotionally and feels noble and inspirational, why not live that purpose? Set aside those who assert myopically that deep purpose is impossibly idealistic. Stop making excuses. Stop embracing false promises. Step up and go deep. If you don't, you're doing a disservice not just to your organization and its stakeholders, but to your entire industry. Facebook's struggles with purpose damage the reputation and fortunes of the entire technology sector, while Bühler's pursuit of purpose lifts the entire food value chain. What legacy do *you* want to leave?

So far, we've focused on definitional issues that prevent leaders and companies from going deep with purpose. I've argued that leaders must change how they think about purpose and how they approach decision-making. But as my research found, deep purpose leaders are also much better at activating purpose within the organization than the vast majority of leaders. Going beyond standard change management techniques on which leaders typically rely, deep purpose leaders deploy more nuanced strategies that orient processes and structures far more fully around the reason for being.

The first of these strategies concerns the articulation of purpose itself. Where does purpose come from? How do organizations imbue it with a sense of the sacred? We can turn back here for inspiration to the concept of moral community. Religions often create meaning for believers by grounding their beliefs and practices in rich historical traditions.

Deep purpose leaders do something quite similar. If purpose enables an organization to look forward confidently toward a desired future, deep purpose leaders imbue the purpose with authenticity by grounding it in the company's past. They help organizations reconnect with that most fundamental, animating, and timeless part of themselves: their ineffable "soul."

CHAPTER 4

WHERE PURPOSE *REALLY* COMES FROM

Looking Backward While Looking Forward

In defining purpose, deep purpose leaders look to the past, immersing themselves in the intentions of founders and early employees, scouring for themes that capture the firm's ineffable soul or essence. This attention to history lends purpose an extra weightiness, resulting in deeper emotional connections and more commitment to the reason for being. Paradoxically, it also serves as a bridge to the future, helping leaders to chart a path ahead that is meaningful, coherent, and grounded.

Imagine, if you will, a bird that flies forward but, strangely enough, looks behind it as it soars through the air. Ghanaian folklore depicts precisely such a creature, a mythological bird called Sankofa. With the body directed forward but the bird's head looking in reverse, the Sankofa symbolizes how past wisdom can help us address future obstacles.[1]

The Sankofa captures something important about deep purpose organizations and the mindset of their leaders. They, too, look backward as they fly forward. To understand how, let's examine one of these companies and their pursuit of purpose.

We start with a scenario. Not long ago, you worked as a kindergarten teacher teaching kids to raise their hands and share toys with one another. Unsatisfied, you went on to earn a PhD in economics and to work in consulting for a few years. Then you joined a toy company as its head of strategy. It's now three years later, and the billionaire family that signs your paycheck has some big news for you. They're making you CEO and giving you full authority to run the company as you wish. You're all of thirty-five years old.

Pretty cool, right?

Not exactly. The company, which has been around for almost one hundred years and is one of the world's most recognizable brands, is on life support. Struggling over the past decade to adapt to kids' shifting preference for new kinds of video games and electronic toys, the company lost focus and pursued opportunities in too many directions, neglecting profitability. Margins tanked, and the company suffered its first-ever loss. The existing CEO, a scion of the owning family, stayed in his role, but he brought in a leader known for turning around troubled firms (Mr. Fix-it, the media called him) and installed him as COO, authorizing him to make big changes. Unfortunately, the measures this new COO took—layoffs, centralization of product design, streamlining of production, and development of direct retail sales to customers—weren't enough. The year before you became CEO, sales declined 26 percent and the company lost over $300 million.

In replacing Mr. Fix-it with you, the owning family made a radical move, staking their fortune on someone with more experience wiping running noses than leading large organizations. Outside observers couldn't believe it. Were these owners crazy? Maybe, but what's done is done, and now the fate of a venerable company and thousands of employees rests in *your* hands. If you can't reverse the company's fortunes, the family might have to sell it to one of its global competitors, and you might go back to consulting or even teaching kindergarten. What do you do?

Jørgen Vig Knudstorp faced this quandary upon becoming CEO of the Danish company LEGO in October 2004.[2] Initially hired as head of strategic development, he had spent the previous few years consulting on specific assignments around the company and, more recently, filling an informal role as chief operating officer. As he struggled to understand the extent of the company's challenges, he found that they were daunting. Between 1993 and 2002, LEGO had turned profits on paper but "had lost some $1.6 billion of economic value" (if you compared actual return on equity with low-risk government bonds).[3] When Knudstorp reported this to the board, offering dire forecasts for the future, he thought they'd fire him. But board members and owners had little choice but to face reality. "It's hard to describe how bad things were," one employee said. "There was this feeling that LEGO wouldn't exist in another year."[4] Instead of firing him or selling the business as Knudstorp recommended, the owners named him CEO and asked him to help craft a last-ditch plan to rescue the company.

Knudstorp first moved to stabilize the company, realizing that the firm would have to "fight for survival" before it could grow.[5] He recalls that "80% to 90% of [LEGO's] problems were the result of internal factors," not external ones. Excessive product complexity, exploding inventories and write-offs, runaway costs, inefficiencies, and a lack of accountability—all of these posed problems.[6] Knudstorp decided to radically simplify the product portfolio and streamline the organization. He took the company out of non-core ventures, outsourced its manufacturing processes (in the process laying off thousands of workers), and attended to relationships with its retailers. The point was to staunch the company's bleeding, and he succeeded. By the end of 2005, LEGO became profitable again thanks not only to cost savings but improved sales of the company's simplified products. Profits tripled year over year in 2006, and sales growth continued as well.[7]

With the economics of the business under control, Knudstorp set about making internal changes designed to position the company for sustainable growth. In 2006, he launched a strategic and organizational overhaul to improve consumer connections, increase innovation, overhaul manufacturing capabilities, and further embed simplicity into the company's products. But Knudstorp also looked deeper, seeking to reconnect the company with its abiding purpose, or as Knudstorp called it, its "spirit," "essence," or "identity." "If you want to transform—not just turn around—a company," Knudstorp observed, "you need to find the essence of the brand, your unique identity. . . . finding that identity is just like finding out your purpose in life—it's not up to you, not up to management, to decide that. It's not a rational choice. You don't 'decide' what your calling is. You *detect* it."[8]

Knudstorp and his team embarked on a journey of intellectual discovery to detect the company's animating spirit. "This was not something I cooked up with an advertising agency because it would make a great advertising campaign," Knudstorp says. "It was a two-year journey of asking questions—and since then it's been a constant, never-ending journey of continuing to ask, 'Is this really true? Do we really believe in that?'"[9] As Knudstorp told me, he spoke during this process not only with a large number of employees but with hundreds of adult fans of LEGO products, listening to "what they felt was essential about the brand and the product."[10] He also consulted with external experts such as Mitch Resnick, a professor at the MIT Media Lab whom Knudstorp regards as "a bit of an oracle of the theory of learning through play."[11]

Alongside these investigations, Knudstorp probed in a direction many innovative, forward-looking leaders might find surprising: he immersed himself in LEGO's history. He aspired to help LEGO fly forward by looking backward, very much like a Sankofa bird. As organizational scholars Majken Schultz and Tor Hernes documented, LEGO had looked toward its past before. In 2000, the firm had produced a pamphlet called "Remembering Why We Are Here" that reminded readers of the company's core focus on children's creativity and learning.[12] This time, leaders probed further back into LEGO's history to understand what the company was all about. Knudstorp recalls that he consulted primary sources and "spent a lot of time with the third-generation owner, who in some sense is the founder, because he was eleven years old when the LEGO brick was invented [in 1958]. I spent a lot of time trying to understand his journey." He also met with "people who have been in product design for more than thirty years" to understand the thinking at the root of LEGO's core products.[13]

Knudstorp realized that the company's reason for being encompassed far more than a particular toy such as the LEGO brick. It had to do with the foundational idea of providing "good play," a concept that was elaborated at LEGO's founding and that evolved into the notion of a "system of play" during the 1950s. When Ole Kirk Kristiansen started LEGO in 1932, selling wooden toys he had hand-crafted in his workshop, he sought to provide children with play opportunities that enabled creativity and growth (the name "LEGO" itself merged two Danish words that mean "play well").[14] As Knudstorp realized, LEGO's enduring purpose was to serve humanity by providing healthy opportunities for children to learn and grow and to engage both creatively and logically.[15] It was a purpose with which he personally identified. Not only had he grown up near LEGO's headquarters playing with LEGO toys; his parents' household merged logic and creativity thanks to his engineer father (who emphasized a methodical and rational approach to life) and schoolteacher mother (who instilled a free-ranging creativity).

Knudstorp's forays into the past cast additional light on the company's founding values and mission. As he was intrigued to discover, Kristiansen's son had hand-carved a mantra into a block of wood intended to guide the company and its work: "Only the best is good enough."[16] To Knudstorp, this phrase represented the spirit or mindset with which the company pursued its mission, borne out in what company old-timers remembered of the early ethos.[17] The phrase had fallen out of favor, construed to mean an unhelpful perfectionism and over-engineering of products. Knudstorp interpreted it differently. "I decided that, to me [this phrase] meant a constant striving, or continuous improvement, or that we should always be [providing] the best play material for children. We should always be the best supplier to the retailers we served. We should always be the best place to work. So for me it was an obsession with being a great company, as opposed to a good company."[18] Knudstorp also construed "only the best is good enough" more broadly as committing the company to be "good enough not just for children, but for all of our stakeholders."[19]

The motto was more than just a deft turn of phrase. Linked closely to the purpose, it was both the ideological core of the company and the foundation for its future prosperity. In short, it was key to developing LEGO's distinct, Sankofa way of flying. Convinced that the company had lost sight of its deeper mission, Knudstorp made "only the best is good enough" a central tenet in his leadership and proceeded to institutionalize it, making sure that everyone understood its meaning. He referenced "only the best is good enough" constantly in his speeches, emails, and other communications. He also displayed the motto in his office and even purchased the founder's house, transforming it into a museum of the company's history. "I went on a journey of actually telling people, 'Let's not forget about this spirit which came directly from 1932 and the founding of the company. Let's give it a modern-day interpretation.'"[20]

Paradoxically, this awareness of LEGO's past served to catapult the company more decisively toward its future. Rediscovering the company's historic purpose seemed to galvanize employees and other stakeholders, altering their impressions of the company and intensifying their commitment to its strategies. Understanding itself as an enterprise that delivered a unique and premium "system of play," LEGO went on over the next several years to pursue a wide-ranging growth strategy. It developed closer bonds with customers and retailers, enhanced its innovation around its core product, returned to in-house manufacturing (the company had formerly outsourced production), and managed complexity better, executing with newfound passion and determination. The results were astonishing. Over a four-year period starting in 2007 (and spanning the Great Recession of 2008), LEGO grew pretax profits by 400 percent, dwarfing rivals like Hasbro and Mattel.

Like Knudstorp, the deep purpose leaders I studied turned their companies into Sankofa-like enterprises that flew forward by looking backward. These leaders discovered or "detected" purpose statements for their organizations rather than dreaming them up themselves and imposing them arbitrarily.[21] They tended to look to the past when defining the company's existential intent. Instead of just running the typical interviews, focus groups, or town hall meetings, deep purpose leaders immersed themselves in the intentions of founders and early employees, scouring for themes that captured the firm's ineffable soul or essence. This attention to history lent the purpose an extra weightiness and even sacredness. The organization forged a deeper emotional connection between stakeholders and the enterprise, binding everyone together into a moral community that was defined, cohesive, and inspired.[22] In this way, it developed an ability to move ever more forcefully toward a desirable future.

The Business Enterprise as Moral Community

We don't hear the term "moral community" a lot in the business world, so it's worth lingering over it for a moment. The sociologist Émile Durkheim used the term to describe small, premodern, nonurban communities whose inhabitants knew one another personally and also shared a common moral sensibility.[23] In modern times, we can spot moral communities of our own if we know how to look for them. They're small faith communities whose members stick together, support one another, and fervently share the same basic beliefs. They're groups of local political activists who share common values, meet frequently, and work together to spread their views among disbelieving others. They're groups of health-care workers who "are bound to each other through common ethical commitments" and who work through ethical quandaries with one another.[24]

People in moral communities experience a sense of camaraderie and belonging thanks to their shared moral perspective on the world; they possess a "unified system of beliefs and practices relative to sacred things."[25] They also "demonstrate supportive relationships in pursuit of a common moral goal."[26] And they come to possess a shared sense of *commitment* not just to the group and its larger cause, but to its efforts to tackle specific external challenges that might arise.[27] To participants in a moral community, the group's ongoing struggles take on a personal feel rather than being something abstract or distanced. As they see it, the group's success or failure is theirs as well.

The personal nature of these attachments doesn't mean that moral communities are always small or intimate. We can observe something akin to moral communities in larger, more anonymous settings, including among premodern ethnic groups. The ancient Hebrews believed that God chose them from among the other nations, freed them from slavery in Egypt, and settled them in the promised land of Canaan.[28] "To be chosen is to be placed under moral obligations," wrote the late Anthony D. Smith, a leading scholar of nationalism. "One is chosen on condition that one observes certain moral, ritual, and legal codes, and only for as long as one continues to do so. The privilege of election is accorded only to those who are sanctified, whose life-style is an expression of sacred values."[29]

Modern nations also create identities and moral communities via mythmaking, defining sacred purposes or missions for themselves related to their identities. "Nationalism is the secular, modern equivalent of the pre-modern, sacred myth of ethnic election," Smith wrote. "Nationalism, as an ideological movement that seeks autonomy, unity, and identity for a population deemed to be a nation, draws much of its passion, conviction, and intensity from the belief in a national mission and destiny; and this belief in turn owes much to a powerful religious myth of ethnic election."[30] Invented traditions such as festivals, ceremonies, pastimes, folksongs, anthems, and so on root national communities in the past, giving flesh and blood to the group identity.[31]

Most companies and business leaders ignore the past, preferring to focus on the future. Some worry the past will cast a shadow over the organization, holding it back from embracing change and moving boldly toward its future. It's one thing for a nation or ethnic group to build solidarity through a shared history, quite another for an organization struggling to survive in a dynamic and competitive landscape. But some leaders, spotting hidden benefits in the organization's history, turn to mythmaking and imagined traditions just as nations do to establish identities and corresponding moral communities.[32] Consider the Carlsberg Group brewing company.[33] Looking to thrive in a competitive market flooded with craft beers, Carlsberg during the late 1990s rediscovered a Latin phrase adopted by an early patriarch of the company: *semper ardens* [always burning]. The patriarch had carved this phrase in stone for use as a corporate motto, and now a team within the company took the phrase as the name of a new line of handcrafted, microbrewed beers.

Immersing themselves in the company's historical archives, employees learned more about the company's founder, his beer recipes, and even the art created about him by contemporaries. They used this material to create and market the new products, producing specially designed bottles, labels, and recipes. For team members, resurrecting the semper ardens motto in product form meant reconnecting the company with a founding story and transcendent values. As one explained, "Passion and pride and commitment, those things are what Semper Ardens told me. And also the heritage, so what the old brewer intended to do with this company. So for me there was also an obligation to be aligned to the bigger picture of what he wanted to do with this company [which] is also in the name of Semper Ardens."[34]

About a decade later, the company incorporated semper ardens into a document spelling out its corporate identity as an enterprise united by a common spirit of determination and daring: "Founded on the motto, Semper Ardens—Always Burning—we never settle but always thirst for the better. We are stronger together because we share best practices, ideas, and successes. We brand as many, but stand as one. With the courage to dare, to try, to take risks, we constantly raise the bar. We don't stop at brewing great beer. We brew a greater future—for our consumers and customers, our communities, and our people."[35] Although this statement doesn't define a clear purpose per se, the last line comes close, articulating an intention as well as a social logic. Implicit in that social logic are moral values—a sense of what a "greater future" is—as well as a commitment to realizing them. Some employees in fact perceived semper ardens as a purpose. As one remarked, "You need to have a purpose, a higher purpose. And I think the [identity document] is the higher purpose that was formulated and now starting to be used."[36]

Moral communities typically share a sense of collective identity that forms not just around values, but a common purpose.[37] In business contexts, we can think of identity as those elements of an organization that seem to persist over time and render it distinct.[38] With this definition in mind, it's hard to think about purpose and identity in isolation from each other. Identity answers the existential question, *"Who are we as an organization?"* while purpose answers the question, *"Why is our organization here?"* When your company ponders who it is, the conversation naturally winds its way toward the future and a values-laden mission or intention that binds everyone together. Likewise, members of an organization who deeply ponder its purpose, posing and answering the question, "Why are we here?" will often feel a sense of uniqueness and perceive themselves as part of something larger, enduring, and distinct.

It might seem a stretch to describe a purpose-driven beer company as a moral community akin to a church, temple, or synagogue, but in a broad sociological sense it can be, or at least come close. By delving into its past, the Carlsberg Group unearthed a set of moral values and a related purpose that had been lost in time and that could stand as sacred or elevated in the minds of employees and other stakeholders. This purpose and these values formed the basis for an identity to which employees and other stakeholders could subscribe, and that could inspire action on the community's behalf. Carlsberg certainly wasn't a "church" that gave existential clarity, meaning, focus, and purpose to every last part of employees' lives. But thanks to semper ardens, it could function as a place where employees could transcend the mundane through daily work and do it in communion with others.

Finding the Sacred in the Past

The sort of mythmaking Carlsberg attempted tends to elevate and sacralize companies in the minds of stakeholders by imbuing them with "authenticity"—a sense that they remain true to early craftsmanship standards and the moral values of a company's founders.[39] Deep purpose leaders understand the sacredness that derives from authenticity, and they apply it specifically to the reason for being. Like LEGO's Jørgen Vig Knudstorp, these leaders arrive at authenticity by sifting through the company's history, researching foundational truths about the company's early mission, vision, and moral values, and chronicling the heroic measures leaders took at peak moments to overcome adversity and realize their vision. If possible, deep purpose leaders involve retired founders in these efforts (as Microsoft CEO Satya Nadella did, speaking with Bill Gates). Once they've distilled a purpose rooted in the past, deep purpose leaders not only promote the purpose internally; they take pains to educate the company about its past, instilling reverence for the authentic moral values, practices, and ambitions of founders and early employees. They make use of authentic physical artifacts and corporate museums, like Knudstorp did at LEGO, and they personally promote a sense of the company's past in their communications.

Such efforts tend to yield strong emotional ties. At Carlsberg, one HR leader suggested the power of the motto to elevate people and connect them with one another. "I just think that they were reminded about what they're actually a part of. They're part of something really big. So I think that was the feeling. You said 'Wow!'" At an extreme, an authentic, historically grounded purpose transforms the employee-firm relationship. Instead of regarding this relationship as transactional, impersonal, and "flat," employees perceive it as meaningful and emotional. We've seen that organizational scholars have long evoked the potential of companies to bring people together on the basis of emotional ties rather than merely economic ones. Others have verged beyond an economic view of "relational contracts" by speaking of "psychological contracts" existing between companies and employees[40] and by studying how employees inject personal meaning into their work via "job crafting."[41]

The ability of the firm to feel personal to employees is especially relevant here. By arousing emotion, an "authentic," historically rooted purpose encourages personal affinities within the organization to take root and blossom. As such, purpose potentially transforms companies from impersonal groups into something approaching small, intimate communities. In one of his interviews with me, Knudstorp attested that LEGO's purpose "had and continues to have a huge impact" inside the company, serving as a "game changer" in terms of employee engagement and "the mood of the organization." The historical connection to the founder and the notion of "only the best is good enough" instilled "a completely different level of camaraderie and sense of belonging and commitment and passion. . . . I know of many people who feel a very strong connection to the brand and the company and its authenticity."[42] Employee engagement scores that ran considerably higher than corporate benchmarks evoke the level of excitement that exists among the workforce, at least in part due to the company's purpose and values.[43]

We'll have occasion in chapter 6 to explore more fully how deep purpose helps create more intimate, personal bonds. For now, we should note that these bonds don't come without cost. Knudstorp describes how LEGO employees expect him and other leaders to live up to the values embodied in the history. The company now means so much to employees—they're so invested in its purpose—that they feel protective of it, and they let leaders know. "There's certain things you can do and can't do" as a leader, Knudstorp says. "And your actions on difficult decisions . . . people look for confirmation or the opposite in those decisions and can quickly grow cynical that you're living up to it." Employees also don't hesitate to hold leaders to account. "They will say 'I think we should have behaved differently' or 'I think that communications lacked authenticity.'"[44] Linked to the distant past, purpose becomes serious business for stakeholders. Leaders must attend closely to their job as stewards of the moral community and its values.

Looking Backward While Looking Forward

As we've seen, deep purpose leaders fly forward but look backward. They don't interpret their companies' pasts in purely nostalgic ways, seeing the founders or early employees as uniformly wise and trying to replicate their thinking and practices. Rather, they recognize that in distilling a reason for being they must connect with the past and also break with it. We can discern *three key strategies* deep purpose leaders follow to root the purpose in the past without becoming imprisoned by it:

STRATEGY #1: FOCUS EXPLICITLY ON THE NOSTALGIA-POSTALGIA TENSION

The organizational scholar Sierk Ybema distinguishes between two different but familiar kinds of stories that leaders tell about the organization's relationship with the past. In the *nostalgic view*, the past was a "golden age" from which the company has unfortunately strayed. Leaders and employees often take such a view to resist change and critique present-day ideas and practices. A second kind of narrative, what Ybema calls *postalgic*, flips this logic somewhat, presenting the past as "bad" and the future as "good." Progressive leaders often emphasize the limitations or deficiencies of the enterprise up to the present moment, evoking the company's potential decline because of its rootedness in the past, but also the prospect of a glorious future if the enterprise can break with the past and make change real. As they suggest, the company can write its own epic tale of rescue and redemption if it chooses to shake off the shackles of tradition and forge a bold path forward.[45]

Studying deliberations inside a Dutch newspaper struggling with digital disruption, Ybema found staff members spinning both nostalgic and postalgic narratives as they debated the newspaper's identity, its current prospects, and its future direction. Similarly, I found deep purpose leaders incorporating elements of both narratives when deriving a reason for being. They portrayed themselves as bridging or balancing between the past and the future. In their hands, the past inspired a purpose that would engender a future both consistent with and different from its heritage.

As Microsoft's Satya Nadella recalls in his book *Hit Refresh*, the company explored its purpose following his appointment as CEO in 2014 as part of an effort not simply to resurrect a fabled past (nostalgia) or break with an inglorious one (postalgia), but to do both in the course of regenerating the enterprise. The very subtitle of Nadella's book in which he recounted his efforts to transform Microsoft—*The Quest to Rediscover Microsoft's Soul and Imagine a Better Future for Everyone*—captures both sides of the nostalgia/postalgia equation. As Nadella explains, he was on a quest to take Microsoft into a future of "mobile-first and cloud-first." But executing well on this would require that Microsoft bring out its strategy from within, rediscovering its founding mission as a company that democratized and personalized technology for the masses.[46] The company sought not merely to connect with a "soul" that it had lost over time, but also to look ahead to a future that would be different from and "better" than what had come before.

Kathleen Hogan, Microsoft's chief people officer, recalls that throughout the nine-month process of defining the purpose Nadella sought to balance a progressive mindset with veneration of Microsoft's heritage. He wanted "to honor our past while we charted our future."[47] Hogan counts this posture toward the past and the future as among the most important of the lessons she gleaned from this process. She notes that a key factor was Nadella himself. Whereas other executives leading a turnaround might have felt tempted to frame past norms and decisions as uniformly "bad" and their own thinking as smart and correct by comparison, Nadella was capable of taking a more nuanced view. He could see both the good and the bad in the past, and in turn could chart a purpose and a broader path forward that both connected with and broke with Microsoft's legacy.

STRATEGY #2: FOSTER CRITICAL DIALOGUE ABOUT THE PAST

During the final years of his life, Steve Jobs became concerned with how to perpetuate his legacy and knowledge base inside the company. Interestingly, he didn't place much emphasis on defining a formal company purpose. Although he cared deeply that employees *lived* the company's mission (he would often challenge leaders by asking them, "Is this what we're put on this planet to do?"), the exercise of creating and communicating a formal mission or purpose statement held little interest for him. Jobs felt that if employees bothered to write down such a statement, the ideas it contained would lose their power. Employees would slap the statement up on the wall and forget all about it. The closest Apple seems to have come to publicly disseminating a mission statement during these years was Chief Operating Officer Tim Cook's apparently spontaneous disclosure of some basic principles informing Apple's operations during a 2009 investor call. (These included the line: "We believe that we are on the face of the earth to make great products and that's not changing."[48]) Jobs reportedly frowned on Cook's disclosure, fearing that he'd made public the "secret sauce" behind the company's success.

But Jobs had other ideas about how to perpetuate his legacy and a moral community by fostering a shared understanding of the firm's reason for being (what he'd described years earlier as honoring "people with passion" and helping them "change the world for the better"[49]). In 2008, a few years before he succumbed to pancreatic cancer, he started

Apple University, an internal unit charged with developing course materials and running training programs that exposed employees to the company's heritage. As one former employee remarked, "Steve was looking to his legacy. The idea was to take what is unique about Apple and create a forum that can impart that DNA to future generations of Apple employees. No other company has a university charged with probing so deeply into the roots of what makes the company so successful."[50]

And yet, Jobs sought to design this forum in ways that would prevent people from reverting to veneration of "the good old days." Having served on Disney's board, Jobs was struck by how often leaders asked, "What would Walt have done?" To his mind, leaders deferred too often to the founder, a stance that impeded innovation. He coached his own successor, Tim Cook, to chart his own path rather than to constantly be asking what he, Jobs, would have done.[51] And he wanted other employees at Apple to take a more critical and balanced approach as well.

Rather than pounding a crisply defined purpose into employees' heads directly, or venerating every last profound utterance of Jobs, Apple University took a more indirect approach. As one observer put it, the company sought to convey not just a purpose but a "unique culture where people there believe they're making the best products that change people's lives."[52] To that end, Apple University asked employees to critically analyze a series of past actions and decisions undertaken by company leaders.[53] Interpreting historical case studies, employees could deconstruct and contextualize Jobs's decisions, considering how their underlying logic might or might not apply to situations they currently face.

Jobs wanted employees to perpetuate Apple's purpose and core principles such as radical simplicity or thinking differently by immersing themselves in past decisions and their rationales. If they chose to deviate from any of those principles, they would at least understand the tradeoffs they were making. By fostering critical engagement with history, employees could stake out an intellectual space outside the past even as they exposed themselves to the company's unique, purpose-infused culture. Perhaps from all this they would distill the company's purpose and core values for themselves.

STRATEGY #3: STRESS-TEST THE PURPOSE

In 1943, Robert Wood "General" Johnson, son of the founder of Johnson & Johnson, forged a corporate credo to guide the company. The document, which has since become one of the most famous corporate expressions of purpose,[54] doesn't lay out a single, overarching purpose or intention as described in chapter 1. Instead, it outlines the company's obligations to its respective stakeholders.[55] As the credo makes clear, the company sees itself as responsible primarily to its customers: "We believe our first responsibility is to the patients, doctors and nurses, to mothers and fathers and all others who use our products and services." Last on the list are shareholders, to whom the company declares an intention to provide a "fair return."[56] In addition to the credo, the company has more recently adopted a formal purpose statement, described as follows by current CEO, Alex Gorsky: "We blend heart, science and ingenuity to change the trajectory of health for humanity."[57]

To this day, Robert Wood Johnson's credo remains sacred at Johnson & Johnson. It is, for example, carved into a massive, six-ton block of quartz and limestone and displayed at the company's New Jersey corporate headquarters.[58] But the credo has hardly gone unchallenged. In 1975, incoming CEO James Burke wanted to know whether the credo still meant something, or whether the company should jettison it. He convened formal meetings inside the company in which leaders debated the credo's value and in particular whether they could run businesses that served all the stakeholders provided for in the credo. Noting that the credo then hung on the walls at between 150 and 200 company facilities, Burke remarked, "I think if it's there as an act of pretention it's not only valueless but has a negative effect" and should be discarded.[59]

As a result of Burke's "credo challenge," the company committed itself more deeply to its credo, although it did make some minor modifications to the document (the company would make further tweaks in 1979 and 1987 to reflect concern about the environment and broader social changes related to gender and families).[60] The act of testing the credo clarified its relevance for leaders and gave them a sense of ownership over it. The credo was no longer some dusty document they had to uphold because "this is how we've always done it." Testing the credo also seems to have inculcated an ethic of self-critique that fostered striving and commitment to the credo. As one of Burke's successors as CEO put it, "It's about constantly asking ourselves if we're living up to our values and thinking of ways to build for the future."[61]

The wisdom of recommitting to the credo under Burke became apparent less than a decade later when the company suffered a potentially devastating crisis. In 1982, someone in the Chicago area laced Tylenol capsules manufactured by Johnson & Johnson with cyanide and left them on the shelves of several local retailers. Seven people died and a nationwide scandal ensued. Guided by the credo, Johnson & Johnson under Burke took quick action. Concerned first and foremost to protect customers' well-being, as the credo requires, they immediately warned consumers across the country to stop consuming Tylenol. A recall of Tylenol from Chicago-area stores led to the discovery of two more bottles. Although the chances of finding more contaminated product elsewhere in the country was slim, the company spent in excess of $100 million formally recalling its product nationwide as a precaution.[62] The company also communicated extensively and transparently throughout the crisis, inspired again by the credo. Within six months, the company introduced new packaging that made tampering more difficult. Today, scholars regard the company's response as "the most exemplary case ever known in the history of crisis communications."[63]

More recently, questioning and recommitting to the credo helped the company recover after losing its way. During the 2000s, Johnson & Johnson experienced quality issues with a number of its popular consumer products, including Children's Tylenol, Motrin, and Benadryl. Rather than act swiftly as it had under Burke, the company apparently waited almost two years to recall products after first receiving quality complaints.[64] Among other issues, the company allegedly tried to cover up product lapses by hiring people to go to retail stores and covertly buy up questionable packages of Motrin.[65] A congressional committee in 2010 hauled in a senior Johnson & Johnson executive for questioning. At a second hearing months later, then-CEO William Weldon appeared before a congressional panel and apologized for the company's delays in recalls, accepting "full accountability" and claiming that Johnson & Johnson had "learned a very important lesson."[66]

Following these scandals, the company's stock performance lagged and commentators questioned whether the credo still meant anything. Some observers blamed Weldon for taking his eye off the credo and running the business instead with an eye toward profit above all else. "There was a time when people really believed in [the credo] and took great pride in it," this observer argued. "But those days are long gone." Instead, "the major function of the credo is similar to mommy's skirt—which you hid behind—or like wrapping yourself in the American flag. It is to distract people from what is going on."[67]

Following Weldon's retirement in 2012, it fell to incoming CEO Alex Gorsky to turn around Johnson & Johnson. One of his early moves was to refocus the company on the credo—not by venerating or celebrating it, but by returning to Burke's practice of critically evaluating it and questioning its continued relevance. In 2013, to commemorate the company's seventieth anniversary, Gorsky had the boards of Johnson & Johnson's 250 constituent businesses conduct a "credo challenge session" to critically examine the credo line by line.[68] In 2017, the company held focus groups with over two thousand employees to discuss the credo and solicit further suggestions for refining it. After this latter round of discussion, Gorsky and his team made updates to the document, inserting language to reflect a new emphasis on patients, highlight the importance of inclusion and diversity at the company, address the workforce's changing needs, and express an intention to help improve "the health of humanity."[69]

As Johnson & Johnson's history suggests, companies will face dilemmas and crises that call their purpose into question. Indeed, J&J's recent involvement in the opioid crisis represents a new test of the company's purpose. Given these challenges, a purpose statement must be, as Gorsky says of the credo, "a living and breathing document," one that is "both timely and timeless."[70] In this regard, a purpose statement can serve as a bridge between the past and the future, one that allows the company to both honor the past (nostalgia) and chart new paths (postalgia). As Gorsky put it in the company's annual report: "Our Credo is the moral compass that we use to guide our business decisions, and it's the blueprint that outlines how we operate and care for the world. Our Credo is the 'red thread' that connects our rich heritage, thriving workplace culture, and the corporate DNA that continues to shape our present and future."[71]

Lessons for Leaders

When established companies find themselves on the brink of failure, they often respond by bringing in outsiders as CEOs, leaving these "turnaround artists" to implement new frameworks or approaches with little concern for the company's rich past. Such radical, tough-love approaches seem smart at the time, much-needed shocks to the system. But they often fail, as they did in the case of LEGO prior to Knudstorp. This chapter has examined another, more effective pathway toward reinvigorating a troubled company: recommitting it to a purpose rooted in the past. Deep purpose leaders like Knudstorp and Nadella turn around companies by identifying a reason for being that seems timeless, transcendent, and sacred. Treating the past as a bridge to the future, they recover the company's early energy or "soul," transforming the enterprise into a moral community dedicated to a unique mission that they aspire one day to achieve. These leaders create deep, emotional, and personal connections while also providing the organization with a guidepost for principled innovation and change, as well as the motivation to leap toward the future. In effect, they teach their organizations to fly in the unique and powerful way of the Sankofa bird.

Does your company's purpose derive either wholly or partially from its past? Have you spent time probing into the company's early history and the beliefs, principles, and spirit of its founders? Although it might seem counterintuitive and even a bit arduous, journeying back into the past might be precisely what your company needs to deepen its understanding and commitment to an existing purpose or, alternately, to develop an entirely new, more meaningful, and more authentic one. In good times, such a journey can push organizations onward to even higher levels of innovation and performance. As was true of Johnson &

Johnson during the 1970s, it can improve resilience and readiness for a future crisis. If your company is already struggling, like LEGO during the early 2000s, you can follow Jørgen Vig Knudstorp's lead and use thoughtful exploration of the past to drive a full-scale and long-term regeneration of the company from within.

In excavating the past, you shouldn't simply report historical facts as you found them, nor should you allow the past to subsume you. Rather, you should engage the way Knudstorp did: as an active interpreter of the past, with one eye always fixed on the future. You want to discover elements of the early business that, articulated in the form of a purpose statement, might continue to inspire, animate, and guide people toward the future, giving the organization meaning and a sense of having been chosen for an important mission. At the same time, it's in your interest to look at past failures squarely in the face. As corporate historian Line Højgaard, who oversees LEGO's historical museum, emphasizes, the company tells inspiring stories that illustrate the motto "only the best is good enough," but it also happily talks about past mistakes.[72] Such honesty doesn't erode LEGO's image. On the contrary, it humanizes the organization and its founders while rendering the company's overall engagement with its past more credible. Visitors to LEGO's museum forge a more personal and meaningful connection with the company's founders and early employees by seeing them as imperfect people who still managed to triumph over adversity.

LEGO's museum alerts us to another facet of the deep purpose company's engagement with history: its nature as an ongoing, never-ending process. Well over a decade after Knudstorp began exploring LEGO's history, the company's museum continues to play an important role, educating consumers about the company's enduring spirit and serving as an important touchpoint for onboarding new employees. The company's effort to define its purpose continues as well. In 2019, LEGO further elaborated its reason for being and sharpened its future orientation by articulating a "vision" alongside its stated mission ("inspire and develop the builders of tomorrow") and its "spirit" ("Only the best is good enough"). According to this vision, the company now sought to serve as "a global force for establishing and innovating learning-through-play."[73]

Rooted in an awareness of LEGO's past, the vision has spurred the company to emphasize its broader social contribution across all of its businesses by advocating publicly for learning-through-play.[74]

LEGO continues to reap the benefits of its exploration of its purpose. Its revenues grew dramatically over the past decade, reaching 5.16 billion euros in 2019, up from 2.2 billion in 2010 (the company saw a revenue dip in 2017 but has since recovered).[75] Net profits more than doubled,[76] and the company was recognized as one of the world's most reputable brands, topping one ranking four years in a row and beating companies like Disney, Rolex, and Ferrari.[77] Although Knudstorp stepped down as CEO in 2017 to become chairman, the company under his successor, Niels B. Christiansen, continues to infuse its decision-making with a strong sense of purpose.

Once leaders define a purpose, conventional wisdom holds they must embed that reason for being into the organization, in large part by communicating it well. And yet, such communication all too often falls flat, striking internal and external audiences as forced, inauthentic, and forgettable—yet another "feel good" but ultimately meaningless directive from the executive suite. How can we convey purpose to organizations in ways that truly connect, reaffirming that powerful sense of the sacred and sustaining a cohesive moral community? The key is for leaders to make fuller use of that most ancient and enduring communication technique: storytelling.

CHAPTER 5

ARE YOU A POET, OR JUST A PLUMBER?

In communicating the purpose, deep purpose leaders go beyond slogans and rallying cries, telling a grand, foundational story about the company that lends depth, meaning, and even poetry to the enterprise. In conveying this story, they discuss purpose in personal terms, establish a sense of shared ownership, and evoke urgency to embrace purpose in the present. Through their storytelling, they convene diverse stakeholders as a moral community, allowing intense bonds between them and the company to form.

Imagine you're a senior leader at a global health-care company. You and two hundred of your peers from around the world have gathered at a luxurious tropical resort for your company's annual leadership summit. Your agenda: to eat and drink too much, network, celebrate the past year's solid performance, and preview the coming year's strategy.

At the opening session, held with great fanfare in the resort's grand ballroom, your CEO takes the stage to deliver the keynote address, their face illuminated by a spotlight. They make a few jokes, welcome everyone, and announce how proud they are of the prior year's results and how excited they are about the strategy they're about to unveil. "But before we begin," they say, their face growing somber, "let's remind ourselves of why we show up for work each day. Let's shine the spotlight on the people who really matter most: our customers."

A hush falls over the room and a massive projection screen behind them illuminates. You watch a brief video about "Sam," an attorney in his early thirties. As a narrator reveals, Sam visited his doctor a few years earlier complaining of a number of concerning symptoms. A vegetarian and self-described "fitness nut" training for his fifth marathon, Sam had been feeling sluggish and unwell for most of the past year. At first, he figured he was just rundown from his stressful job and the strain of helping to care for his rambunctious two-year-old. He didn't have time to go to the doctor and couldn't imagine anything could be seriously wrong.

Months passed, and his sluggishness persisted, often accompanied by nausea and constipation. Sam also found he was getting sick more often. Twice or more a month, he stayed home from work with chills and a low-grade fever. He still neglected to visit the doctor, reasoning he'd just had a spate of bad luck. He would "tough it out" as he always did. Over the past month, though, his body seemed to be crashing. He could barely run a few miles without having to stop and take a breath. Normally he could make do on seven hours of sleep, but now he woke up exhausted and lethargic after nine hours.

His doctor advised that Sam undergo a series of tests to "see what we're dealing with." Sam agreed, registering the concerned look on his doctor's face. The next day, his doctor's assistant called and asked Sam to come back in right away. It was bad news: Sam had a rare form of cancer. A biopsy later that week confirmed that the cancer was quite advanced. Sam had two years to live, possibly less.

Sam and his wife, who was seven months pregnant, were devastated. Sam took time off from work and began a series of standard treatments, desperate to beat the odds. Unfortunately, the treatments didn't work. Six months later, Sam was feeling worse than ever, sleeping all the time and feeling pain throughout his body. Simply walking down stairs exhausted him. Tests revealed that his cancer hadn't only worsened; it had spread much more quickly than his doctors expected. Sam seemed unlikely to survive the year.

Through his online research, Sam learned of an innovative new treatment engineered by your health-care company and currently in phase 2 clinical trials. With his doctor's encouragement, Sam relocated temporarily across the country and enrolled in the trials. For three months, he received the treatment. Almost immediately, he found that he was feeling better. A month into the treatment, he could walk around the block. Three months into it, he was well enough to exercise. Scans showed that his cancer was almost gone. At the six-month mark, his cancer was undetectable. "I can't tell you how grateful I am," Sam says on camera. "I was once so sick, but now I have my life back." The video ends with images of Sam in his living room playing with his toddler as his thankful wife looks on.

"And now," your CEO says, "meet Sam." A tanned and vigorous young man takes the stage, carrying a toddler in his arms. His wife walks behind him, holding their preschooler by the hand. The whole room rises to its feet and applauds. Cheers and whoops fill the air. Glancing around, you see usually hardened, old guard leaders wiping tears from their eyes. You feel the emotion, too. Your boss is challenging, your organization isn't perfect, and you spend more time away from your own family than you'd like. But *this* is why you show up for work each day. This is why your company exists. To help people like Sam.

If you've worked at a large organization, you've probably encountered some version of a "Sam" story. I've heard such stories dozens of times at formal corporate gatherings, and not just at health-care firms. A software company might bring in the CEO of a large customer and have them extoll the company's products and services and the critical difference they make. Hospitality and other service firms recount how dedicated employees went to extraordinary lengths to satisfy customer needs and win their undying loyalty. Manufacturing conglomerates tell stories about cutting-edge technologies created by engineers and the impact they have on their industrial customers and even on entire economies. Companies also frequently portray the social good employees do as part of CSR initiatives—how they give of themselves to help the underprivileged, respond to crises, help younger generations, and make the world a better place.

Companies tell such stories for a reason: because they motivate employees and other stakeholders, stoking passion and enthusiasm. We all want to feel we're doing good for the world, not just logging more hours, booking more revenue, or generating more profit. Inspiring stories about customers and employees soften and humanize organizations, conveying that they serve some purpose that transcends financial performance. And these stories don't simply describe the organization's purpose—they *dramatize* it. Compelling storytelling—defined in the broadest sense as the depiction of one or more events transpiring over time—helps us *feel* the purpose by letting us watch it come to life before our eyes.[1]

As engaging as stories about employees and customers are, they usually don't convey a sense of *deep* purpose, an existential intent that informs all that an organization does. It's wonderful as a health-care executive to see your product helping people like Sam. But watching a video like this, you might find yourself struggling to understand the organization's existential intent.[2] Does your company exist to eradicate all disease? To help human beings live longer? To keep people well in addition to helping them when they're sick? What kind of far-reaching change does your company seek to bring into the world, and what values inform that intention? Lacking such clarity, you might not feel a strong, enduring moral connection to the company and your colleagues. You and your colleagues might all wish to help customers, but you aren't united in a true *quest*, working together to achieve an ambitious goal that will deliver social and commercial benefits.

Not Just an Anecdote—A *Big Story*

You might respond that this is where senior leaders should intervene, reminding us of the organization's existential intent and expounding on it. Somehow, leaders must go beyond specific, feel-good stories, to convey the purpose in a broader way that elevates the company, convenes diverse stakeholders as a moral community, and sparks intense emotional bonds between them and the company. Leaders must tell a grand, foundational story about the company that lends depth, meaning, and even *poetry* to the enterprise. They must evoke the company's values, trajectory, and destiny in a way that sticks with people and provides them with an enduring context in which to understand their daily operational realities.

Deep purpose leaders do precisely this. Although they do tell one-off, feel-good stories, they craft a compelling *master narrative*—a "Big Story," as I call it—depicting a coherent and ambitious change the enterprise intends to bring about in the outside world.[3] As part of this narrative, they critique the status quo (including the enterprise itself, the industry, or capitalism at large), establishing the magnitude of the change required. They evoke a future that reflects moral values and captures how the world *ought* to be. And they issue a rallying cry, asking the entire enterprise to band together and fight valiantly to realize the existential intent. Linking the present with a desired future as well as with the company's distant past (chapter 4), deep purpose leaders portray the company and its stakeholders as pursuing a sacred, transcendent quest.

They convene stakeholders as a moral community, unleashing what some have called "moral potency," an ability to behave valiantly and overcome challenges in service to a noble ambition.[4] Solid in their values and fired up by their future vision, stakeholders become bolder, prouder, more determined, and more unified. Instead of just talking about the collective quest, they're inspired to take meaningful *action*—together.

Deep purpose leaders regard dissemination of a Big Story about the future as a fundamental task of leadership. Unlike convenient purpose leaders, who often perceive the task of mobilizing people around the purpose as a short-term branding exercise, deep purpose leaders devote themselves to reinforcing the master narrative over a period of years, making it a defining feature of their tenure. They reiterate elements of their narratives on a variety of occasions and tell smaller, supportive stories that illustrate particular parts of the Big Story. They become so absorbed in their role as narrative builders and believe so fully in their Big Story that they infuse it into their leadership generally, behaving in ways that conform with and support the unfolding story of change.

Performance with Purpose

Business icon Indra Nooyi has broken many barriers in her life. Born into a conservative Indian family, she grew up in a traditional culture that restricted the opportunities open to girls and expected them to land a good husband by age eighteen. That didn't stop her from playing cricket on an all-girls team as a teenager, or from joining a rock band made up entirely of girls. Some years later, she asked her parents to let her travel to the United States and attend graduate school at Yale on a scholarship. "It was unheard of for a good, conservative, South Indian Brahmin girl to do this," she recalled. "It would make her an absolutely unmarriageable commodity after that."[5]

But Nooyi's parents agreed, allowing her to go to Yale so long as she consented to having friends look in on her in the United States.[6] She went on to graduate and build an enormously successful corporate career. After stints at Boston Consulting Group and Motorola, she joined PepsiCo in 1994 as a senior strategist and in 2001 became the company's chief financial officer and president. In these roles, Nooyi helped orchestrate PepsiCo's successful restructuring, including its spinoff of its fast-food franchises Pizza Hut, Taco Bell, and KFC into a separate company (Yum! Brands) and its nearly $14 billion acquisition of Quaker Oats in 2001.

All along, Nooyi remained grounded in her culture, in part because her mother, a powerful figure in her life, wouldn't have it any other way. Nooyi recounts that when she informed her family of her big promotion to CFO and president, her mother didn't seem all that impressed at first. Instead of congratulating her and expressing pride in her daughter's accomplishments, she asked Nooyi to run an errand. When Nooyi returned home, her mother informed her that regardless of her business success, she still retained her traditional female roles and should "leave that damned crown in the garage."[7]

Nooyi would soon have a much larger crown to leave in the garage. In 2006, PepsiCo made national news by naming her the first female CEO in its history. Fewer than a dozen other Fortune 500 companies had women CEOs at the time, and Indian-born executives were rarely seen among the top corporate ranks. Observers lauded PepsiCo's decision, and not just because it advanced the cause of diversity.[8] Working alongside her predecessor Steven Reinemund, Nooyi had played a critical role in leading PepsiCo through what had been an enormously successful run. Between 2001 and 2005, PepsiCo's total revenues and net income for the company had soared, and market capitalization had surmounted $97 billion, up from $85 billion in 2001.[9]

And yet for all Nooyi's prior success, it was unclear whether she would manage to keep the company on its exceptional growth track. In the United States and other markets, an outcry was mounting about rising rates of obesity and other chronic illnesses. Public health officials and other observers pegged snack and soda companies as villains, accusing them of hooking consumers on addictive foods filled with fat, sugar, and calories.[10] Consumer tastes were also shifting, with sales of PepsiCo's core soda products declining in favor of other beverages perceived to be healthier, such as sports drinks and waters (consumption of soda peaked in 2004 and has since been declining).[11] In addition, there was a growing awareness nationally and internationally of a looming climate crisis that businesses along with governments would somehow need to address. In taking the top job at PepsiCo, Nooyi would have to find ways to get ahead of these trends, while also outpacing the company's archrival Coca-Cola.

As it turned out, Nooyi had a plan, one that she would champion until her retirement in 2018 and that would put her on the vanguard of multi-stakeholder capitalism. In 2006, shortly after becoming CEO, and well before terms like "purpose-driven" and "conscious capitalism" had gone mainstream, Nooyi announced that she was reorienting PepsiCo around a new strategy called "Performance with Purpose."[12] Under the strategy, PepsiCo would remake its operating model to pursue both a commercial and a social logic at once.

Financial performance remained paramount under her new strategy, which is why performance came first in the strategy's name rather than the other way around. But a broad-based purpose that included adjusting the company's product portfolio and addressing environmental concerns would also be essential. It would help to instill pride among employees while allowing the entire enterprise to respond to changing customer needs. Hence Performance *with* Purpose.

Performance with Purpose had four parts: "financial sustainability" (sustainable financial performance for shareholders); "human sustainability" (a new emphasis on supporting human health by making the company's product offerings more nutritious); "environmental sustainability" (a drive to make operations more sustainable); and "talent sustainability" (investment in PepsiCo's workforce).[13] As part of this strategy, the company aimed to make its snack foods healthier, cutting sodium, sugar, and saturated fats. But just as important, it hoped to offer more products—such as Quaker oatmeal—that were healthy or "good for you," as opposed to "fun for you" snacks like Doritos and Fritos and "better for you" products like Diet Pepsi or Baked Doritos.[14] The company would also take steps such as including more nutritional information and refraining from selling sugary drinks in educational settings.[15]

As Nooyi later explained, PepsiCo's purpose was rooted in an understanding that "We have a profound role to play in society, and we have to make sure that we are constructive members of society."[16] This broad formulation translated into making the company's products more nutritious and easier on the environment to produce while overall being a good corporate citizen. But as attractive as that message sounded, it aroused considerable controversy among PepsiCo's stakeholders. When PepsiCo's independent bottlers first learned about Performance with Purpose, some of them feared the company would now sell less soda and book less revenue.[17] Investors were upset, feeling that PepsiCo had lost its way by investing too heavily in a long-term strategy and too little in its existing products. One analyst urged PepsiCo "to realize that at their core they are a sugary, fatty cola company, and people like that."[18]

Some health advocates dismissed PepsiCo's efforts to behave more responsibly, accusing the company of what today we would call purpose-washing.[19] Meanwhile, some employees had trouble breaking old habits and allowing the new purpose to guide their decision-making. Nooyi relates how one team that bore responsibility for Tropicana, the company's brand of orange juice, planned to introduce a "sugary carbonated orange drink" under that name. "The team hadn't yet understood that PepsiCo needed to limit the introduction of treatlike products."[20]

Telling PepsiCo's Big Story

To surmount this entrenched resistance, Nooyi promoted the new strategy throughout her tenure, speaking about purpose at every opportunity and publicizing it in internal and external communications. Former Chief Marketing Officer for Global Consumer Engagement Frank Cooper recalls that Nooyi debuted Performance with Purpose in her first major speech as CEO, following it up with emails, discussions of the strategy at town hall meetings, banners around the office, messaging on the company's website, and other communications ("Performance with Purpose" apparently even emblazoned screen savers in the company's headquarters).[21] She charged her direct reports with promoting Performance with Purpose to their own teams, explaining how it translated to their respective businesses. "It was a complete surround sound performance," Cooper says, "to the point where eventually people knew Performance with Purpose so well they called it by its abbreviation, PwP."[22]

In conveying PepsiCo's new purpose, Nooyi didn't just tell one-off emotional stories about, say, a consumer who lost weight because they consumed some of the company's healthier offerings. Rather, her presentation of Performance with Purpose came embedded with a broader, foundational narrative about the company and its destiny. The gist of this Big Story went like this: "We've long been a responsible, well-managed company that sought to behave responsibly. But the world is changing, and we have to take our social responsibilities to a new level. We'll become a different kind of company in the years ahead, changing our portfolio to make our products healthier and changing our core operations to do social good."[23]

Ever the strategist, Nooyi grounded her Big Story in data and analysis. She had asked her team to research global trends that threatened PepsiCo's business, including consumer desires for healthier diets, rising environmental pressures such as increasing water scarcity, and shifts in what employees were seeking from their work. In her communications, Nooyi drew on these trends to argue that the company had to not just give money away but change how it made money. It had to deepen its sense of why it existed, recognizing a mission beyond just supplying the world with snacks and drinks.[24] If PepsiCo did so, it could create a future in which it was more relevant than ever to consumers *and* more responsive to society's needs. As Nooyi puts it in a 2007 interview, it could make PepsiCo "among the defining corporations" of "the first two or three decades of the twenty-first century."[25] It would be a future in which the company earned more of its revenues from healthy foods, reduced its impact on the environment, and did more to fulfill workers' needs.

If Nooyi's Big Story was desirable and morally resonant, it was also attainable. In that same 2007 interview, given when Nooyi's team had just begun to socialize the new purpose internally and develop concrete goals, Nooyi emphasizes that the company won't realize the noble goals of Performance with Purpose right away. When it comes to environmental sustainability, for instance, it will have to strike a balance between progress in that area and financial demands. But with careful planning and discipline, PepsiCo can make solid progress over time. "We want to lay out a program and deliberately [work] toward it," she says.[26]

Nooyi also acknowledges that purpose and performance will require difficult tradeoffs between short-term profit and long-term social good. When customer or investor demands arise, "every time it happens, we have to very, very thoughtfully think through it, and then decide what action to take without losing sight of long-term purpose. Because, if we give up completely and say performance is paramount, that's wrong. It's carefully walking through these minefields."[27] Performance with Purpose is a delicate business, but it's a morally resonant vision that the company can achieve with concerted effort.

Nooyi is hardly alone in articulating a Big Story with moral overtones. In presenting Danone's purpose of "bringing health through food to as many people as possible," the company's former CEO Emmanuel Faber issued a resounding call for a "food revolution." In a 2017 speech at the Consumer Goods Forum, for instance, he observes that the industry has done a lot of good, giving masses of people access to food and "barring hunger from many places around the world." At the same time, progress had brought about unexpected side effects, including "the explosion of non-communicable diseases and the depletions of the resources of the planet."[28] For years, the industry has been denying the harms it has caused. Now, consumers around the world were demanding change, and the food industry needed to choose: Would it battle consumers, or would it recognize "that its ultimate goal is to serve the sovereignty for people on their food"? Danone, Faber notes, has opted to help lead a far-reaching "food revolution." He suggests that his fellow food executives should listen to consumers as well as their own employees, join the fight, and help "create lasting food sovereignty for all."[29]

Calls for a food revolution appeared in other of Faber's speeches, press appearances, corporate communications, and social media postings. Faber told smaller stories that illustrate or connect with the purpose and impact stakeholders emotionally, but he advocated for a compelling master narrative, one that was desirable, potentially attainable, and morally relevant. He dramatized an existential intent for the company and linked it to the past and the present.

The Stories Behind the "Big Story"

Although we can summarize Big Stories simply in just a few lines, these narratives aren't as simple as they seem. Deep purpose leaders communicate them tirelessly over an extended period in different settings and formats. Rather than hewing to a fixed script, they keep the basic narrative but tend to adjust and elaborate on it, emphasizing certain elements, approaching the narrative from different angles, and illustrating specific points in new ways, depending on the occasion. What might at first seem like a single Big Story is in fact, upon closer inspection, a *constellation* of similar, overlapping, and related narratives. It's a seemingly haphazard approach to communications, with details shifting in the retelling and leaders incorporating personal anecdotes, stories about the organization and its history, and accounts of current challenges facing the enterprise.

Why do deep purpose leaders introduce such complexity? It's not imprecision, but rather an effort to heighten the Big Story's motivational power. Leaders adept at communicating often deploy rich, highly visual language to sear a shared sense of organizational purpose into stakeholders' minds.[30] Although deep purpose leaders deploy sensory language, they also allow the Big Story to unfold and develop in ways that further enhance its emotive power. Their seemingly diffuse elaborations of the story serve to establish a sense of intimacy with audiences while highlighting and dramatizing the narrative's moral dimensions. Connecting with stakeholders personally, deep purpose leaders mobilize stakeholders into a vital, morally charged *movement* around the purpose.

The political organizer Marshall Ganz lays out a powerful, three-part model of narratives designed to help leaders arouse emotion and rally people to purposeful action.[31] A veteran of the civil rights era who also worked alongside social activists like Cesar Chavez to organize farm workers in California, Ganz seeks to explain how "discontented, but compliant, publics can mobilize to demand political change."[32] Noting that such change "does not 'just happen,'" he describes narrative as "the discursive means we use to access values that equip us with the courage to make choices under conditions of uncertainty, to exercise agency."[33] Narrative conveys our values, but it does so in a more direct, emotional way. In particular, Ganz argues that "public narrative" motivates people to act by telling three levels of interwoven stories: "self," "us," and "now." As I found, deep purpose leaders function as social activists in their own way, telling these three kinds of stories and moving stakeholders to take action.

SELF

In crafting public narratives, Ganz observes, leaders must put the focus squarely on themselves and evoke their origins, motives, and desired destination. Doing so establishes leaders' credibility, conveying their moral values to inspire followers and connect with them on a human level. When Ganz talks about stories of self, he doesn't mean any old stories but rather accounts of dramatic and defining decisions we've made in our lives, "moments when we faced a challenge, made a choice, experienced an outcome, and learned a moral. We communicate values that motivate us by selecting from among those choice points, and recounting what happened."[34]

Deep purpose leaders similarly tell morally revealing stories of "choice points" they've faced. By sharing these difficult moments, they not only show their own vulnerability but reveal their own values and beliefs through their choices. In a 2016 commencement speech, Danone's former CEO Emmanuel Faber describes how a tragedy—his brother's schizophrenia diagnosis and eventual death—transformed his view of leadership and spurred his belief in purpose. He found himself dealing with psychiatric hospitals, spending time with homeless people, and, eventually, coping with his brother's death, all of which shook his sense of normality and shifted his values.

In effect, Faber faced a choice. Would he recoil at embarrassment or disgust at his brother, rejecting or distancing himself from him? Or would he love his brother enough to stretch as a person, accept him, and take the time to care for him and learn from him? To his credit, Faber did the latter. Instead of the usual cravings for glory, money, and power, he came to appreciate the central importance of service in business. The leader's task, Faber tells the graduating students, is to "find a way to serve a purpose. Purposes that will make you become who you truly are. Purposes that will make you become your very best, in ways you do not even know yourself."[35]

Faber's "choice point" of how to grapple with his brother's illness reveals the depth of his values and moral awareness, both of which he is now applying to the task of furthering Danone's purpose. Stakeholders encountering Faber's speech or learning about his story in other venues understand that he doesn't come to Danone's purpose lightly—it ties back to the core of who he is. They thus likely view him as more credible and are more inspired to follow him on the quest toward Danone's future.

Stories of self needn't depict an actual choice point to convey values. During her tenure as PepsiCo's CEO, Nooyi strongly emphasized her personal connection with the purpose without always pointing to a single, morally revealing moment. On some occasions, she referenced her childhood experiences growing up in a house lacking ready access to running water, noting that it left her with a conviction that companies had to act responsibly toward local communities. "Every morning my mom would get up at 3:00 or 4:00 am in the morning," she recounts in a 2011 appearance. "She'd wait for the taps to start releasing water because the corporation would release water from the central reservoir, and water would trickle in. And my mom would find every pot and pan to fill water in and to give the kids and my dad three containers of water, which was your quota for the day."[36]

As harsh as this circumstance was, Nooyi says, she had a harder time accepting it knowing that large multinational companies had built plants in the city that used vast amounts of water. For all the good these companies did to support the local economy and create jobs, it didn't seem right that they could operate in ways that so clearly also damaged the local community's interests and welfare.

On one occasion in 2007, Nooyi related that while she was growing up her mother would ask her what she intended to do to change the world. "Today," she said, "I know my answer would be that I want to lead a company that is a force for good in the world. A company that delivers strong financial performance, while embracing purpose in everything it does."[37] On another occasion, Nooyi spoke more broadly of the impressions she formed early in her life about multinational firms and how they operated: "I saw what they could do to create jobs, bring technology, and improve the quality of life, but also how they could come in and take resources away from the local country. I saw the best and worst and felt very deeply that, as a CEO, I had to make sure that our company would not operate as if we are an inanimate being."[38] In all these ways, Nooyi helped PepsiCo's disparate stakeholders understand her own, personal motivations for pursuing deep purpose, conveying her values and establishing her credibility as a moral leader.

US

Organizations and other groups experience "choice points" as well, moments that reveal the group's identity and core values. It's important for leaders to depict these episodes, telling stories of "Us" that evoke "the values that move us as a community" and that distinguish us from outsiders. As Ganz suggests, "Organizations that lack a 'story' lack an identity, a culture, core values that can be articulated and drawn on to motivate."[39]

Deep purpose leaders tell stories of "Us" in the course of framing Big Stories, eliciting a sense of belonging to the collective and duty to take action on its behalf. In PepsiCo's 2008 annual report, Nooyi sums up what had been a difficult year for the organization. There was a recession, volatile commodity prices, and market pressures on Pepsi's share price. "All told," she says, "I can't recall a more eventful or trying year." And yet, "The ingenuity of our company showed through again. All our teams of extraordinary people applied their can-do spirit and must-do sense of responsibility to meet the economic and market challenges head on." Even more important, the organization remained focused on its purpose: "2008 was a year in which our mission could easily have been abandoned. The extraordinary circumstances would have resulted in it being abandoned if it were not already embedded into our culture. So, during 2008 we stayed true to our beliefs, even as the backdrop got tougher."

The company had experienced a choice point, and its actions had revealed just how committed to its values it really was. Nooyi closes by explicitly positioning the company as a moral community bound by shared values: "A great company is a place where people come together, with a purpose in common. By defining that purpose, by trying to bottle it, we are bound together. That is the message you see on every page of this report." Remarkably, Nooyi turns adversity into an opportunity to reestablish the company's identity as a strong and resilient moral community. The cover page of the report says it all with a single, clear message: "We are performance with purpose."[40]

NOW

To articulate compelling public narratives, Ganz argues, leaders must tell a story about a *current* challenge the group faces and how action in the present might lead to a positive future. "Stories of Now," he writes, "articulate the challenges we face now, the choices we are called upon to make, and the meaning of making the right choice. Stories of Now are set in the past, present, and future. The challenge is now; we are called on to act because of our legacy and who we have become, and the action that we take now can shape our desired future."[41] As this formulation suggests, and as Ganz confirms, stories of now arouse hope because they come embedded with a strategy for overcoming challenges. The group must decide to embrace hope and commit to the strategy: that's the morally revealing choice at hand. And they must not only decide, but take immediate action.

In a 2017 LinkedIn article entitled "Food Is a Human Right, Not a Commodity," Faber articulates what we might interpret as a story of Now, one seemingly aimed at a variety of audiences, including potential or actual employees, consumers, other food manufacturers, and the general public.[42] Referencing systemic problems like climate change, malnutrition, environmental degradation, and inhumane labor practices, he observes their interconnectedness and ties them back to a fundamental challenge: a "global industrial food system" that disconnects people from what they eat and how it's produced. Using language evocative of urgency, Faber observes that this food system is "reaching its limits," confronting the company and the world with an imminent choice: Will we take this challenge seriously and reform the food system, or will we continue to ignore it and allow systemic problems to worsen?

Faber connects his Story of Now with the past, suggesting that Danone's own history invited action because the company's founder, Antoine Riboud, envisioned "a dual project of both economic value creation and social progress." Faber also indicates a way forward, presenting not a formal strategy per se but a series of meaningful measures Danone has begun to undertake: seeking third-party certifications such as becoming a B Corp, providing progressive employee benefits and policies, devising programs to benefit local communities, and striving to become carbon neutral. Faber notes that market shifts are putting new pressures on food companies, which might incline them to short-term profit maximization. This heightens the moral choice facing the industry: Will it persist with the food revolution and move the world toward a healthier, more sustainable future?

Faber calls on the industry and consumers to push harder toward the food revolution. "Now is the time," he says, when concerned industry players "should start to more broadly support and be catalysts of change for people to reconnect with their food." He continues: "Another world is possible. I believe that every day, each time we eat and drink, we can vote for the world we want to live in. And as CEOs, as leaders, we will have the responsibility to adjust the way our companies operate, the way our brands interact with their communities. This is full of risks and opportunities. Our business models, our companies' organizations could be—will be—disrupted. But this is the only way out, off the limits. Set food free."

Faber calls upon food companies to step up right now to be "catalysts of change." If they do, working together with consumers and other stakeholders, "we can be collectively remembered as the generation that harnessed its accumulated experience, its access to disruptive technology, its collective intelligence to create true, lasting food sovereignty for our world." It's a glorious vision, a meaningful one, and a potentially viable one. By telling a Story of Now, Faber mobilizes a social movement by defining a quest and calling stakeholders to advance it— *right now*.

TO CONVEY DEEP PURPOSE, USE MARSHALL GANZ'S "SELF-US-NOW" FRAMEWORK

Talk about *Self* ...
Establish personal credibility, delineate moral values, evoke morally revealing "choice points" from your life.

Talk about *Us* ...
Evoke collective identity and moral values; convey collective "choice points" that reveal these values and cement identity. Arouse emotional attachments to the group.

Talk about *Now* ...
Connect audiences to a current challenge or choice point. Evoke what's at stake in the present day; arouse a sense of hopefulness; suggest a strategy for resolving a challenge.

Embodying the Big Story

You're enjoying your golden years, and your children are all grown and spread out across the world. Between the demands of work and raising young families of their own, you don't hear from them as often as you'd like. You know they care about their jobs, but you have only a foggy idea of the work they do. One day, you open your mail to find a personal note. It's a thank-you card, and you realize to your shock that it comes from the CEO of the company where one of your children works—one of the world's largest and best-known. This CEO spends a good paragraph describing what your child contributes to the company, thanking you for giving the company the gift of your child. Imagine the pride you would feel upon receiving such a note, the delight at knowing that the child you raised and helped form was having a positive impact on the world.

Nooyi wrote hundreds of such notes to the parents of senior officers at PepsiCo, relating the impact their children were making at the company and thanking them for the role they played as parents. As she related in her public appearances, the letters had a tremendous emotional impact, not just on the parents but on the executives, who were happy to see their parents so delighted.[43] Nooyi began writing these letters after a 2006 trip to India during which her mother had brought her to her living room and a long line of visitors stopped by. "They'd go to my mom and say, 'You did such a good job with your daughter. Compliments to you. She's CEO.' But not a word to me." Reflecting on this episode, Nooyi recognized that her parents had helped set her up for success and that they deserved recognition for it.[44] She resolved to give such recognition to the parents of PepsiCo's senior leaders. Such gestures seem to have contributed to Nooyi's popularity as a leader. As of 2017, prior to stepping down as CEO, she enjoyed a 75 percent approval rating on Glassdoor.[45]

Nooyi's epistolary practice reflects a basic awareness on her part that people take pride in where they work, and that their pride only intensifies when they know that the company cares about their loved ones. Nooyi's letter-writing also connects back to Performance with Purpose, and particularly its devotion to "talent sustainability" and "building a work environment where all of our associates can achieve a better quality of life and know that, as a business, we cherish them."[46] Intentionally or not, Nooyi's heartfelt actions brought this dimension of the purpose to life in an unforgettable way, modeling it for the rest of the organization. She wasn't just talking about Performance with Purpose or even illustrating it with a story. She was *doing* it, without drawing special attention to her actions and tying them explicitly to the purpose. Since her actions seemed so authentic and unprompted, and since she consistently undertook them, they became part and parcel of her identity as a leader.

Other deep purpose leaders I studied took steps to embody the Big Story, not simply communicate it verbally. That's not surprising: leaders believe in their master narratives, perceiving them as wholly consistent with their personal values and purpose. Deep purpose leaders are also keenly aware of leadership's performative nature. They know stakeholders are watching them, taking cues from their behavior and words and holding them accountable for any inconsistencies. Determined to remain compelling and effective spokespeople, they project the Big Story in their person so that stakeholders perceive them as true, credible, and aspirational carriers of it.

To adopt the terms of a popular management framework, deep purpose leaders seek to *be* the Big Story, not simply *know* it (understand it intellectually) or *do* it (behave in accordance with it).[47] They live the Big Story as fully as possible, tapping into the deepest part of themselves. Ultimately, they become what Bill George has called "authentic leaders," keenly self-aware and in touch with their most deeply felt beliefs, values, and principles.[48]

As Danone's Faber told me prior to stepping down as CEO, he never approached his communications around purpose with a strategic frame of mind. Rather, he did so spontaneously and from the heart. His starting point was simply an attempt to connect with his deepest, innermost convictions. "I'm talking with the whole of myself. I'm not reading a script that's been prepared by a nice team that says, 'You know, boss, you should be talking about sustainability.' I can't do that. I'm super bad at that. I'm just speaking what I truly believe."[49] In truth, Faber didn't need to draw attention to this openness and authenticity. As I saw for myself, it was immediately evident. And because of that, he seemed to powerfully embody the organizational purpose.

Similarly, Nooyi suggested that it wasn't the content of her message alone that allowed her to connect with audiences but also her ability to internalize it. "If the CEO doesn't feel the change," she relates, "as opposed to just talking about the change, people will see right through it."[50] It seems clear that Nooyi did indeed "feel" Performance with Purpose. On one occasion, after learning about the plight of a disabled veteran living in Pepsi's birthplace in New Bern, North Carolina, Nooyi felt so moved that she asked a local Pepsi representative to send company products to the veteran's family, accompanied by a personal note. The Pepsi representative was moved in turn, expressing how proud he felt to work for a company like Pepsi. If that employee had any doubt about the authenticity of Nooyi's commitment to the purpose, it ended right there.[51]

Deep purpose leaders complement their narrative building with *management actions* that signal their enthusiasm and seriousness about embedding the reason for being. When Nooyi adopted Performance with Purpose, she highlighted her seriousness by ushering out leaders who rejected the new strategy and by making several key senior hires, including a former Mayo Clinic endocrinologist as the company's new chief scientific officer and a former executive director of the World Health Organization as vice president of global health policy. As she notes, her willingness to fund new R&D capabilities under the new chief scientific officer during the 2008 recession "reinforced the message throughout the organization that [Performance with Purpose] was here to stay."[52]

Character in leadership isn't just about possessing moral sensitivity and judgment—you also must be willing to take action and display moral courage.[53] In realizing the existential intent through their actions, deep purpose leaders embody it in the eyes of followers by taking *meaningful personal risks*. Research has found that a "self-sacrificial" style of leadership serves to rally followers, assuming that the leader doesn't behave in an overly autocratic manner.[54] Whereas some leaders prefer to watch from the sidelines as team members take the bullet, deep purpose leaders lead the charge, showing courage themselves and in the process building unique credibility among team members.

Nooyi showed courage during the early 2010s when investors grew upset with the company's disappointing short-term results. "Indra Nooyi's job is on the line," the *Economist* reported then, summarizing the company's approach as "good for you, not for shareholders."[55] Nooyi might have scaled back her efforts, but she stuck doggedly by Performance with Purpose, a move that solidified her position as a steward of the purpose and enabled her to embody it in the eyes of stakeholders. Years later, as Nooyi's approach began paying off commercially, investors and analysts acknowledged that she had been correct in staying the course.

Lessons for Leaders

The organizational theorist James March and a colleague memorably distinguished between the "plumbing" and "poetry" of leadership.[56] Leaders must make rational, economic decisions in running their businesses day-to-day to achieve efficiency and optimal performance—that's the "plumbing," the technical or operational side of business. But they must also attend to meaning, values, and purpose—the "poetry" of business. As other scholars have since remarked, "leaders must therefore build values and purpose into the social structure of the organization" and ensure that the organization's commitment to them are real and enduring, not a passing fancy.[57] The goal is to embed purpose and values so deeply that stakeholders internalize them and act spontaneously to realize them.

Although my study of deep purpose as a whole elaborates on the "softer" emotional and moral dimensions of the leader's role, this chapter has shown deep purpose leaders operating as literary creators to convey existential intent to their organizations. They don't write poems about the purpose (at least, none that I'm aware of). But they do tell master narratives, calling upon the organization to pursue a noble quest and function as a moral community.[58]

Assess your own leadership and whether you currently serve as your organization's chief storyteller. Yes, you might offer up stories to illustrate the purpose, but have you articulated a Big Story? If you have articulated the rough outlines or essence of such a narrative, do you continue to rehearse, adapt, enhance, and elaborate on that narrative year after year, even in the face of hardened opposition? And like inspiring leaders in the political realm, do you tell a variety of subordinate or embedded stories that evoke your moral values, help your stakeholders feel that they belong to a moral community, and set the stage for moral action *now*?

Be honest about your commitment to and affinity for the Big Story. Do you regard storytelling as primarily a short-term brand-building exercise, or do you conceive of it as a core part of your role? How deeply do you *really* subscribe to the Big Story? Does it reflect the essence of who you are as a leader? For that matter, have you bothered to reflect enough to understand your core? If your Big Story truly is rooted in your core beliefs, do you behave consistently in ways that exemplify the master narrative and its underlying values to stakeholders? Do others perceive you as embodying your organization's purpose?

Even if they do, your work communicating the purpose is by no means done. You must also manage a basic tension, that between generality and specificity. One scholar has observed that "The messages leaders use to convey the organization's ultimate aspirations present a paradox: the very properties that make ultimate aspirations meaningful are those that leave employees unable to sense how their daily responsibilities are associated with them."[59] The loftier a purpose seems, the more distanced it seems from individual employees and their work.

Something similar holds for the rhetorical exercise of crafting a master narrative. Big Stories define a quest and position it in moral terms, but they don't fully convey its meaning for individuals. To do that, you'll have to tailor the message for specific audiences, connecting it directly with their challenges and needs. Deep purpose leaders I interviewed tweaked the Big Story when speaking with specific business units and geographies, using language and incorporating themes that *they* would understand. Over the long term, these leaders cultivated a careful balance between the general and the specific, the soaring and the tangible, poetry and prose.

Nooyi stuck with her communication efforts, promoting Performance with Purpose throughout her twelve-year tenure as CEO. She argued consistently for the company's urgent need to transform its businesses, tapping into widespread concerns about diet and the environment as well as evolving expectations of the social role of businesses. She continued to field skepticism from shareholders and activists, but employees and the board bought in, allowing the company to execute well on the strategy. According to one leader, "We've really seen Performance with Purpose kind of woven into the fabric of our company and really very much now a guiding mantra—something that all of our employees feel so proud of."[60]

During Nooyi's tenure, the company saw an 80 percent increase in sales and a total shareholder return that outperformed that of the S&P 500.[61] Although PepsiCo is today hardly a health food company, its healthier food portfolio accounted for a greater percentage of the company's revenue in 2017 than it did in 2006 (50 percent as opposed to only 38 percent).[62] Its Fun for You snack products also became healthier (as Nooyi noted in 2019, Lay's potato chips had "20 to 25 percent less salt than they did a decade ago").[63] The company slashed its water usage by a quarter, gave twenty-two million people access to safe drinking water, and rendered its leadership ranks more diverse (women in 2018 made up almost 40 percent of top managers), among other accomplishments.[64] Observers regard Nooyi's tenure quite favorably, with one noting that she had a "sterling reputation" and had "plenty to be proud of."[65]

Big Stories can indeed inject poetry into an organization, rallying people around an existential intent. But to inspire people to live the organizational purpose in their daily work, leaders must also connect it with each employee's personal purpose, so that they, too, can bring it out spontaneously from within in a way that feels authentic and natural. Deep purpose leaders do this by becoming more thoughtful than their peers about a key managerial tool at their disposal: culture.

CHAPTER 6

THE "ME" IN PURPOSE

Deep purpose leaders bind organizational purpose to team members' personal development and growth, firing up intrinsic motivation and unleashing new levels of commitment and performance. Deep purpose leaders craft humane and inclusive cultures that emphasize self-expression, growth, and individual purpose. Further, these leaders provide opportunities for individual employees to live the organizational purpose by connecting it with their own personal reasons for being.

The National Football League (NFL) holds a "media day" prior to its annual Super Bowl championship game, making players on the competing teams available to meet with journalists for up to an hour each. The event is a spectacle, "nothing short of a circus of entertainment," in the words of one observer.[1] Players let their personalities shine, cracking jokes and making colorful statements that help to build excitement around the game.

The event held in early 2015 before Super Bowl XLIX, a showdown between the Seattle Seahawks and the New England Patriots, was especially memorable thanks to one particular encounter. Video footage shows a superstar player emerging on the far side of the crowded arena.

He's a muscular, dreadlocked Black man wearing sunglasses with white plastic rims, a baseball hat with a flat, high-profile visor, and a heavy chain over his white sweatshirt. It takes several minutes for him to make his way through the crowd to the podium. At every turn, journalists snap pictures of him. Anticipation mounts as he nears the podium. "We'll see if he provides us with some surprising answers," a commentator says.

The athlete sits before the microphone and confirms it's time to begin. Leaning into the microphone, his eyes obscured by those sunglasses, he says, "Hey, I'm just here so I don't get fined. So y'all can sit here and ask me all the questions y'all want to, I'm going to answer with the same answer, so y'all can shoot if y'all please. I'm here so I won't get fined." Journalists begin shouting out questions. Each time the answer is some variant of "I'm here so I won't get fined." Twenty-nine questions over a four- to five-minute period. Twenty-nine replies of "I'm here so I won't get fined." And then he unceremoniously stands up and walks off.[2] Not exactly the most illuminating press appearance, but one that few people present would soon forget.

If you're a fan of American football, you know this athlete is Seattle's Marshawn Lynch. During that year's media day, other players showed up and performed as expected. Patriots' star Rob Gronkowski revealed he once had a crush on television star Pamela Anderson. The Seahawks' Michael Bennett proclaimed himself the world's second most handsome guy after actor Denzel Washington. But Lynch refused to offer meaningful answers to reporters' queries. His multimillion-dollar contract obliged him to speak to the media, and the NFL had fined him $100,000 for failing to do so during the regular season.[3] Now, with the NFL threatening to impose a half-million dollar fine if he skipped media day, he devised a work-around that apparently satisfied his contract requirements.[4]

Such nonconformist behavior was vintage Lynch. Nicknamed "Beast Mode" for his aggressive, highly physical style of play, Lynch was one of the National Football League's preeminent running backs (for non-football fans, a running back is the player who takes the ball and tries to run it down the field, avoiding tacklers).[5] Lynch had literally sparked seismic activity during his game-winning "Beast Quake" run in a 2010–

2011 playoffs game—the sound of celebrating Seattle fans was so loud that it registered on seismographs.[6] In 2014, he helped lead Seattle to its first-ever Super Bowl victory with a trouncing of the Denver Broncos.

But as impressive as Lynch was on the field, the media often disparaged his off-the-field behavior, casting him as a disruptive player who refused to abide by the rules. During his first three NFL seasons with the Buffalo Bills, he performed well in his position but also was arrested twice, for a hit-and-run charge in 2008 and a weapons charge in 2009.[7] The Bills and the media perceived him, as one journalist recalled, "as a disappointment and somewhat of a liability."[8]

In Seattle, Lynch's mystifying practice of avoiding the media struck some as deeply disrespectful.[9] "All he has to do is mutter a few short answers," one observer complained, "throw in a cliché or two, and he's out the door. It really isn't that difficult. Instead, Lynch's defiant behavior simply calls more attention to himself. His postgame antics now are a story."[10] Observers also weren't impressed by his practice of grabbing his crotch to celebrate a touchdown score, which garnered him tens of thousands in fines.[11] Some in the media, mindful no doubt of his previous criminal record, called him a "thug."[12]

There was one person who didn't seem overly bothered by Lynch's behavior: Seahawks coach Pete Carroll. Following Lynch's "I'm here so I won't get fined" performance, Carroll was asked whether he found Lynch's conduct "frustrating." Carroll reportedly laughed and said, "No, it's not frustrating. He's just being who he is. . . . It's really not a burden to us."[13]

Unleashing the "Me"

Carroll's response went to the heart of the Seahawks' team culture and Carroll's highly successful leadership practices. Whereas football coaches traditionally drive performance by adopting an authoritarian, even military-style approach, demanding strict discipline and conformity from players and levying harsh penalties when they slip up, Carroll does precisely the opposite. He relishes and supports his players' individuality, even if it leads to nonconformist behavior. Within certain bounds, he creates a welcoming, inclusive organizational culture that allows people to express themselves openly.

As Carroll professes, team performance begins with *individual* performance. Unleash team members to thrive as human beings, set them free to exercise their creative power and to grow, and they will help advance collective goals. "Our culture," he says, "is about recognizing the extraordinary value in the individuals that are in it and supporting their development throughout."[14] To that end, Carroll strives to see his players as individuals. Far more than the typical football coach, he engages players in ongoing dialogue, including about their personal philosophies and sense of purpose, and aims to satisfy their individual needs and desires. "He was able to have great conversations with us," one player attests. "Whenever you were going through something personal, he would come to you and you wouldn't feel like it was somebody who was trying to get you back on the field. It was more like he was trying to understand where you were coming from and what happened and what your emotions were."[15]

Carroll sought to build trusting personal *relationships* with players that fostered their growth, supported their self-expression, and laid the foundation for optimal performance. Players certainly had to work hard and meet demanding performance expectations, but Carroll saw value in showing kindness and empathy. As he told me, "When you feel comfortable about where you are and you're accepted and you belong, now you're open to allow for yourself to express your best abilities, your best potential. . . . We're trying to build an environment that is conducive to that kind of ability to tap into what you're best at."[16]

Carroll's emphasis on nurturing a culture of individuality and personal relationships has important implications for leaders interested in embedding deep purpose. As Carroll told me, an organization's willingness to nurture employees' individuality is critical to galvanizing them around the collective purpose. "If someone feels you're recognizing who they are and what they're all about, you've opened up the connection to introduce them to the collective purpose."[17] It's important as well, Carroll notes, for organizations to not merely affirm team members' individuality but to help them explore and deepen their own sense of who they are, including their personal purpose. We've spoken so far of organizational purpose in this book, but individuals also have their own, personal reasons for being. They develop deeply felt notions of the impact they intend to have on the world, notions that in turn imbue their work efforts with meaning.

The virtuous connection between individual and organizational purpose is cemented by a culture that provides clear guardrails while celebrating individual expression. Carroll understood how an organization's culture could unlock tremendous motivational power by *connecting* personal and organizational purpose. In his view, the more deeply the organization helped team members to understand their own, personal philosophies, identities, and reasons for being, the more fully team members could further the organization's purpose. Carroll himself became far more effective as a coach, he told me, when he came to develop a personal philosophy. There's "magic," he suggests, when organizations can inspire people to align their own personal passion, self-understanding, and desire for growth with a common, organizational ambition.

Deep purpose leaders relish this magic and work to unleash it. Although many companies implement rigorous cultural change programs to support purpose, conceiving of culture and the reason for being as tightly linked, deep purpose leaders go further. They understand that even the strongest, top-down culture isn't enough to mobilize the workforce around an organizational purpose, nor are the usual steps to "cascade" the purpose and culture down through the organization by having managers communicate it. Breaking from traditional notions of culture as a means of enforcing conformity, these leaders craft more humane and inclusive cultures that emphasize self-expression, growth, and individual purpose. They also provide specific opportunities for individual employees to live the organizational purpose by connecting it with their own personal reasons for being. Forging an unlikely *synthesis* between employees' highest ambitions and the company's, deep purpose cultures enable people to feel both deeply fulfilled on the job and personally committed to the company's Big Story.

"Be Yourself, Be Candid, Be Kind"

Generations of scholars have seen culture as a powerful *control* system within organizations, a means of subduing individuality and ensuring conformity.[18] Culture offers an inexpensive and informal way of regulating behavior that is all the more effective because it occurs inside the minds of employees and relies on peer pressure as a mechanism.[19] "When we care about those with whom we work and have a common set of expectations," one scholarly article observes, "we are 'under control' whenever we are in their presence. If we want to be accepted, we try to live up to their expectations."[20] In companies with strong cultures, norms of behavior are pronounced and widely accepted without constant oversight on the part of managers. Individuals voluntarily regulate themselves, refraining from behaviors that clash with the culture.

Over the past few decades, many corporate leaders have sought to build strong cultures that define their organizations for stakeholders. In addition, they've paid attention to the specific *content* of their cultures, shaping them to inculcate specific behaviors relevant to strategic execution. Eager to support goals like innovation, quality, growth, and excellence in customer service, companies like Southwest and IBM became famous for their finely tuned cultures, which many took as the key to their business success.[21]

More recently, the limitations of "strong" cultures have come into focus.[22] As important as conformity is, leaders and companies have recognized that organizational performance hinges on the ability of employees to project *individuality* in the workplace, at least to some extent. Organizations understand that they must become more diverse, equitable, and inclusive places, and that they must reach out to people as individuals of different backgrounds, engage with them on *their* terms, and make space for them. In addition, organizations want *all* workers to feel engaged and highly motivated, and they want those workers to muster creativity and diverse perspectives to solve problems. If workers have latitude to express themselves, they'll feel more inspired and do better work—not because of a boss dangling a carrot or leveling a stick, but because they themselves feel an internal desire to excel.

The question, though, is how to inject more individuality into the workplace without inviting chaos. Some companies and leaders have tried to graft individuality and related values like authenticity, creativity, and diversity/inclusivity onto their existing, conformist cultures. The results are not terribly compelling. These organizational cultures seem mismatched and contradictory—like a car whose front door has been replaced with one of a different color. But many other companies haven't even tried to accommodate more individuality. One study of companies' formal statements about their cultures reveals that most don't proclaim concepts related to individuality as core values. Only 22 percent listed "diversity" as an official value, only 11 percent listed "creativity," only 8 percent listed "boldness," and only 3 percent listed "authenticity."[23]

Rather than modifying an old-fashioned, conformist culture, the deep purpose leaders I studied try to reinvent their organizational cultures more fully as bastions of individuality. They aren't going to the opposite extreme, allowing their organizations to become individualistic free-for-alls in which anything goes in the name of "being yourself." Rather, they clear space for individuality *alongside* conformity. They even adopt a somewhat paradoxical stance, seeking to generate collective alignment and ensure a measure of conformity *through* individuality. They develop inclusive cultures that encourage individuals to contribute in their own, unique ways to the common purpose, within certain bounds defined by leaders and with the expectation that individuals will meet rigorous performance expectations. These cultures include a strong emphasis on allyship and a sense that everyone should support their teammates in their personal development, no matter who they are or what their background.

The Boston-based women's technology company Ovia Health is the leading digital health platform in the United States for women and families, with some fourteen million women using its mobile apps to improve their and their children's health outcomes.[24] Ovia seeks to improve poor maternal health outcomes, particularly among women and children of color, adopting as its existential intent the provision of "equal care, longitudinal support, lifesaving interventions" to "every woman, parent, and child" so that they can enjoy "a healthy, happy family."[25] In building its culture, the firm focuses squarely on recognizing and affirming employees' individuality. One of Ovia's core values is "Be your-self, be candid, be kind." Elaborating on this, an internal company doc-ument related that "We are a team of agile, imaginative and analytical *individuals*."[26]

Ovia's CEO, Paris Wallace, grew up on government assistance in California's Marin County, one of the wealthiest areas in the United States. Raised by a mother who was single and disabled, he managed to gain admission to elite local schools and to attend on scholarship. "It was always very clear that I was different," Wallace told me, not just because his family was poor but because he was also one of the few Black students.[27] Talk to Wallace for more than a few minutes, and you realize that he's unusually comfortable in his difference and unabashed about expressing his individuality. He speaks passionately and directly, unafraid to let his personality shine and to make himself vulnerable.

But Wallace wants *everyone* in his company to feel and behave like this. As he recognizes, it's very difficult for employees to engage fully with an organizational purpose—or, frankly, with anything related to their jobs—if they're holding back important parts of their identities or personalities. "Who are those people who can't wait to leave work every day, who are leaving right at five p.m.? And why are they leaving? To be someone else, right? That's the only answer. If you've been pretend-ing not to be gay all day or changing your accent, then when five p.m. comes, you're out of there."

Wallace knows he can't simply model individuality at work—he must build it into the culture. As a result, Ovia espouses individualism at every turn, starting with recruiting. "We're very clear that in an inter-view, and just in general, one of our core beliefs is be yourself," Wallace says.[28] Relatedly, the company places a strong emphasis on inclusivity. As COO Molly Howard notes, interviewers ask every prospective hire about their gender identification and the pronouns they use. "That ques-tion says from the beginning that we choose to value our employees as *individuals*."[29]

In daily meetings and communications, leaders and coworkers pro-mote the value of diverse opinions and the notion that every employee has a stake in the organization. They also draw people out, so that they can feel accepted and their coworkers can get to know them more deeply. During the COVID-19 pandemic, the company ended every meeting by inviting participants to discuss "moments of joy" in their lives. Some employees discussed the small daily pleasures that made life worth living, while others took the opportunity to divulge very personal information. In one case, a female employee shocked her colleagues by relating that she had breast cancer and had been having treatments for months. On that particular day, her oncologist had told her that her cancer was in remission. That was her moment of joy.

Ovia encourages people not just to bring their personal lives into work, but to share their opinions about substantive business issues. Wallace explains that the company operates as a meritocracy, with leaders publicly acknowledging that they don't have all the answers and that employees often are better equipped to come up with answers to pressing questions. "It's really about saying, 'I care about what you're interested in and you can help set the direction of this company and you're contributing to what we're about and what we're doing and where we're going and really able to make a meaningful contribution, and I'm interested in your diverse thoughts and backgrounds and helping us get there.'" The company also provides employee-led online forums that allow people to express and pursue their unique passions and interests—book clubs, cooking clubs, a skin-care group, and the like. And it holds "innovation days" during which employees can pursue their own work-related projects.

Another fast-growing health-care start-up that I studied, Livongo, also made the pursuit of personal and organizational purpose a central theme. Livongo, short for "Live Life on the Go," was founded to provide real-time advice to diabetics on how to manage their fluctuating blood sugar levels. Glen Tullman, the founder, had a personal motivation as his son was diabetic and he had personally seen how such a service could benefit other people with diabetes. Tullman and the leadership team were deliberate from the outset to build a company centered on a purpose of using technology to make the lives of those with chronic conditions like diabetes much easier. From the beginning the pursuit of this purpose was personal not only for Tullman but also those on his team.

It was surprising for them to see that a number of talented individuals joining them had a personal connection to diabetes. Very quickly the firm became a magnet for top talent even in the extremely competitive market in Silicon Valley. At one point the majority of employees either had diabetes or had someone in their family impacted by it. Aligning their personal and organizational purpose came naturally to them.

As the stories of the Seattle Seahawks, Ovia Health, and Livongo reveal, deep purpose leaders engineer cultures of individuality because they understand that commitment to the organization's purpose rests on its connection to each employee's self-knowledge and sense of personal purpose. Underlying that connection is something even more fundamental: a heightened recognition of each employee's uniqueness. It's one thing for employees to buy in intellectually to the company's existential intent. But if they feel free to express themselves and see work as an opportunity to thrive as individuals, they'll inject even more of their passion and exuberance, resulting in the best possible performance. Not every employee is as fiercely and publicly individual as a Marshawn Lynch, but most of them do come to work seeking to learn, grow, and express themselves as human beings. By welcoming in employees' basic humanity and helping them to thrive, deep purpose leaders galvanize them to rally even more powerfully behind the organization's unifying purpose.

Why Do *You* Come to Work?

Gender-friendly tech start-ups aren't the only ones saving the world. Traditional accounting firms are, too. In 2014, leaders at the professional services firm KPMG adopted a new purpose statement for the organization: "Inspire confidence. Empower change." To promote the purpose, the company released a video and created posters that revealed the broader significance that KPMG's services have in the world. "We champion democracy," the video proclaimed, describing the role the firm played during World War II in helping the Allied powers defeat Nazism. "We reunite families," the video further observed, noting the behind-the-scenes work the firm did to help resolve the 1979 Iran hostage crisis and bring the American hostages home.

As inspiring as this messaging was, leaders realized that a traditional, top-down approach to communicating the new purpose wouldn't suffice. They went deeper, asking everyone in the company to create posters that conveyed the purpose *they* see themselves pursuing in their roles. Leaders sought to gather ten thousand employee stories, and they offered employees two extra vacation days if the company reached that goal. The response was overwhelming. KPMG logged forty-two thousand employee stories, including many that flowed in after leaders had announced that the initiative had succeeded and everyone would receive their extra time off. "I combat terrorism," one employee responded, observing that her work on behalf of financial institutions helped guard against money laundering, in the process "keeping financial resources out of the hands of terrorists and criminals." In another entry, an employee proclaimed, "I help farms grow," referencing his work helping facilitate loans to small family farms.[30]

Coupled with top-down efforts to communicate the purpose, the 10,000 Stories Challenge, as the initiative was called, was immensely successful. In a survey, virtually all of the firm's partners—90 percent—agreed that the pride the workforce took in the company increased because of the firm's purpose-related efforts. Employee engagement rose to unprecedented highs. A year later, 89 percent of employees reported feeling that KPMG was a "great place to work," up seven points. Over three-quarters of employees agreed that their "job had special meaning (and was not just a job)," a four-point gain over the previous year. Employees felt much more positively about their jobs and their meaning if their managers had talked about purpose with them.[31]

Bruce Pfau, former vice chair of human resources and communications, masterminded the 10,000 Stories Challenge. When I asked him why the company had thought to prompt employees to contemplate their own role- or work-related purposes, he noted that KPMG had previously made rapid gains in employee engagement, but that those gains were leveling off. He and his team thought a new focus on purpose could boost engagement further, helping the company compete for talent with its peers. While KPMG needed traditional top-down communications to communicate the corporate purpose, Bruce felt it essential for employees to *translate* the corporate purpose into a personal work-related purpose of some kind. If they did, the purpose would seem real to them, not just some meaningless formulation that corporate had dreamed up.

Bruce was shocked at the campaign's impact. "What really amazed me was the pent-up appetite for this to work." Visiting offices around the world, he routinely spotted posters in employees' cubicles relaying their personal purpose. Employees, it seemed, had a burning desire not just to experience more purpose on the job, but to project their own, *personal* reason for being. After 2015, KPMG continued to build on the 10,000 Stories Challenge, and continued to see gains in its key metrics. By 2018, when Pfau left the firm, KPMG had surged up the ranks of companies on *Fortune*'s Best Places to Work list, ultimately reaching as high as twelve, the best ranking of any Big Four accounting firm.[32]

What Can Your Company Do for You?

In his book *Hit Refresh*, Microsoft CEO Satya Nadella recounts convening his team for a special session in 2014 when he was contemplating a renewal of the company's culture. It was early in his tenure, and he wanted to see if he could get his team to engage at a whole different level than they had been. "I felt that we needed to deepen our understanding of one another—to delve into what really makes each of us tick—and to connect our personal philosophies to our jobs as leaders of the company," he writes. Nadella hoped that this deeper understanding would enable the team to pursue a new mission that was bold and inspiring but that also tapped into the original intent of Microsoft's founders.

Getting more personal was a risky experiment. Nadella's team comprised serious, high-powered people, including several career Microsoft leaders, a former investment banker, a PhD in robotics, and a former partner at a prestigious law firm. As Kathleen Hogan, chief people officer at Microsoft and an architect of the company's cultural transformation, told me, many of those present hadn't ever engaged in this way with their peers at Microsoft. "I thought half of these folks were going to roll their eyes and go, 'Kathleen, are you kidding me? We're going to have to talk about our purpose and we're going to have to sit in couches and you're going to ask me to put my laptop down?"[33] Kathleen enlisted Dr. Michael Gervais, a well-known mindset coach and psychologist who was hardly a newbie, to facilitate the day.[34]

Members of Nadella's team did start to open up. As Hogan remembers, "People connected their personal mission to the work we do. They brought in their upbringing, their religion, be it Confucianism or Catholicism."[35] Nadella led the way, describing his childhood growing up in India, his personal philosophy built around empathy and learning, and, most movingly, his experiences raising a child with special needs. As portrayed in Nadella's book, this conversation marked the beginning of a years-long journey to create a new culture at Microsoft, one that sought to galvanize people around the purpose by empowering people to grow as individuals.

Nadella's biggest challenge upon becoming CEO was to turn around the company, which in recent years had become smug and sluggish.[36] As he told me, he couldn't hope to succeed if he simply picked a new strategy for the enterprise. He had to delve deeper to something more fundamental—a purpose—that could serve as an anchor and a guide to strategy formation. "We were doing a lot of things out of envy just because our competition had some success," he explained. "We felt, 'Oh, we have to do this just to keep up with them.' And I said, 'Hey, let's go back. I believe companies have a sense of purpose and identity.'"[37]

But purpose on its own wasn't enough. It would be superficial and ultimately meaningless if it wasn't supported by a culture that brought it to life inside the organization. Companies need purpose, Nadella remarked, but they also need "the culture that allows you to pursue your sense of purpose." The psychologist Carol Dweck's research influenced Nadella to build a culture grounded in a growth mindset, where employees could use the company platform to fulfill their own sense of purpose.

This approach led him, Hogan, and others on his team to a novel, even radical idea. Instead of building a culture in which people performed better because they construed what they did as personally meaningful, they sought to build one in which people explored their own deepest life purposes, whatever those might be, and used the company as a platform for realizing them. As Hogan notes, "You won't fully work for Microsoft until you make Microsoft work for you." It was this notion of the company as platform that first began to take root during that unorthodox 2014 meeting. "Our roles on the [senior leadership team] started to change that day," Nadella writes. "Each leader was no longer solely employed by Microsoft, they had tapped into a higher calling—to employ Microsoft in pursuit of their personal passions to empower others."[38]

Research in organizational psychology points to the wisdom of spurring employees to consider and express personal purpose on the job. Scholars have postulated that the meaning of our work isn't locked in place or beyond our control. We can take steps to *shape* our jobs so that they hold more meaning for us. We can change any number of elements, including how we conceive of what we do, the nature and scope of our activities, and how we relate to others around us. Through such "job crafting," as scholars call it, we can greatly increase the satisfaction and joy our work brings us. More than a job or even a career, job crafting can turn our careers into deeply purposeful callings.[39]

By prompting Microsoft's leaders to contemplate and identify their own, personal purpose on the job, Nadella was *spurring* job crafting, guiding leaders to attach deeper personal meaning to what they do—to see their jobs as callings on account of the social good they perform. Other deep purpose leaders I interviewed have made similar moves.

Recognizing that individual expression and the personalization of work lead to greater motivation and engagement, they encourage others to heighten their own understandings of work and its significance. They presume that employees who are more motivated in general and better capable of performing will also serve the organization's purpose more fully. Research suggests they're on to something. A survey of more than three hundred senior leaders found that, in their view, inspired workers vastly outperform those who are merely satisfied. In fact, "it would take two and a quarter satisfied employees to generate the same output as one inspired employee." Researchers tie inspiration back to a sense of mission or purpose.[40]

As some deep purpose leaders told me, prompting individuals to think about their personal purpose serves organizational purpose in another way. Employees who ascribe a higher purpose to their jobs or roles are *temperamentally* more inclined to respond to and pursue an organizational purpose. Matt Breitfelder, global head of human capital and senior partner at the private equity firm Apollo Global Management, put it this way: "If I'm in the zone of purpose, I'm very clear about my craft and what I'm trying to accomplish. I wake up in the morning excited to get better at it and to have impact. So naturally, I become receptive to others in my company who think like this. And I'm really receptive to my company's expression of purpose. Not only receptive to it, but I want to be part of it. I want to shape it and contribute to it."[41]

Microsoft has since created opportunities for *all* employees to explore their life purposes through their work and to communicate it to their peers. The idea isn't to make Microsoft a playground for people's pet projects. It's to spur them to connect their personal desire to contribute to society with Microsoft's purpose of empowering others. As Kathleen Hogan puts it, "We focus on fostering a workplace where everyone can use the power of the Microsoft platform to pursue their passions, fulfill their purpose, and empower others. It's core to our mission as well as our culture."[42]

In speeches and other communications, Microsoft's leaders emphasize how important they feel it is for a synthesis to exist between life purpose and the organization's purpose of "empower[ing] every person and every organization on the planet to achieve more." Microsoft trains its thousands of leaders to help their team members connect the company's purpose with their own life purpose.[43] The company also affirms the importance of life purpose by maintaining a portal called Microsoft Life, which contains deeply personal stories about employees, their worldviews and personal missions, and their connection with their work at Microsoft. Finally, Microsoft provides financial and logistical support to employees who are using the company as a platform for pursuing life purpose.

John Kahan, general manager of customer data and analytics at Microsoft, tragically lost his infant son to sudden infant death syndrome

(SIDS), which kills thousands in the United States each year. Since then, he's raised hundreds of thousands of dollars for the medical institution where his son received care. A member of his team learned of his tragedy and felt so moved that they organized other data scientists on Kahan's team to see if they could create a new tool that would aid medical researchers. They discovered that researchers around the world could access only relatively small sets of epidemiological data. Using Azure, Microsoft's cloud computing platform, the team created a tool that allowed scientists to glean insights from millions of datapoints from an as-yet untapped federal health database.[44]

The team donated this tool, which required 450 hours of staff time to build, to Seattle Children's Research Institute. Through a matching program designed to encourage staff to pursue these kinds of projects, Microsoft made a cash donation of $11,250. Scientists welcomed the tool as an asset that would help them probe deeper into the complexities of SIDS. Kahan described himself as feeling "incredibly blessed" not only to work with such skilled and compassionate colleagues, but to work for "a company that encourages us to use our skills to solve world problems."

Unleashing the Power of Life Purpose

As the Microsoft example suggests, people forge multiple kinds of personal purpose. We might ascribe purpose to a specific job role (job or role purpose) as well as to our entire careers (career purpose). At the deepest level, we might perceive our entire lives, not simply our work or careers, as bearing an existential intent (life purpose).[45] If we're emergency room physicians, we might identify our job purpose as "saving patient lives" and our career purpose as "making emergency medicine safer and more humane." Our life purpose, which we might pursue only in part through our work, might be broader and more profound. Perhaps we wish to "project more caring and compassion into the world." Or if we're religious, perhaps we dedicate ourselves, both as doctors and as human beings, to "helping to realize God's spirit on Earth." If we belong to a historically underrepresented group, we might regard our

THREE DIMENSIONS OF PURPOSE

life's purpose as helping to strengthen our community and create opportunities for the next generation. Life purpose goes to the core of who we are as people, and we arrive at our ultimate reason for being thanks to hard-won experiences or after prolonged searching or contemplation.

Some deep purpose leaders and companies seeking to embed organizational purpose only prompt employees to consider their job or career purpose. But others go further, asking employees to look inward and contemplate their life purpose. These leaders have entirely different conversations with team members than leaders usually do—intense, searching dialogues about the kind of people team members are and what ultimately matters to them. At first glance, delving into life purpose might seem daring and even ill-advised. It's one thing to challenge employees to find deeper meaning in their jobs, but there's no guarantee that a given worker's life purpose will align well with the organizational purpose and its supporting culture. If people show up at work focused on their own, individual purposes, they might not pull together as readily to achieve common, organizational objectives. Coordination and commitment could break down, contributing to chaos and confusion in the workplace.

Employees' personal purposes might also turn out to conflict with the company's existential intent. In the National Football League, teams focus on the simple purpose of winning games and making it to the Super Bowl.[46] The Kansas City Chiefs fulfilled this purpose in 2019–2020, going 15–4 and defeating the San Francisco 49ers in Super

Bowl LIV. During the 2020–2021 season, the Chiefs again reached the Super Bowl, but they did it without offensive lineman Laurent Duvernay-Tardif. When he's not blocking tacklers, Duvernay-Tardif is also pursuing a career as a physician—one of the few in league history to do that. In July 2020, with the COVID-19 pandemic raging, he made the difficult personal choice to skip the entire upcoming autumn season to take care of patients at a facility in his native Quebec. Announcing the decision, he noted that if he continued to play that year, he would risk transmitting the virus to patients.[47] Duvernay-Tardif's personal purpose conflicted with the organizational purpose. Personal purpose won.

Duvernay-Tardif's team accommodated the deviation from the organizational purpose. "I just think it's tremendous dedication to his profession, what his future is going to be, and mainly to the people that he gets to help," Chiefs' head coach Andy Reid said.[48] If such deviation became more common, however, it could easily prove disruptive to the team. Deep purpose leaders understand this risk and yet still seek to help team members explore their life purpose. They take this stance for three reasons. First, they can mitigate risk by screening prospective hires to gauge whether their personal purpose conflicts with that of the organization, and by ushering out current employees whose personal purposes pose a problem. Second, deep purpose leaders believe that in most cases it *will* be possible to find an overlap or synthesis between employees' personal agendas and that of the organization. Third, they perceive the upsides of encouraging employees' pursuit of life purpose to be so extraordinary that they are worth the risk.

As Pete Carroll suggests, self-knowledge including a sense of our life purpose is the very engine of exceptional performance. "It's being in connection with your true self that's so powerful," he says. "And when you consistently do what you believe in, then you just have the opportunity to be all you can possibly be."[49] Leaders at Microsoft have come to a similar conclusion about life purpose. "You need to think of Microsoft as a platform to achieve your purpose, empowered by your colleagues who share the company culture and values," Kathleen Hogan remarked.[50] Elsewhere, Hogan noted that Microsoft employees who use the company as a platform for realizing their own life purpose will find "deep meaning in what they do—and solutions for some of the world's biggest challenges result."[51] Satya Nadella put it to me succinctly: the organizational purpose will only feel compelling to you "if you feel that it's connected to you. Otherwise, it feels like you're doing it for somebody else."[52]

In his understanding of human motivation and the role of life purpose, Pete Carroll was profoundly influenced by the work of the pioneering psychologist Abraham Maslow. Many know Maslow for his famous hierarchy of needs, depicted as a pyramid with more basic needs at the bottom and our highest need—self-actualization—at the top. According to this schema, we must first satisfy our lower order needs before we can go on to achieve the higher order ones.

As I was surprised to learn, Maslow never conceived of his hierarchy of needs as a pyramid—that was the work of a management consultant, who reinterpreted key aspects of Maslow's theory. Analyzing Maslow's published and unpublished works, the psychologist Scott Barry Kaufman observes that Maslow conceived of human needs as interrelated and integrated with one another. Further, he believed that we worked on our needs on an ongoing and overlapping basis over time, not in a rigid, stepwise way. In place of a pyramid, Kaufman argues that Maslow's hierarchy better resembles a sailboat. Some of our needs—those for physical safety, connection with others, and self-esteem—relate to our basic sense of *security* as human beings. These make up the hard, protective hull of the sailboat. Other needs of ours—including those for exploration and love—relate to our *growth* as human beings. These are the sail that powers the boat's motion. At the very pinnacle of the sail, Kaufman argues, is our need for purpose in life. We humans cannot live to our full potential unless we pursue an "overarching aspiration that energizes one's efforts and provides a central source of meaning and significance in one's life."[53]

Importantly for our discussion, Maslow didn't regard mere self-actualization as the highest potential of human beings, but rather as a pathway to something still higher: a movement beyond self and personal identity and toward others and their needs. "Self-actualization . . . paradoxically makes more possible the transcendence of self, and of self-consciousness and of selfishness," he wrote.[54] The highest human need, Maslow seems to have believed, was the purposeful pursuit of higher, socially minded ambitions, not selfish ones. True self-actualization entailed, Kaufman notes, the "harmonious integration of one's whole self in the service of cultivating the good society."[55]

By engaging in a dialogue about employees' own life purposes and helping to connect those with organizational purpose, deep purpose leaders and companies cue into our highest yearnings and strivings. They create cultures in which individuals can be their fullest possible selves, understanding that the drive to self-actualize and ultimately transcend will unleash the highest levels of motivation, dedication, and creativity, and that these in turn will better help the organization achieve *its* purpose.

Lessons for Leaders

You might shudder at the thought of conversing intimately with your colleagues about personal purpose, identity, and values. It feels too "mushy," too far removed from the business of your company. Contending with competitive and volatile markets, you lack the time or energy to spend on getting to know people and indulging their individuality. Everyone would be better off if employees and managers just focused on performing well at the tasks before them rather than focusing on themselves.

A traditional, no-nonsense approach to culture can certainly work: witness the success of the New England Patriots, which under coach Bill Belichick have employed exactly that approach under the mantra "Do your job."[56] But a more humanistic approach oriented toward the needs of individual team members can work too, far more effectively than many might think. Microsoft, the Seahawks, Ovia Health, Livongo, and KPMG all realized important gains by building cultures of "me." By changing their basic assumptions about people and their psychological needs, they managed to unlock human potential.

Between 2014 and 2020, Microsoft's revenues rose from $86.8 billion to $143 billion.[57] Its valuation surpassed $1 trillion for the first time in what one commentator called a "Nadellaissance."[58] Leaders at the company regard cultural transformation as integral to these results, with one noting that the alignment of personal and organizational purpose "drove a wave of engagement. People started giving us more of their discretionary free time than ever before."[59] Likewise, Pete Carroll compiled an impressive 145–94 record and one Super Bowl win during his NFL coaching career, leading the Seahawks to the playoffs in nine out of his eleven seasons with the team and sparking speculation that he was on track for election to the Pro Football Hall of Fame.[60] As for KPMG, we've already described the great success of the company's 10,000 Stories Challenge campaign.

Connecting organizational purpose with the individual's own, personal purpose isn't easy. You might balk at allowing individuals to "be themselves," worrying that you're ceding too much control and that performance will suffer. That fear is not unfounded: a member of Carroll's staff relates that the team environment at the Seahawks resembles a "controlled chaos" at times given the liberty team members feel to express their individuality. The paradox, though, is that by ceding control over individuals, you ultimately unlock individual performance. You obtain that high performance not by compelling or incenting team members, but by firing up intrinsic motivation. As an important additional benefit, you create an environment more welcoming to diverse employees, one that enables them to feel included and valued.

This doesn't mean there's no room for a more authoritative stance. Previous chapters have explored the pursuit of deep purpose as a primarily top-down process of injecting more soul, meaning, values, and community into the company and the experience of work. In giving employees a voice, you must continue to show strong leadership by defining, promoting, and activating a transcendent purpose around which the organization can rally. Apple University Dean Joel Podolny observes that people often discover personal purpose "through the actual pursuit of an extraordinary organizational purpose."[61] Lacking an inspiring organizational purpose, they might never become aware of their own, individual reasons for being. As a leader, it's your job to convene a moral community around a transcendent purpose and to provide space for both individuality in general and the pursuit of personal purpose.

In the end, embedding purpose through a more personalized culture means changing how you perceive employees. You must truly empathize with them, seeing them not as a means to an end but as people seeking self-actualization and transcendence. The management thinker Douglas McGregor famously expounded on his Theory Y, a notion some managers have that employees potentially enjoy work, are self-directed, and are self-motivated to achieve their highest limits as humans. By contrast, Theory X, as McGregor defined it, holds that employees are uninterested in work, responsive only to coercion, and motivated only by money and other external rewards.

To move toward deep purpose and build the kinds of cultures that activate people deeply around a common reason for being, you must embrace Theory Y to the fullest, developing a collaborative style rather than an authoritative one. You must also embrace what Abraham Maslow late in life called Theory Z, the idea that some people seek to transcend their own self-actualization and devote themselves to higher, humanistic values like beauty, justice, or excellence for their own sake.[62] Leaders like Pete Carroll and Satya Nadella tend toward Theory Z when prompting team members to think about their loftiest personal ambitions, which might include devotion to the humanistic values. Underlying their devotion to both Theory Y and Theory Z is a basic and pervasive empathy toward others, which all leaders must cultivate to take purpose deeper. As Pete Carroll notes, his approach "is simply about caring for people. If you care about people, you elevate their own self-worth, you coach up their strengths and that makes them more powerful than they already are. This isn't a new age deal. This isn't rocket science. This is just humanness."[63]

If you take away nothing else from this chapter, make it this: *the best way to activate deep purpose is to increase the care you show to individual employees.* Caring leaders elevate employees' uniqueness by acknowledging and engaging with them as individuals. They show true curiosity about individuals and their experiences, restraining their impulse to judge. They encourage and support employees in their development, helping them feel confident. They encourage employees to deepen their own self-understanding and to explore their own, personal reasons for being, engaging them in deeper conversations about their philosophies or life purpose. Rather than simply mentoring them and offering advice, they serve as committed, long-term sponsors of their careers. To help employees feel passionate about their work, they connect them with the purpose as a common, transcendent cause. When employees' performance suffers, caring leaders don't rush to levy penalties but instead look to the underlying causes and consider how they might help. In large organizations, caring leaders train managers to take these actions at scale. In each of these ways, caring leaders unlock human potential to its fullest, unleashing high performance.

But we would do well to take an even broader view of caring. In large organizations, caring about employees isn't just about interacting personally with employees in humane, compassionate ways. It's also about rethinking how work is organized and structured. Many companies retain old-fashioned, command-and-control operating norms that thwart the individual's pursuit of life purpose and make a commitment to organizational purpose both frustrating and fruitless. Empathizing with employees and their needs, deep purpose leaders dismantle these norms and grant more discretion and autonomy to employees. Realizing purpose's potential as a humane, noncoercive leadership philosophy, they unleash people to pursue their and the organization's highest ambitions and, in turn, to perform at their best.

CHAPTER 7

ESCAPING THE IRON CAGE

Leaders who go deepest on purpose seem unusually dedicated to tearing up the conventional bureaucratic playbook and positioning their companies for innovation, agility, and growth. They take two key steps. First, they give lower-level employees and managers more autonomy, flattening their hierarchies. Second, they nurture collaboration across functions, business units, geographies, and other traditional silos. These organizational moves fuel trust in the workforce and commitment to the purpose. At the same time, purpose itself enables trust to flourish, facilitating the departure from traditional bureaucratic structures.

What killed sixteen-year-old Amber Marie Rose wasn't a dread disease or an active shooter at her school. It wasn't suicide or an accidental overdose. It was a small device in her car's steering column that most people probably haven't even heard of. A device called an ignition switch.

Amber went to a party one Friday night in late July 2005. She was driving home at around 4 a.m. when she lost control of her new Chevy Cobalt and hit a tree. The impact killed her. She'd been drinking, was driving over twice the speed limit, and wasn't wearing a seat belt.[1] But another factor played a role in her death: her car's airbag hadn't deployed. As a close relative of Amber's later recounted, she had spoken with first responders who had attended to Amber following the crash. "They told me that had the airbags deployed she would have been injured, but she would have been alive today."[2]

We can trace her airbag's failure back to that ignition switch. When you slip a key into a car's ignition and turn it on, you must apply a certain amount of force. Ditto for when you turn the car off. That's not a coincidence: if the switch inside the steering column didn't require much force to turn off, a car that was running might suddenly turn off or slip into "accessory mode"[3] if you hit it with your knee or go over a bump or if keys or other objects weigh down your key ring. Your car might stall at an inopportune time, leading to an accident. Or if you crashed your car, the airbags and other safety features might not work as expected.[4] The latter is what happened in Amber's case. As a private investigator found, her car had been in "accessory" mode when her accident occurred.[5]

Amber wasn't the only person harmed by a faulty ignition switch in a Chevy Cobalt. In 2014, nine years after Amber died, General Motors (GM), maker of the Cobalt and other cars with the same ignition switch, publicly acknowledged that flaws in its switches had led to many fatal accidents. The company recalled 2.6 million cars for ignition switch problems and allotted $625 million to provide compensation for 124 deaths and 275 injuries.[6] A settlement in 2015 compensated over 1,300 additional death and injury claims. GM also agreed that year to pay $900 million to end a federal criminal investigation.[7] In 2020, GM paid out $120 million as compensation for economic harms caused by its faulty ignition switches.[8]

Following its recall announcements in 2014, it emerged that GM had known of issues with the ignition switch since 2001, and that since 2007 it had known of about four fatal crashes possibly linked to the switch.[9] Initially, GM employees dismissed the ignition switch issues as unrelated to safety and failed to take serious action. After 2007, GM's internal investigators failed to trace the fatal crashes back to the faulty ignition switch. Only in mid-2013 did GM bring in an external consultant who pegged the ignition switch as the Cobalt accidents' root cause. In early 2014, Mary Barra, at the time GM's incoming CEO, finally learned about serious issues with the ignition switches.[10] A committee of the US House of Representatives summoned Barra for a hearing, wanting to understand how GM could have waited so long to recall the defective cars. The question seemed especially apt given that the part itself only cost $10 and took less than an hour to replace.[11]

"One Ugly Mess"

In a 1909 speech, the great German sociologist Max Weber lauded bureaucratic organizations—those that are rational, rule- and process-bound, hierarchical, impersonal, professionally managed, and marked by a sharp division of labor—for their unrivaled accuracy and efficiency. "There is nothing," he said, "no machinery in the world, which works so precisely as does this human machine—so cheaply! . . . The technical superiority of the bureaucratic mechanism stands unshaken, as does the technical superiority of the machine over the handworker."[12] By regulating behavior and removing variation born of personal emotions, prejudices, and quirks, bureaucracies ensure accountability and consistency.

Think for a moment what life would be like without bureaucracy. If you went to the airport to catch a flight, you wouldn't necessarily know what documents you'd need in order to clear security and board the plane. The experience might be something like what partygoers experience when trying to get past the bouncer at a nightclub. Whoever is on duty at the airport that day might have their own rules about whom to admit—rules that might be arbitrary or unrelated to your own best interests as a traveler. Is your physical appearance deemed attractive? Do you slip the TSA agent a twenty? Do they happen to be in a good mood that day? Then they might let you in. Otherwise, they might not. And they also might not be paying all that much attention to security because there are no formal regulations governing their work or formal mechanisms for holding them accountable, as there are in bureaucracies. The TSA agent might decide to scan every bag for hidden weapons, or they might not.

This is but one small example. Think of how unsettling it would be to know that there's no bureaucracy organizing the mechanics working on the plane, the pilots flying it, or the mechanics fixing it. Think of how unsettling it would be to have no consistency or formality governing the functioning of organizations in health-care settings, or in education, or in government. A world without bureaucracy would be a very unfamiliar one for most of us, and one that most of us probably wouldn't want to inhabit.

At the same time, as Weber recognized, the very rationality and machine-like constancy that made bureaucracies so efficient also rendered them soul-destroying. By squeezing out human expression and judgment, bureaucracies turn workers into mere functionaries, "a little cog in the machine." It was "horrible to think that the world could one day be filled with nothing but those little cogs, little men clinging to little jobs and striving towards bigger ones." This would be a world, Weber suggested, of individuals terrified of taking risks and thinking for themselves. "The great question," he concluded, was not how to advance bureaucracy, but rather how to "keep a portion of mankind free from this parceling-out of the soul, from this supreme mastery of the bureaucratic way of life." Elsewhere, Weber and other sociologists that came after him famously described the rationality underpinning bureaucratic life as disenchanting and imprisoning, an "iron cage."[13]

If you've worked in a large organization, you know that bureaucracies remain every bit as soul-destroying as Weber suggests. But as you might also have gathered, the benefits of bureaucracies are no longer as apparent as they once were. Built for efficiency and regularity rather than speed and adaptability, bureaucracies languish under their own weight in today's digital world. My own research has tracked how bureaucracy can make firms look inward and ignore their customers, even when their very survival is at stake.[14] These and many other effects of iron cages take an immense toll. By one calculation, bureaucratic companies are blowing $2.6 *trillion* on "unnecessary bloat and busywork."[15] And this doesn't begin to account for bureaucracy's broader societal costs. People *die* because companies are too freighted with rules, processes, silos, hierarchy, and top-down decision-making to solve problems expeditiously. Indeed, what ultimately killed Amber Marie Rose and so many others wasn't a defective car part but something far more insidious: entrenched corporate bureaucracy.

When the Cobalt crisis blew up in early 2014, newly minted CEO Mary Barra struggled to explain how the ignition switch debacle could have happened,[16] so she brought in former US Attorney Anton Valukas to investigate. Valukas's scathing June 2014 report revealed a number of problems, including, in the words of one commentator, "an organization mired in bureaucracy and unable to take responsibility for its mistakes."[17] There was, Valukas contended,

> *a proliferation of committees and a lack of accountability. The Cobalt Ignition Switch issue passed through an astonishing number of committees. We repeatedly heard from witnesses that they flagged the issue, proposed a solution, and the solution died in a committee or with some other* ad hoc *group exploring the issue. But determining the identity of any actual decision-maker was impenetrable. No single person owned any decision. Indeed, it was often difficult to determine who sat on the committees or what they considered, as there are rarely minutes of meetings.*[18]

The silos that existed in GM's big, top-down bureaucracy also posed a problem. As Valukas noted, internal investigations of the ignition switches floundered because information didn't flow readily among different groups. For example, when engineers in 2004–2005 considered reports of vehicles stalling while in motion, nobody bothered to tell them that "the vehicle was designed so that the airbags would not deploy when the ignition switch was in Accessory [mode]. As a consequence, the engineers failed to recognize the stalls as a safety issue and resolve the problem quickly. Even the committees . . . that were designed to have cross-disciplinary members did not connect the dots."[19] Leaders also told Valukas they hadn't taken the airbag problems as seriously as they might have because nobody had communicated that fatal accidents had occurred.[20]

General Motors was well known for its lumbering bureaucracy. After the company declared bankruptcy in 2008 and received a bailout from the US government, a task force assembled by President Barack Obama encountered the company's organization up close, and it wasn't pretty. "Everyone knew Detroit's reputation for insular, slow-moving cultures," one of the task force members observed. "Even by that low standard, I was shocked by the stunningly poor management that we found."[21] But as the Valukas report revealed, bureaucracy was so out of control at GM that it gave rise to a dangerous culture of lassitude and inaction. Valukas documented a practice called the salute, in which leaders pointed at others to deflect blame when problems arose. There was also the "GM nod," in which "everyone nods in agreement to a proposed plan of action, but then leaves the room with no intention to follow through, and the nod is an empty gesture."[22]

Such a nod took place at a 2011 meeting when GM's lawyers, concerned about mounting lawsuits, prodded investigators to take swift action. A manager of the investigative team was allegedly present, and by some accounts he didn't want to "investigate the airbag non-deployment issue because the incident rate was not high." The manager apparently agreed to assign a team member to investigate, but when he did so he failed to convey any sense of urgency. As a result, little was done.[23] Overall, the Valukas report stands, in the words of one legal expert, as "a classic study of the dangers of bureaucracy: divided responsibility, lack of initiative, failure to seize problems and solve them, failure to see the larger issues for the company, perhaps fear of surfacing bad news."[24] Another media account put it succinctly: "One ugly mess."[25]

The Purpose Connection

Mary Barra has since moved to clean up the mess, slashing red tape and making GM more responsive and nimbler. She began paring back on bureaucracy before becoming CEO,[26] but the ignition switch crisis hardened her resolve, as did the need to reimagine the business to stay ahead of disruptions (including electric cars, car sharing, and digitally connected cars). GM couldn't suddenly eradicate key elements of bureaucracy. Still, Barra and her team took important steps to moderate their effects. To prevent safety issues from becoming buried down in the hierarchy, GM implemented programs that allowed employees to easily alert superiors to safety issues and that trained employees to speak up when they saw problems. To break down silos, GM created an organization within the company that took a systems approach to engineering, connecting individual parts with the whole product.[27]

GM later introduced additional programs to make the company more collaborative, transparent, and innovative, including the GM 2020 initiative, which convenes employees in hackathon-style "Co:Labs" to solve problems, and the Tipping Forward initiative, which enables employees to share their work in a live presentation before their peers.[28] For Barra, reducing bureaucracy and making the organization more fluid remains a top priority, not just on account of safety but as a means of enhancing overall performance. "If you believe that most people come to work every day and want to do a good job," she said, "then what's getting in their way? Do we have an environment, a collaborative environment, and the tools that are necessary so they can do their best work? Or is it painful to get the most simple task done?"[29]

Interestingly, GM's reform of its bureaucracy coincided with a new commitment to purpose. While the company had once merely sought to lead its industry,[30] now it adopted a corporate "promise" that resembled an existential intent: GM committed "to deliver safer, better and more sustainable solutions for our customers. We are transforming personal mobility and improving communities around the world."[31] Relatedly, the company in 2017 adopted as its vision "to create a world with zero crashes, zero emissions, and zero congestion."[32] The following year, Barra was among the 181 CEO signatories of the Business Roundtable's "Statement on the Purpose of a Corporation."[33] Barra has stated that the company is "fully committed to an all-electric future,"[34] and in 2021, the company made news by publicly committing to a goal of achieving carbon neutrality by 2040.[35]

It's too early to tell if GM has become a deep purpose company, but the company's trajectory points to an intriguing pattern. As my research revealed, leaders who go deepest on purpose seem unusually dedicated to tearing up the conventional corporate bureaucratic playbook and positioning their companies for innovation, agility, and growth. Further, they shake their companies free of the iron cage in two primary ways. They solve what I call the "Too Many Bosses" problem, flattening their hierarchies and giving lower-level employees and managers more autonomy. And they solve what I call the "Entrenched Silos" problem, nurturing collaboration across functions, business units, geographies, and so on.

But what is the precise connection between breaking free of the iron cage and deep purpose? It is twofold. On the one hand, the presence of purpose itself fosters trust, enabling better, more humane ways of organizing to take root. On the other, addressing the Too Many Bosses and Entrenched Silos problems also helps to build trust, and in turn, embed deep purpose into an organization. For deep purpose leaders, sustaining purpose goes hand in hand with building innovative, high-performance organizations marked by an ever-deepening dynamic of trust.

Solving the "Too Many Bosses" Problem

It was 2020, and small farmers in the Indian state of Haryana had a problem. Their crops were ready for harvesting, but there weren't enough agricultural workers to do the work. These local farmers weren't wealthy. Each harvest could make the difference between a small measure of prosperity and poverty. If the farmers couldn't find a way to get their crops out of the ground, they, their families, and the communities that relied on them would be ruined.

A heroine came to the rescue: a team member at the global Indian firm Mahindra's farming equipment business (FES) named Shipra Kumari.[36] A $19.4 billion conglomerate founded in 1945, Mahindra operated in one hundred countries and maintained a large portfolio of businesses spanning the automobile, financial services, IT, and real estate industries, to name a few. Its FES sold tractors, harvesters, and other machinery, claiming a 40 percent market share in India.[37] On this occasion, Kumari learned of the farmers' plights and felt moved to act. "The crop was ready, and the farmers were helpless," she told me. "Everything can wait but not agriculture, so it was a huge concern for me as a Mahindraite. It was time to step up and act."

On her own initiative, Shipra called the local department of agriculture to track down how many harvester machines were available in the area, where they were located, and where exactly their owners would be taking them to perform harvesting tasks. With this information, Shipra could connect farmers to available equipment in their immediate areas that could harvest their crops. "It wasn't an easy task," she recalled, "but I thought that no, I have to do it, like it was a big thing I wanted to do for the farmers."[38] Shipra didn't expect to book any revenue as a result of her efforts—it just seemed like the right thing to do. And indeed, it was. Thanks to her quick thinking, over a dozen local farmers salvaged their crops.

This act of goodwill wasn't an isolated incident. As a business, FES strove to use technology to make a difference in the lives of small farmers—a mission whose pursuit, as one employee told me, gives him "immense pleasure."[39] FES developed a new farming-as-a-service (FaaS) offering that would increase farmers' productivity and improve their livelihoods.[40] Unlike other companies, FES initially offered FaaS for free to farmers—a strategic move that differentiated their offerings while also allowing small farmers access to state-of-the-art technology. To help more women succeed in farming, FES began an initiative to help them build their farming skills, secure low-cost tools, and find ways to supplement their incomes.

FES's enlightened business practices didn't spawn from some high-level corporate directive. They were local actions taken independently as interpretations of Mahindra's broader corporate purpose. During the late 1990s, under the leadership of then-managing director and now chairman Anand Mahindra, Mahindra adopted a limited purpose: to show the world that an Indian company could produce world-class products and services. Few at the company understood this purpose or utilized it in their business activities. During the 2000s, as the company globalized, Anand realized that Mahindra needed to institute a new, broader reason for being to unify and embolden its far-flung operations. In 2010, the company adopted a purpose captured in a single word—

"Rise"—and articulated in the following statement: "We will challenge conventional thinking and innovatively use all their resources to drive positive change in the lives of stakeholders and communities across the world to enable them to Rise."[41]

Delivering on Rise meant pursuing three themes: "Accept no limits," "Alternative thinking," and "Driving positive change," all of which defined the overarching concept of rising up to transcend obstacles, challenges, or conventional wisdom. As Anand explained to me, Rise entailed a new, much more profound awareness of work and its meaning. It meant "seeing our work as an intrinsic part of who we are and what we want to be," not just doing a good job but "doing a job that impacts people's lives and helps other people to Rise."

Once Rise launched in 2011, Anand and his leadership team spent the next several years exhaustively communicating, embedding, and sustaining it across Mahindra. Studying these efforts, I noticed an impulse on the part of leaders to depart from a rigid command-and-control mentality and allow for more autonomy. Leaders drove the Rise initiative, but they never wanted the purpose to feel like a top-down directive. Rather, they intended to inspire business units across the company to make decisions as they saw fit, but in a consistent way built around a clear vision of the company's intentions. Anand remarked, "My style is to delegate. I don't want people saying they are carrying out Anand's orders, that's not Rise. They have to Rise first and they have to believe what they say. My job is just to make sure that people understand Rise and are in line with its philosophy."[42] Because Rise was much more of a general philosophy and approach to operating, the company opted not to measure it too closely, monitoring overall business and external branding metrics rather than holding leaders accountable to a new array of Rise-specific metrics.

Mahindra's leaders allowed each business to implement and sustain Rise internally as it saw fit. As Ramesh Iyer, managing director of Mahindra and Mahindra Financial Services, told me, "None of us as sector heads or CEOs was pressured to communicate Rise or told how we should use Rise."[43] Over time, as Rise became embedded, leaders and business units began to interpret it in their own ways to drive action. The farm equipment business interpreted Rise as "democratizing technology for small land holding farmers globally" so that they could enjoy more economic prosperity. Mahindra Auto lived Rise by fostering long-term relationships with stakeholders, helping suppliers and dealers that ran into financial trouble and declining to lay off employees at one of its manufacturing subsidiaries. Mahindra Finance not only marketed products to formerly unserved rural customers; it also hired local employees, offering them new growth opportunities. As Rise became more firmly embedded, one leader told me, "We were living the Rise pillars consciously and in a more widespread way. Many leaders were taking initiatives in their own areas, independent of process and structure. People were consciously making choices aligned with Rise."[44]

Autonomy linked to and enabled by the purpose injected palpable energy into Mahindra and enhanced its performance. The company's profits more than doubled between 2011 and 2018, gains leaders partly attribute to employees' enthusiasm for Rise. Several employees I interviewed spoke with obvious excitement about Rise. They told me the purpose energized them not only at work but in their personal lives, inspiring them to exercise more and cultivate other positive changes.

From a psychological standpoint, this response is hardly surprising. Research suggests autonomy does indeed motivate and engage employees.[45] We act voluntarily and enthusiastically when we tap intrinsic motivations, chief among them our need for autonomy.[46] A body of work in psychology called self-determination theory highlights autonomy alongside our needs for social connectedness and a sense of competence.[47] When we exercise "choice or volition" at work, we are well on our way to feeling a healthy sense of well-being grounded in a sense of agency. As the theory holds, humans are naturally primed to realize their potential, but their social environment can nourish or squelch their development. Undermine autonomy, and humans won't flourish. Support it, and they thrive. At Mahindra, largely autonomous business units drive the agenda under the umbrella of a purpose—and it shows. A commitment to purpose has led the company to loosen the grip of the iron cage.

The Purpose-Autonomy-Trust Nexus

But what precisely links autonomy and purpose? In describing how personally meaningful they found Rise and how gratifying it was to bring the purpose to life, a number of interviewees evoked the concept of trust. They liked that the company was trusting them, and they in turn trusted the company. Trust had arisen in my discussions at other deep purpose firms as well. On one level, the connection between trust and autonomy seems fairly obvious, but analyzing it I found some interesting connections not only between trust and autonomy, but between these concepts and purpose. The links between these three were so nuanced and multidirectional that I came to conceive of a veritable *nexus* of purpose, autonomy, and trust.

AUTONOMY-TRUST-PURPOSE NEXUS

To glimpse this nexus at work, consider the fast-growing American eyewear retailer Warby Parker. Founded in 2010, Warby Parker seeks to make eyewear affordable for everyone and to advance the cause of "socially conscious business."[48] To make good on this existential intent, Warby Parker adopted a signature policy of giving away a pair of glasses for each one sold—what it calls "buy a pair, give a pair."[49] As of this writing, Warby Parker has given away some eight million pairs of glasses[50] and sends every three-year veteran of the company to a developing country to see its glasses donation programs in action. The company also broadened its social contributions, running programs that seek to expand access to eyecare in general among those who lack it.[51] At one time a B Corp,[52] Warby Parker is carbon neutral and advocates publicly on behalf of social issues, including immigrants' rights, LGBTQ+ protection, and net neutrality.[53]

Like Mahindra, Warby Parker addressed the Too Many Bosses problem in the course of pursuing deep purpose. During the company's early days, Warby Parker's four founders "had no hierarchy between themselves, committed to consensus-based decision-making and agreed that clear communication should be a core value of their start-up, going as far as to conduct regular 360-degree reviews of one another."[54] As the company grew rapidly during the 2010s, leaders emphasized autonomy as an operating norm, to the point where employees who had worked in more conventional organizations found the transition jarring.[55] Leaders integrated crowdsourcing into decision-making, most notably in the firm's product development group. Warby Parker created a system called Warbles that allowed employees to propose new projects to work on in accordance with the firm's strategy. Employees, managers, and leaders voted to determine which projects the company would prioritize. Afterward, employees could decide which projects to work on. If they wished, they could choose projects that didn't make it to the top of the priorities list.[56]

As cofounder and co-CEO Neil Blumenthal told me, such autonomy presumed the existence of trusting relationships. "If you have trust in one another," he said, "particularly if leadership has trust in the team, they can grant autonomy to team members."[57] He and other leaders explicitly communicated confidence in their employees, enshrining trust as one of the company's core values.[58] But for autonomy to blossom, employees also had to trust leaders. They had to have faith that leaders would support them if they made decisions that later turned out to be misguided. Warby Parker went out of its way to win this trust by explicitly welcoming employees to take risks, show creativity, and express themselves (another of the company's stated core values, for instance, was to "pursue new and creative ideas").[59] Leaders felt that their willingness to trust employees in turn induced employees to trust the company more. "To earn trust you have to give trust," cofounder and co-CEO Dave Gilboa says. "Trust is a two-way street."[60]

Purpose greatly intensified this connection between trust and autonomy. Scholars have argued that purpose benefits companies in part by prompting employees to trust the company more. Some theorize that purpose fosters trust inside companies because it clarifies the company's decision-making and enhances its credibility.[61] Such trust in turn comes to pervade the organization, underpinning, I argue, the granting of autonomy. Purpose transforms the entire basis for cooperation inside the workplace, turning the enterprise from a nexus of contracts between self-interested individuals into a nexus of *commitments*.[62] As my research confirmed, the trust that deep purpose companies inspire in employees not only forms such bonds; it's visceral and experiential—a stark contrast with the absence of trust that exists in most organizations.[63]

At Warby Parker, Director of Social Innovation Jesse Sneath told me of a memorable story shared by one of its veteran employees. To help employees connect with the purpose, Warby Parker sends them into the field to help distribute glasses to children in need. The departing team member went to a school in a tough neighborhood in the Bronx to present a new pair of eyeglasses to an eighth grader with severely impaired vision. "Have you ever gotten glasses before?" this employee asked the child. "No," she replied, "this is my first pair. Sometimes my mom lets me borrow her glasses."

This brief exchange made a strong impression on that employee. The thought of a child who desperately needed glasses having to go without them and to borrow their mother's glasses on occasion was heartbreaking. And to understand firsthand what it meant for a child's life prospects to finally have glasses—well, that was amazing. This experience stood out years later as one of the most powerful moments of this employee's career. It shaped his view of the company, inspiring him to embrace its mission. "A lot of team members have really similar experiences," Sneath said. "They feel connected, engaged, and proud of what we're building."[64] They come to *trust* the company, its leadership, and the moral community of which they are a part, for they can see that the company delivers on its lofty aspirations.

If a reason for being allows deep purpose leaders to nourish employees' trust in the company, these leaders cement that trust by granting employees more autonomy in actualizing the purpose. When employees encounter autonomy on the job, they understand that deep purpose leaders possess an entirely different conception of the enterprise than most leaders do. This validates the purpose in their eyes—they perceive it as real and worthy of their own commitment. We might further observe that purpose *presumes* the existence of considerable autonomy. Purpose offers an alternative to rigid control—it creates an environment in which individuals regulate *themselves* in ways helpful to the organization and to themselves. But empowering individuals to self-regulate requires that the company *trust* them and grant them a measure of autonomy—otherwise self-regulation would mean little.

Warby Parker and other deep purpose companies create a *virtuous circle* of trust: by establishing a purpose and trusting employees to bring it to life, they prompt employees to trust the company even more and to engage even more energetically on the purpose's behalf. A nexus of mutual trust, autonomy, and purpose emerges, with each of the elements undergirding and enhancing the other.[65] The result is a very different kind of organization, one that has freed itself to some extent from the iron cage and become more dynamic, nimble, and innovative.

There is one wrinkle: the autonomy that purpose helps to fuel isn't absolute. It usually comes with guardrails that instill a degree of control and render greater autonomy possible. Some might think of control and autonomy as opposites, antagonists in a zero-sum game. My research has shown that we can deploy constraints to *pave the way* for the healthy exercise of autonomy.[66] Total freedom seems desirable, but it frequently proves a burden, leading to confusion, chaos, and overwhelming choice for employees as well as diminished performance.[67] By providing a framework that helpfully bounds action, leaders and companies can liberate them to make choices autonomously and perform at their best.

Such "freedom within a framework," as I've called it, resembles jazz improvisation. Seasoned musicians don't play whatever they want. Rather, they give their improvisations form by adhering to some basic structural elements, such as a song's melody, rhythm, and chord changes. For businesses, freedom within a framework requires mobilizing three overriding structural elements: a *purpose* or mission; *priorities* or rules derived

from the organization's business goals; and *principles* derived from the
purpose and priorities that translate them for daily work.[68] The existence
of a purpose implies a *responsibility* to act intentionally. The specific language of the purpose as well as the priorities and rules incorporate positive prescriptions for behavior (*thou shalt*, in the parlance of the Bible's
Ten Commandments) as well as negative rules (*thou shalt not*). Purpose
gives rise to restrictions on behaviors (certain business opportunities the
company won't pursue, for example, or certain human resource policies
it won't adopt) as well as suggesting more positively the kinds of pro-
social behaviors employees and managers *should* take.

Solving the "Entrenched Silos" Problem

On September 12, 2001, the day after terrorists attacked the Twin
Towers in New York City and the Pentagon, it was the job of recently
installed Director of the Federal Bureau of Investigation (FBI) Robert Mueller to brief President George W. Bush on the government's
response. This historic, high-pressure briefing took place in the Oval
Office with the vice president, the head of the Central Intelligence
Agency, and other senior leaders in attendance. Almost immediately, it
was clear that it wouldn't go as Mueller had planned.

Mueller began by informing the president that the FBI had established command centers at the sites of the attacks and was working to
identify the precise identities of those responsible. A couple of minutes
into his presentation, the president interrupted him. "Hold on, Bob," he
said. "I understand you're doing that. I expect you to do that—it's what
the FBI has been doing for any number of years, and I've got confidence
in your ability to do it. My question to you today is: What is the FBI
doing to prevent the next terrorist attack?"[69]

Mueller was flummoxed. "I felt like an eighteen-year-old high school
student who had gotten the wrong assignment," he remembered during
a visit to one of my classes. "I had not thought about that. I had no
answer. It was not in my lexicon." Up until that point, the FBI's mission had been very simple: to investigate crimes once they had occurred
and enforce the law. Bush was asking the FBI to do something very

different: to *anticipate* national security threats and prevent them from happening.

At the time, some critics thought the FBI should stick to fighting crime, and that another agency should gather domestic intelligence about future threats. Not Mueller—he thought the agency should do both. When Attorney General John Ashcroft ordered him to prioritize preventing future attacks over investigating past crimes, Mueller moved aggressively to comply, defining prevention as the FBI's new purpose. But as he recognized, the FBI couldn't hope to succeed with its existing organization. Prior to the 9/11 attacks, the FBI was run as a series of silos, with fifty-six local field offices bearing responsibility for investigating crimes in their geographic areas. Still other silos existed at the FBI's headquarters, with teams dedicated to specific kinds of crimes, such as white collar or narcotics. Collaboration across offices and with other federal, state, and local law enforcement bodies and intelligence agencies was sparse (a failing that might well have led to the 9/11 Commission's post-mortem observation that "the FBI lacked the ability to know what it knew").[70] Local offices began investigations and continued to run them even when they sprawled into other local jurisdictions. To prevent attacks, the FBI would have to share information and resources across geographies and agencies. It would have to break down silos and the competition that they engendered. How would it make the shift?[71]

Business leaders everywhere face a similar challenge. It's one thing to inject more autonomy into an organization, but to become more innovative and agile in a complex, dynamic environment, leaders must also bridge the silos that constrain information flows and impede coordinated efforts.[72] Among today's hierarchy-heavy companies, lack of collaboration and alignment is endemic. As organizations try to align their structures with their strategies, silos proliferate around geography, product, function, customer, and a whole host of other axes. Matrix structures are everywhere, with boxes and arrows running amok.

Leaders also feel a huge temptation to create new boxes or silos. In their eyes, each box becomes a self-contained unit with clearly defined tasks and metrics. With a box in place, leaders can more easily hold people accountable while concentrating expertise and focus. But although organizations unquestionably need such units, they often have unhealthy downstream effects. Employees wind up turning their gaze inward, identifying with their unit more than the organization and impeding collaboration across units. One survey of thousands of managers found that the vast majority of them (84 percent) regarded their bosses or subordinates as reliable, but fewer than 60 percent felt they could rely on colleagues in other departments to deliver on promises either all the time or on a majority of occasions.[73]

Companies seek to solve the Entrenched Silos problem by building "bridges" between the silos, but often their efforts fail because they don't grasp the full scope of organizational collaboration. Firms put out catchy slogans like "one firm" and refer loosely to building a culture of "teamwork." But organizational silos activate an almost primal tribalism within us—again, we feel loyalty to our little silo. Exacerbating such loyalty is the need for silos to compete for scarce resources and leadership attention. This internal warfare can become so distracting that firms lose sight of markets and customers.

Infusing a purpose into an organization can foster greater collaboration across its disparate silos. But simply announcing a purpose won't do it. To get people to work together across silos, companies and leaders must take two distinct but reinforcing actions. They must find ways to facilitate joint activities and the flow of information across silos (*coordination*). And they must foster an inclination among the silos to work together (*cooperation*).[74] In other words, they must build bridges across the chasms separating different functions, business units, or teams internally, and they must motivate people to walk across those bridges. Coordination aligns people's actions across the organization, while cooperation aligns their interests.

Most companies seeking to bridge silos focus primarily on enhancing coordination, taking steps such as increasing the number of people who report to individual managers, creating short-term task forces that cut across silos, and establishing ongoing committees and councils. Companies typically neglect cooperation, which they regard as too "soft." To foster cooperation, companies must undertake the arduous task of building it into the culture and creating financial and nonfinancial incentives to reinforce it. A shared purpose can powerfully complement such culture-work, but companies often overlook it as a possible platform for cooperation. As a result, talk about "one firm" doesn't translate powerfully into employees' lived experience.

Deep purpose leaders take a more balanced approach, embracing both coordination and cooperation as powerful levers to activate the elusive "one-firm" mindset. These leaders create cross-disciplinary teams and mechanisms for smooth information flows across internal boundaries *and* they foster a spirit of cooperation, emphasizing purpose as well as culture and incentives.

To improve coordination at the FBI, Mueller centralized control over counterterrorism activities, no longer allowing the originating field office to retain control over a case and assigning "flying squads" at headquarters "to coordinate national and international investigations."[75] He sought to create greater coordination within local field offices by creating new teams—called Field Intelligence Groups (FIGs)—residing in each local office and charged them with gathering intelligence, interfacing with headquarters, and working with other offices. In 2007, Mueller created a team that standardized operations for the FIGs, identifying best practices, detailing a common operating model, and training FIG personnel.[76]

In the course of instituting these reforms, Mueller moved to improve cooperation. He took a multipronged approach, leveraging the bureau's new purpose to align everyone's interests. In the years after 9/11, people felt a sense of urgency relating to national security, and the agency's purpose was foremost in people's minds. But would it persist? To ensure that it did, Mueller reminded stakeholders of the new purpose. As he remarked, "It is a substantial shift and an understanding that our mission, our responsibility in the future is to prevent additional terrorist attacks in the United States. And there is not an agent out there, there is not a support person, there is not an analyst that does not understand that."[77]

Explicitly referencing "a paradigm shift in the FBI's cultural mindset," Mueller sought to instill partnership and sharing between intelligence officers and operational agents.[78] As one FBI internal document put it, "The new field intelligence model challenges us to begin a new way of thinking about ourselves, and our roles and responsibilities for conducting domestic intelligence. We need to start thinking about ourselves as part of a national security organization. . . . This is not the job of one 'side of the house,' but of the entire Bureau. Operational activities feed information into the intelligence process, and the intelligence process informs operations. . . ."[79] Intelligence officers and operational agents had to work well together as members of the same team, and they had to trust one another.

To help the new cooperation mindset stick, Mueller instituted periodic Strategy Performance Sessions (SPS) in which leaders evaluated how well agents were collaborating and provided feedback. "Utilizing the SPS sessions," he noted, "management has systematically led the cultural transition from a Bureau focused on cases and successful prosecutions to an intelligence-driven organization focused on comprehensive domain awareness and network disruptions."[80] Finally, Mueller included better cooperation and coordination with external partners at various levels of government on a list of ten priorities he circulated in the wake of 9/11 that he intended to serve as a guiding mandate for the organization.[81] Among other measures, the agency formed regional joint terrorism task forces with local law enforcement that met regularly to ensure smooth transfers of information about potential threats.[82] As I saw firsthand while lecturing to several of these task forces, these interactions functioned specifically to build rapport and trust among the agencies so that they could collaborate effectively in times of future crises.

The Purpose-Trust-Collaboration Nexus

In my study of other deep purpose organizations, purpose emerged as an especially important impetus to collaboration by aligning not only the activities of disparate silos but also their interests. The lynchpin once again was *trust*. In deep purpose companies, trusting relationships naturally facilitate both coordination and cooperation. As members of the same moral community, people trust that their colleagues in different silos are "on the same team" and pursuing the same goal according to the same values. People more readily cooperate, since they perceive their interests are aligned and that it is psychologically "safe" to contribute.[83] They more readily coordinate, since they possess a shared orientation toward the world and a shared identity. More coordination and cooperation fosters even *more* trust between colleagues, reaffirming in their minds their shared commitment to the purpose and membership in a moral community. Employees know that they are "all in this together" and can count on their team to help them surmount challenges.

At Warby Parker, a trusting environment underpinned by the purpose and deliberately cultivated by leaders yielded much more coordination and cooperation across silos, as well as a general ethic of collaboration. As Neil Blumenthal confirmed, Warby Parker's dedication to its purpose fostered trust *between* colleagues, not just between employees and the company. Serving as a litmus test for hiring employees, it allowed the company to create a community of people with purpose-driven mindsets, which in turn fueled collaboration by giving them a baseline confidence in one another. It also developed ways of assessing applicants for values that matched the company's and designed its onboarding processes to educate new employees about the purpose and values. All of this helped to build a strong culture of teamwork and collaboration— "#teamwarby," as the company refers to it.[84]

As evidence of the collaborative mindset at Warby Parker, Blumenthal points to cross-functional teams the company mobilizes to pursue important priorities. In 2015, the company assembled one such team to imagine a new contact lens product that would extend Warby Parker's brand while staying true to the company's purpose and values. Blumenthal and other leaders had long anticipated entering the contact lens market, and now the strategy team considered seriously whether the company should do so. The strategy team launched a pilot program with help from the product strategy and retail teams. The product, called Scout, was a new, branded contact lens that in keeping with Warby Parker's mission used less packaging than traditional contact lenses and was sold at an affordable price point. As the pilot proved successful and the company moved to launch Scout at scale, other departments such as customer service and marketing became involved. The coordination between departments was smooth, and the sense of cooperation palpable. As Blumenthal reflects, "I think core to [the project's success] is team members recognizing their role, but also that success is dependent on effective handoffs and collaboration here, and taking pride not in 'Hey, I did this myself' but in the collective effort. I set it up, I've passed it along, and I've supported it as it continues to grow."

In addition to nurturing collaboration indirectly by pursuing purpose and the trust that results, Blumenthal and other leaders nurture coordination and cooperation directly. Like many technology companies, Warby Parker emphasizes a "fun," inclusive work environment, one where it feels "safe" and desirable to collaborate with others. Leaders signal from the top the importance of a coordinated approach. As suggested earlier, supporting collaboration has a rebound effect, further intensifying both trust and commitment to purpose. A second virtuous cycle takes root—a nexus of purpose, trust, and collaboration—that further embeds the reason for being into the organization. Warby Parker lays the groundwork for employees to feel trusted, to trust others, and to dedicate themselves more intensely to the company's purpose. In this way, it pries itself loose from the iron cage, enhancing its agility and capacity for innovation.

COLLABORATION-TRUST-PURPOSE NEXUS

Lessons for Leaders

As we've seen throughout this book, it *is* possible to lead organizations of any size so that purpose and values motivate action. Deep purpose leaders do it by thinking about purpose more philosophically, negotiating tradeoffs, pulling the key levers of purpose, returning to the firm's roots, telling big stories, and building cultures of individuality. But deep purpose leaders also modify their organizations to support purpose. These leaders don't dispense entirely with top-down hierarchies and the siloed allotment of tasks and responsibilities. They know their companies still need to retain a capacity for directed action and specialization amid the dynamism and fluidity of modern markets. But they understand the close, two-way relationship between purpose and breaking down the iron cage. They recognize that convening a moral community around purpose facilitates autonomy and collaboration. And they understand that by nourishing the latter two elements they can embed purpose even further. Conversely, they sense that by declining to tackle the Too Many Bosses and Entrenched Silos problems their companies risk compromising their positions in employees' eyes as authentic carriers of purpose.

If you've been struggling to escape the iron cage and make your firm nimbler, more innovative, and more relevant, especially in our era of more flexible, remote work, I hope this chapter has alerted you to the virtues of starting with purpose and making it central to your endeavors. It's possible to realize more autonomy and collaboration without emphasizing purpose very much.[85] But lacking a strong purpose, you're not able to cultivate as effectively the trust you need to help autonomy and collaboration flourish. You also can't establish the strongest possible guardrails on behavior that, as we've seen, help to enable autonomy.

External guardrails are one thing, but purpose affords an even more effective means of keeping people "on track" and working toward shared goals. As leaders, we often fall back on policies, procedures, and metrics to ensure compliance, forgetting that the greatest controls any of us experience in the workplace are intrinsic and even instinctual. Purpose activates such instinctual self-regulation. At Mahindra, interviewees talked about how natural and effortless they found it to make decisions in support of Rise, particularly in times of crisis. When the COVID-19 pandemic struck in 2020, the company spontaneously responded in compassionate ways. "As purpose drives our thinking," explains Anish Shah, deputy managing director and group CFO, "we have a deep sense of doing what's right and helpful for the community. It is not about wanting to show who we are; this is who we are and what we do."[86] The Mahindra foundation dispensed funds to small businesses adversely impacted by the pandemic. The company helped build inexpensive ventilators for India, made face shields and sanitizer, and repurposed its Club Mahindra resort properties for use as care facilities. According to Shah, "These initiatives created a lot of optimism because no one had told our people to do this. It was all coming from within people and was a manifestation of Rise."

Starting from deep purpose can also help anyone contemplating a redesign or upgrade of their organization because it can prevent leaders from enacting only superficial change. Many leaders purport to welcome autonomy into their organization, seeking input from others in the organization, when in fact they've already arrived at a decision and merely seek buy-in. Some have observed a "false empowerment epidemic" inside companies, regarding this as "a prevalent form of management malpractice."[87] False collaboration also runs rampant: many companies adopt collaboration as a fashionable buzzword, but as we've seen, they fail to do what it takes to create a truly collaborative environment. If you begin conceptualizing organizational reforms from a place of deep purpose, your reforms will run deep. Fidelity to deep purpose and to a moral community will impel you to approach organizational change not as an abstract intellectual exercise, something you're doing because all of your competitors are, but rather as an urgent and necessary imperative established by your existential intent.

This isn't to say that starting from purpose will make it easy to break free of the iron cage. For leaders, cultivating autonomy and collaboration requires a new mindset—they must move from "managing" the business to empowering it and enabling its success. You might not be as comfortable as you think with autonomy and collaboration. "Freedom within a framework" sounds nice, but do you really trust employees to regulate themselves? Employees and managers might resist more autonomy and collaboration. Autonomy, after all, means more accountability for results as well as a departure from a familiar, rule-bound mindset. Bridging silos means venturing out of comfortable fiefdoms and learning to adapt to different mindsets and ways of working. You'll want to go slowly with purpose, allowing time for trust to form. Create small spaces of autonomy, and as you learn that you can trust employees, gradually expand those spaces. Create a few cross-disciplinary teams or initiatives, adding more if they succeed. Be patient as you nurture mechanisms of coordination as well as a culture of cooperation.

Deep purpose leadership doesn't simply entail sparking employees' trust in the organization, but creating an organization suffused throughout with trust. To become a deep purpose leader, you must begin to conceive of yourself as your organization's chief orchestrator and manager of trust. Consider how your actions and decisions will serve to further instill or diminish trust. Look for opportunities to publicly censure deviations from the purpose, as these cement the notion that the purpose is real and the relationships of trust that spawn from it are well founded.

Above all, remember that purpose isn't a magical fix. You must do the hard work of reimagining your organizational structure and implementing that change, fundamentally reconfiguring how your company operates. Some of the deep purpose companies described in this book haven't yet attempted this. For those like Warby Parker and Mahindra that have, it remains a work in progress, something to continually buttress, enhance, and revisit. Such unfinished business points to a broader question: How *durable* is deep purpose? As companies deepen their commitment to purpose, can they sustain their gains? The answer is yes. Leadership transitions, crises, and growth threaten to diminish commitment to purpose and erode moral community. But deep purpose leaders take a series of steps to ensure that the fires of purpose keep burning strong, in both the best *and* worst of times.

CHAPTER 8

FROM IDEAS TO IDEALS

Future-Proofing Purpose

As powerful as purpose is when fully mobilized, it remains fragile. To sustain purpose, deep purpose leaders proactively address some key purpose-derailers. They attend to succession planning, ensuring that new leaders become recognized carriers of the purpose. They also foster accountability by putting metrics in place; they ensure that they aren't neglecting shareholder expectations; and they moor strategy firmly to purpose. Taking responsibility for keeping their organizations on track and aligned, they work devotedly to prevent their companies from losing sight of their animating reason for being.

On a damp chilly morning in January 2016, some four thousand employees of the aerospace company Boeing clustered excitedly along the sole runway at Renton Municipal Airport in Renton, Washington State. They smiled and waved at cameras, eager to witness the maiden voyage of the company's sparkling new, state-of-the-art jet. A pioneer of modern commercial aviation since its founding in 1916, Boeing was debuting the 737 Max 8, billed as the company's "first airplane of our second century."[1]

Since its introduction in 1967, the 737 had become the workhorse of global commercial aviation. By the time of the Max's inaugural flight, airlines were using incarnations of the 737 in a third of all commercial flights globally.[2] Low-cost carriers found the plane especially attractive—737s made up Southwest Airlines' entire fleet and also served routes for many others. But competition with Boeing's nemesis Airbus and its rival A320 line of aircraft had grown fiercer in recent years.

In 2010, Airbus unveiled a new version of A320—called the A320neo—that outdid the existing 737s in fuel efficiency, weight limit, and range—key parameters for low-cost carriers that lived and died by razor-thin margins. Scrambling to meet the challenge, Boeing in 2011 announced it would manufacture its fourth-generation 737, the Max, which it claimed would beat the A320neo in both fuel efficiency and the costs required to operate it.[3] With Airbus planning to deliver the A320neo beginning in the spring of 2016,[4] and with customers showing interest in Airbus's new plane, Boeing embarked on a quest to produce Max airplanes within five years, an aggressive timeline that would challenge its engineers and force the company to divert resources from other projects.[5]

On that rainy morning in 2016, it seemed Boeing had pulled it off and was poised for success. Cheers erupted from the crowd as the first 737 Max, named *Spirit of Renton*, made a picture-perfect takeoff. When the plane touched back down, its test pilots proclaimed it a success. The president and CEO of Boeing's commercial aircraft division, Ray Conner, declared that the Max's inaugural flight "carries us across the threshold of a new century of innovation, one driven by the same passion and ingenuity that have made this company great for one hundred years."[6]

That narrative seemed to hold over the next couple of years. In the spring of 2017, US regulators formally approved the 737 Max for production, and later that summer Southwest Airlines took delivery of its first Max planes. During 2017 and 2018, Boeing delivered over three hundred planes to customers ranging from low-cost carriers to large, established players like United,[7] and by December 2018 the company had logged over five thousand orders for Max airplanes.[8] In 2018, Boeing remained the world's largest commercial aircraft maker, with over $93 billion in revenues.[9]

But on October 29, 2018, the mythos of the *Spirit of Renton* would be punctured when a 737 Max flown by Lion Air in Indonesia crashed shortly after takeoff. Five months later, on March 10, 2019, a 737 Max flown by Ethiopian Airlines also crashed just after taking off. Between the two crashes, 346 people lost their lives.[10] Observing similarities between the crashes, aviation authorities in various countries grounded the Max until Boeing could identify and fix the underlying problems.[11]

Following the Lion Air crash, Boeing expressed its "heartfelt sympathies" and its willingness to help investigate the cause. It issued a statement noting that a faulty sensor had played a role in the crash and then put out a bulletin to flight crews informing them that a new automated flight control system that used data from the sensor could lead to a crash under certain conditions. Although Boeing claimed that the 737 Max was "as safe as any airplane that has ever flown the skies," pilots wondered why the company hadn't alerted them to this new system before.[12] "It's pretty asinine for them to put a system on an airplane and not tell the pilots who are operating the airplane, especially when it deals with flight controls," complained an official with a large pilots union.[13] Speculation also swirled about whether pilot error might have played a role; Lion Air had a poor safety record and was known for cutting corners on pilot training.[14] Boeing itself suggested that pilots with standard training should have known how to respond if the new automated flight control system malfunctioned.[15]

In October 2019, months after the Ethiopian air crash, investigators in the Lion Air crash concluded that although pilot error played a role, a sensor had indeed malfunctioned, causing an on-board software system, the maneuvering characteristics augmentation system or MCAS, to activate erroneously and bring down the plane.[16] The presence of the MCAS was a story in and of itself. Keen to get Max airplanes flying as quickly as possible, Boeing had certified it with regulators not as a new airplane but as a modification of the existing 737. Expedited certification meant

Boeing couldn't change the previous 737 design very much, and in particular, that it couldn't change the plane's aerodynamic characteristics. Since the Max's more fuel-efficient engines would be bigger than those on earlier 737s, the company had to reposition them on the wings for the plane to fly properly. The alternative—adjusting the airplane's size or wingspan—would have required a new certification. The new engine position worked in most respects, but early tests revealed that under certain conditions it caused the aircraft to stall. To solve this problem, Boeing designed a work-around—the MCAS—that sensed the risk of a stall and dipped the plane's nose to prevent disaster.[17]

In the Lion Air crash, a sensor on the fuselage had malfunctioned and the MCAS had activated for no apparent reason, causing the plane to dive repeatedly and uncontrollably (engineers programmed the MCAS to cause the nose to dip every ten seconds if sensors registered a potential stall).[18] As Indonesian crash investigators noted, Boeing should have included "a fail-safe design concept" (causing minimal or no harm in case of failure) as well as a "redundant system" for the MCAS—but it hadn't. In addition, Boeing should have informed pilots about the MCAS. Observed the investigators: "The absence of information about the MCAS in the aircraft manuals and pilot training made it difficult for the flight crew to diagnose problems and apply the corrective procedures."[19] If pilots had learned about the MCAS in the plane's training materials, they might have performed simple maneuvers to override the system and keep the plane flying normally.[20] It later emerged that Boeing had redacted mentions of the MCAS because it didn't want to turn off customers by making it necessary for pilots to train on a new system at considerable cost.[21]

In the wake of the Ethiopian Airlines crash in March 2019, when it seemed likely that the MCAS system had caused that disaster as well, Boeing initially pressed regulators in the United States not to ground the plane, arguing that better training for pilots would suffice.[22] CEO Dennis Muilenburg, a longtime engineer at the company who had arrived at his post months before the Max's inaugural flight, appeared to partially blame pilots in the two crashes, noting that some "procedures were not completely followed."[23] At the same time, Boeing indicated that it would modify the system to prevent a single malfunctioning sensor from dipping the plane's nose down uncontrollably.[24] It would also arm pilots with more instructional materials about the MCAS.

Still, Muilenburg appeared to brush off the seriousness of the problems, offering, in the words of one journalist, "optimistic projections about how quickly the plane would return to service, pushing for speedy approval from regulators."[25] In the months after the Ethiopian Airlines crash, Boeing missed what turned out to be overly ambitious goals for satisfying FAA regulators and returning the Max to service, upsetting airlines who were losing money every day they couldn't fly their airplanes.[26] In October 2019, internal messages emerged showing that Boeing's own test pilot had encountered problems with the MCAS in 2016, but the company had waited months to convey this information to regulators.[27]

Weeks later, in December 2019, Muilenburg clashed with the head of the Federal Aviation Administration (FAA), who chastised him for putting undue pressure on the agency to allow the Max to fly again. At the end of that month, after Boeing announced it would pause production of the Max, wreaking havoc in the supply chain, the company relieved Muilenburg of his post. By early 2020, Boeing estimated it would sustain almost $19 billion in losses thanks to the Max's grounding.[28] Its stock had fallen by 20 percent,[29] and it would be over a year before the Max was cleared again to fly by both the FAA and European regulators.[30] As one observer argued in early 2021, "Boeing's reputation as a manufacturer that produces the highest quality aircraft is tarnished significantly and possibly forever."[31]

Flying Off-Course

What explains such a disastrous product launch? Although market pressure or a poor culture might bear some of the blame, closer scrutiny suggests a deeper cause: purpose-drift. Boeing, it seems, had become so focused on the narrow goal of winning in the marketplace that it abandoned its larger reason for being—the values and sense of purpose that had fueled the firm's success throughout the twentieth century.

Founded in 1916, Boeing initially was open-ended in its purpose and not committed to building airplanes.[32] By the late 1910s, the firm had become focused on airplanes, and by the late 1920s, we can glimpse something that resembles a clear purpose, what we might interpret as deploying science to achieve social progress and improve humankind. "We are embarked as pioneers upon a new science and industry," William E. Boeing remarked in 1929, resolving to "let no new improvement in flying and flying equipment pass us by."[33]

By the middle of the twentieth century, a dedication to scientific progress and technological achievement in aviation seems to have become entrenched at Boeing. The company's 1965 annual report noted that "it is difficult to conceive any other half century in man's history more stimulating, challenging and rewarding than the span from 1916 to 1966. In those fifty years man's scientific and technological progress has surpassed the total of such advancement in all previous history, and Boeing is proud to have played a leading role in that fantastic acceleration."[34] Even into the 1990s, the company seemed cognizant of itself as dedicated primarily to an ideal—technological progress in aviation, in the form of "grand visions of building ever better, faster, bigger aircraft"—with commercial success remaining important but secondary.[35] "For about 80 years," one journalist remarked, "Boeing basically functioned as an association of engineers. Its executives held patents, designed wings, spoke the language of engineering and safety as a mother tongue. Finance wasn't a primary language. Even Boeing's bean counters didn't act the part."[36] Employees took pride in the company and the high-quality, innovative airplanes it produced. They felt personally connected as members of a "family," and trusted in the decision-making of senior leaders who were in the first instance "engineers with a passion for aviation."[37]

This commitment to the purpose of technological progress appears to have shifted following the company's 1997 merger with rival McDonnell Douglas. Former McDonnell Douglas CEO Harry Stonecipher became Boeing's president and COO, bringing with him his former company's emphasis on efficiency and the creation of shareholder value.

A cadre of senior Boeing managers left the company, and those who remained implemented a new regime of cost-cutting, accountability, and financial performance, leading some to note that the company was abandoning its vision and values.[38] After becoming CEO following the resignation of his predecessor amid an ethics scandal, Stonecipher proudly defended the changes he'd wrought at Boeing: "When people say I changed the culture of Boeing, that was the intent, so that it's run like a business rather than a great engineering firm."[39]

Financially, those changes seemed to have paid off. Boeing's revenues skyrocketed from about $58 billion in 2001 to $101 billion in 2018.[40] But nearly two decades later, observers would draw a direct line between Boeing's cultural erosion and the 737 Max debacle, regarding the latter as spawned from management decisions that prioritized profits. The company installed the MCAS rather than redesigning the plane because it could then bring the plane to market more quickly.[41] Leaders, managers, and engineers at Boeing did what their more purpose-driven predecessors would never have dreamed of: in the words of one observer, they "put profits before safety, did not think through the consequences of their actions, or did not speak out loudly enough when they knew something was wrong."[42]

As powerful as purpose is when fully mobilized, it remains fragile. Operating in a world where commercial logic reigns, leaders can find it difficult to run businesses according to both commercial *and* social logics, as described in chapter 2. Confronted with the constant need to make painful short- and long-term tradeoffs, many leaders can't sustain it, and commercial logic wins. Leadership changes, mergers, rapid growth, and other organizational changes can distract leaders and employees from their purpose and dilute the supportive culture that is essential to instilling the reason for being. Even companies like Boeing that have operated purposefully for decades can stumble. To employees and other stakeholders, the loss of purpose can feel demoralizing and tragic—an abandonment of a noble ideal and even the company's very soul.

How can leaders "future-proof" the reason for being, ensuring that it endures? If I'd hoped that my research would lead me to a magic formula, I was disappointed. What I did glean, however, was insight into four key "purpose-derailers" that, when ignored, can trap even the most beloved deep purpose companies. These derailers are insidious and non-obvious. They arise out of good intentions yet ultimately lead companies astray. Still, the decay of purpose isn't inevitable. Taking responsibility for keeping their organizations on track and aligned, deep purpose leaders solve for these traps and prevent their companies from becoming entangled. Their preventative actions aren't foolproof, but as I found, they do make an important difference.

THE FOUR PURPOSE-DERAILERS

#1: The Personification Paradox

#2: Death by (Inadequate) Measurement

#3: The Do-Gooder's Dilemma

#4: The Purpose-Strategy Split

Derailer #1: The Personification Paradox

In early 2007, Howard Schultz, former CEO and chairman of the coffee retailer Starbucks, sent a memo to the company's leadership team entitled "The Commoditization of the Starbucks Experience" in which he raised disturbing questions about the company's path. Since Schultz had stepped down as the company's CEO in 2000, the company had mushroomed in size: it now had about 13,000 stores worldwide, up from about 3,500.[43] But revenue growth, while still impressive, was slowing, as were same-store sales.[44] The year before, while visiting numerous store locations, Schultz noticed that the company's unique store experience seemed to be fading. Excessively high espresso machines blocked customers' views of baristas, preventing them from watching the making of their drinks. The wonderful aroma of the coffee wasn't as strong as before. The stores didn't seem as inviting. As Schultz later wrote in his book *Onward*, he "sensed something intrinsic to Starbucks' brand was missing. An aura. A spirit. At first I couldn't put my finger on it. No one thing was sapping the stores of a certain soul. Rather, the unintended consequences resulting from the absence of several things that had distinguished our brand were, I feared, silently deflating it."[45]

The memo, which leaked to the press, kicked up a firestorm, and Schultz returned as CEO to undertake a wide-ranging transformation of the company. Concluding that Starbucks had strayed from its original mission or purpose, Schultz and his team defined a new one: "To inspire and nurture the human spirit one person, one cup, and one neighborhood at a time." This mission "reflected our heightened ambitions in a world that had changed so much" since the company's founding. As Schultz recounts, the company's leaders were so touched upon first learning about the new mission that they approached him and asked him to sign their copies of it. "I must have written my signature on more than 150 mission statements, the entire time somewhat slack-jawed at the emotional display of commitment unfurling in front of me."[46]

The company's travails following Schultz's departure as CEO in 2000 point to a trap that ensnares companies pursuing deep purpose, what I call the "personification paradox." Deep purpose leaders play an outsized role in establishing purpose inside organizations. In reconnecting firms with their original existential intent, in energetically telling "Big Stories" around the purpose, in forging a culture around the purpose, and in reshaping organizations to enable pursuit of the purpose, leaders come to *embody* the existential intent for the organization as well as the broader moral community. But when these leaders depart, as they inevitably must, what had been a strength becomes a major liability. Because such leaders play such an essential role in animating the purpose, companies find it difficult to sustain fidelity under new leadership. Start-ups in particular tend to lose their "souls" when their founders depart, but so do companies of any size and age whose leader has become closely identified with the purpose.

The solution isn't to downshift leaders' roles as proponents of purpose. Rather, companies can address the Personification Paradox by paying careful attention to leadership succession. Incoming leaders must continue to carry the torch of purpose while also effecting a break with the past to some extent. It's a version of the Sankofa approach described in chapter 4: they have to at once look backward and forward, decoupling purpose from their predecessor and recoupling it to their own personas. They need not decouple purpose from their predecessor entirely, but enough to become effective, inspiring evangelists for the purpose. This requires both confidence and deliberation. Although leaders might feel tempted to simply mimic their predecessor or borrow from successful leaders at other companies, they must project their own voice. "You must have the courage to have the purpose feel different under your leadership [than under your predecessor]," Best Buy CEO Corie Barry remarked to me. "It just won't look the same for me as a leader, as it does for Indra [Nooyi] or as it does for Satya [Nadella] or as it did for [Hubert Joly, her predecessor at Best Buy]. I have to be confident in how it looks and feels with me as a leader."[47]

The approaches taken by leaders to execute the delicate task of taking over from a deep purpose leader can vary. Some new CEOs formally modify or refresh the purpose to signal a sharper break with their predecessor. Ramon Laguarta did this at PepsiCo, unveiling a new strategy called "Winning with Purpose" to replace his predecessor Indra Nooyi's Purpose with Performance. Other leaders take a softer but still effective approach. As Howard Schultz's successor Kevin Johnson told me, he sought to transition Starbucks from "founder-led" to "founder-inspired." As he further explained, "I feel like my responsibility is to have the wisdom to know what to honor and preserve from the past, while at the same time having the courage to boldly reinvent the future."[48] Johnson is explicit about picking up the mantle of purpose, noting that he strives "to constantly evangelize and build that emotional connection to our purpose in each and every partner and inspire them."

Outgoing leaders can lay the groundwork for a company that is "inspired" by their commitment to purpose even while a subsequent leader becomes a new embodiment of the reason for being. As we've seen, Steve Jobs helped create Apple University with the goal of training people not to think exactly as he did, but rather to understand his guiding principles and mindset and apply them using their own judgment in the leader's absence.

Derailer #2: Death by (Inadequate) Measurement

When Vince Forlenza became CEO of the global medical device company Becton, Dickinson and Company (BD) in 2011, one task high on his agenda was to give new life to the company's purpose. Founded in 1897 by Maxwell W. Becton and Fairleigh S. Dickinson, BD had long dedicated its business operations to advancing human health through technology. During the 1980s and 1990s, as the AIDS epidemic raged, the company had taken a lead in protecting health-care workers by developing a broad range of safety needle devices and partnering with academic institutions to develop safety training programs and data surveillance systems. During the 2000s, the company partnered with the Clinton Foundation, the US Centers for Disease Control and Prevention, and national governments to strengthen lab testing capabilities in developing countries. In 2004, the company established a cross-disciplinary Global Health function to forge partnerships with governments and NGOs that would help simultaneously improve global health and develop new business opportunities for BD. During the 2010s, the company worked collaboratively with outside partners to develop the Odon Device, an inexpensive tool that, when distributed at scale and used during childbirth, promised to save hundreds of thousands of newborn lives in Africa alone. As Gary Cohen, executive vice president of global health, remarked, "It is deeply embedded within the company's culture to link big, unmet health needs and societal problems to business practice."[49]

Along the way, purpose became more deeply embedded as well. In 1997, as the company celebrated its centennial, leaders propounded a formal purpose: "Helping all people live healthy lives." They also adopted a vision for the future that explicitly fused commercial and social logics, seeking to "become the organization most known for eliminating unnecessary suffering and death from disease and, in so doing, become one of the best performing companies in the world."[50] As Cohen remembers, "While we didn't explicitly embed the future vision into our formal businesses processes, we communicated it widely, and almost everything identified in our future vision came to fruition by 2005."[51]

Now CEO, Forlenza wanted to take purpose deeper, making it "real for everyone and what they were doing in their daily jobs."[52] He and his team updated the purpose to emphasize the company's strong identity as an innovator, fixing on the phrase "Advancing the world of health" as BD's new existential intent. While socializing this purpose, BD also worked to formalize and enhance its longstanding orientation toward creating shared value. As Cohen notes, he thought of shared value as a business proposition that addressed a "highly important unmet societal need, one that's not just recognized by the company but recognized also more broadly by other stakeholders and is accomplished through business models" that are commercially viable.[53] Forlenza felt that putting more rigor behind shared value would help the company further operationalize its purpose by "getting people to think more broadly and deeply about how they could make an impact."[54]

Executives created a methodology that leaders could use to incorporate social impact when making strategic planning decisions about which R&D projects to fund. Instead of simply asking the two questions they always had before—(1) how financially attractive a potential market opportunity was; and (2) how well the company could execute on it—leaders developed a grid that also took into account a set of social impact metrics for potential new products or services still in the development stage.[55] As Cohen described it, the grid incorporated a scoring system "based on the size of the health problem, the likely reach of the innovation or the technology, how challenging it would be to implement, [and] the economics of it for the customer, particularly if we're looking at a problem that is in a lesser developed market.[56] Unfortunately, despite their hard work and good intentions in creating the grid, it proved too complex and unwieldy to use, and ultimately failed to gain traction. "We didn't figure it out," Forlenza acknowledges, speaking of metrics to gauge social impact. "I was hoping we would because it would be such a nice step forward. But beyond getting to some very basic measures, it just didn't play out."[57]

That BD even tried is worth applauding, a testament to its commitment to deep purpose. Quantitative metrics have become central to the operation of modern businesses. Tools such as the balanced scorecard, introduced during the 1990s, and the more recent objectives and key results (OKRs) serve as popular mechanisms for helping leaders connect strategy with execution.[58] Recognizing that they must "measure what matters,"[59] deep purpose leaders strive to develop reliable ways of gauging their organizations' pursuit of the reason for being. Lacking adequate metrics of commitment to purpose, firms have a harder time delivering on their existential intent, and they might wind up underdelivering on purpose, as we saw in the case of Etsy during the early to mid-2010s. Over time, the absence of clarity might lead to serious lapses in a company's pursuit of its reason for being—what I somewhat dramatically call "Death by (Inadequate) Measurement."

A recent survey of large investors who together managed over $22 trillion in assets revealed that most expect companies to track quantitatively how well they are delivering on their purpose. A full three-quarters of those surveyed felt that companies should develop key performance indicators (KPIs) for purpose, and a majority felt that companies should peg executive incentives to those metrics.[60] So how might companies best measure adherence to purpose?

Companies have well-established methods for measuring the "what" of performance (financial results) or the "how" (process measures that contribute to financial results), but they've struggled to develop methodologies for directly quantifying the "why," which after all is ineffable, subjective, and "soft." Some consulting firms and academics have tried to embrace the subjective by designing surveys to capture sentiment, querying either customers or employees. The marketing consulting firm Strawberry Frog has unveiled its Purpose Power Index, which tracks customer sentiment about brands and their reasons for being. Thousands of customers participated in the research, which covers over two hundred brands. The survey asks four questions: "Is the brand committed to changing the world for the better?"; "Does it do things to benefit all stakeholders, not just shareholders?"; "Does it have a higher purpose that's bigger than profit?"; and "Does it do things to improve the lives of people and their communities?"[61]

A group of Spanish academics has unveiled a methodology for measuring purpose directly that tracks three constituent factors: the extent to which employees understand, identify with, and contribute to the purpose.[62] Likewise, consulting firm BCG has created a survey that measures the "robustness" of purpose across four characteristics: how well it is articulated, how inspirational it is, how deeply it's embedded operationally, and how recognizable employees think the purpose is to outsiders. While attempts to measure subjective phenomena directly can lead to issues of reliability (does the survey produce consistent results?) and validity (does the survey succeed in measuring what it claims?), these two efforts are laudable, and I hope they'll encourage others to experiment as well.[63]

Deep purpose companies like BD, Bühler, Etsy, and Mahindra have also sought to measure commitment to purpose using a range of perceptual measures of customers and employees. None of them have cracked the problem, but as a group they've striven to develop measurement systems that make purpose more tangible and hence actionable. Instead of asking about purpose directly, they do so *indirectly*, taking one of two basic approaches. Some deep purpose companies measure purpose indirectly by monitoring what we might call the *forerunners of purpose*: they track antecedents, actions, or conditions that induce or enable purpose. Alternatively, they measure perceptions of those antecedents. At Mahindra, for instance, leaders collect survey data from employees, asking them to respond to items such as "Sufficient efforts have been made in the organization/sector to bring about awareness and understanding regarding Rise."[64]

A second, seemingly more common approach is to try to make the existential intent more concrete by tracking *purpose outcomes*, various kinds of visible results that might reflect the existential intent's presence. Some firms define principles linked to the purpose and then behaviors associated with those principles. By tracking how much of those behaviors the organization is seeing, leaders get a sense of how deeply the purpose is animating the organization. Mahindra created a "3+5 framework" that combines three "pillars" or principles associated with its purpose and five leadership behaviors, using ratings in 360-reviews to help leaders gauge their progress. Microsoft has something similar as well.

Proceeding further down the chain of cause and effect, many leaders measure end-state outcomes produced by the organization (via workplace behaviors) and linked to the purpose. Here firms are no longer measuring the *why* of performance, but rather inferring their dedication to the purpose by gauging the *what*, expanding their notion of performance to encompass both financial *and* social outcomes (as well as perceptions of those outcomes). To capture the social dimension of performance as a proxy for purpose, some deep purpose companies track end results linked to Environmental, Social, and Governance (ESG) goals. Many frameworks and standards exist, and firms rating companies for their ESG performance diverge in how they define, measure, and weight company results.[65] Given the absence of a universally accepted measurement standard,[66] a number of companies I studied designed their own end-results metrics, emphasizing simplicity. The World Economic Forum's International Business Council has sought to rein in the complexity, creating a standard set of twenty-one "core" metrics and thirty-four additional ones related to the areas of "Governance, Planet, People, and Prosperity" that companies could use to track their progress on sustainability.

Bühler tracks financial performance as well as its execution in three sustainability-related areas: "economy," "nature," and "humanity." The company also fielded a survey asking a range of stakeholders inside the company and beyond to consider four dozen topics related to its purpose, ranking their importance and rating both Bühler's performance in these topics and the impact of these topics on Bühler.[67] This survey allowed the company to gauge *perceptions* of performance outcomes related to purpose. Etsy tracks end-results metrics in three key areas that are similar to Bühler's: economic impact, social impact, and ecological impact. In each area, the company has established measures that are audited and that the company formally communicates alongside financial performance in an integrated annual report.[68] "I definitely think that putting targets out, having third parties audit those numbers, and letting the world hold us accountable is very helpful," CEO Josh Silverman says.[69]

Although a start-up, the flour producer One Mighty Mill, a certified B Corp dedicated to regenerating local food systems, is already very deliberate about measuring purpose. The company is putting in place a system to track results-based metrics related to its core operations, including how much organic wheat it procures, how many mills it constructs, how much wheat it mills and sources locally, how much of its products it delivers to kids who wouldn't normally access it, and how many school systems receive its food and educational support.[70]

One of the most sophisticated methods I encountered for measuring end-state outcomes linked to the purpose was at the EY organization (leave it to the accountants to lead in this area). Defining their purpose as "building a better working world," the company linked it to an "ambition," the provision of "long-term value as the world's most trusted, distinctive, professional services organization." This emphasis on long-term value is critical, highlighting one of the most important features of purpose as a fundamental orientation towards business.

EY teams in turn defined four kinds of long-term value linked to different stakeholder groups and ESG issues: client value (customers), people value (employees), social value (communities and the planet), and financial value (EY's partners). To measure purpose, EY teams measure outcomes across these four forms of value, using ten core metrics.[71] These metrics in turn link up with an additional set of behavioral metrics that allow EY's partners to track their own performance relative to the four kinds of value, and in turn, the purpose. EY teams have used these metrics to set ambitious and concrete goals, track annual progress, and reward partners. The organization has also sought to map internal goals to more conventional ESG measures.

As Carmine Di Sibio, global chairman and CEO of EY, told me, metrics help because they demonstrate to external stakeholders, including potential collaborators and employees, that the company is serious about purpose. "Companies really have to be able to show what they're doing. They get into trouble when they talk a lot about purpose and it's just talk, and what do you really have to show for it in terms of results."[72] Metrics and incentives also help ensure that employees deliver on the purpose. "You've got to measure the outcomes and you've got to measure how you're doing vis-à-vis strategy and if your strategy is long-term value oriented, then if you don't measure it there's no motivation to get there." The following figure summarizes the metrics and specific goals associated with the four types of value.

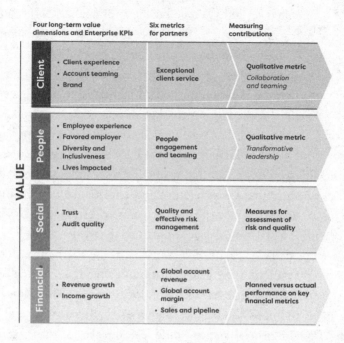

MEASURING PURPOSE AT EY
(Adapted with permission from EY)

	Four long-term value dimensions and Enterprise KPIs	Six metrics for partners	Measuring contributions
Client	• Client experience • Account teaming • Brand	Exceptional client service	**Qualitative metric** *Collaboration and teaming*
People	• Employee experience • Favored employer • Diversity and Inclusiveness • Lives impacted	People engagement and teaming	**Qualitative metric** *Transformative leadership*
Social	• Trust • Audit quality	Quality and effective risk management	Measures for assessment of risk and quality
Financial	• Revenue growth • Income growth	• Global account revenue • Global account margin • Sales and pipeline	Planned versus actual performance on key financial metrics

VALUE

Figure I: EY's Global Ambition

Ultimately, purpose speaks to what some have termed the "human dimension" of business. And as one observer points out, "At least some of that dimension will always be difficult for chief executives to collect, crunch and codify on their digital dashboards. As a result, they must resolve to try harder to manage the things they will never easily measure."[73] In their enthusiasm and dedication to a reason for being, deep purpose leaders make that effort, finding new ways to quantify the organization's pursuit of its existential intent.

Derailer #3: The Do-Gooder's Dilemma

In March 2021, news broke that Emmanuel Faber had been ousted as chairman and CEO of the global food goliath Danone after a challenge by activist investors.[74] Faber had become a prominent advocate of both purpose and multi-stakeholder capitalism, galvanizing Danone behind a purpose of "bringing health through food to as many people as possible." He operated several Danone business units as B Corps, adopted integrated reporting, sought to foster a culture of trust and autonomy, and more.[75] In 2020, Danone became the first public company to be formally designated in France as an Entreprise à Mission, a status (akin to a public benefit corporation in the United States) that obligated it to lay out clear social and environmental goals related to its purpose.[76]

During his tenure, Faber was explicit that pursuing purpose didn't preclude value creation for shareholders. For instance, he promised that the company would see "strong, profitable and sustainable growth"[77] and acknowledged that assessments of his performance would ultimately hinge on his ability to move Danone's stock price higher.[78] Describing the Entreprise à Mission designation to analysts, he noted, "We will not prove our model right until we see that in the share price. It's not a matter of contradicting the value creation, it's really about the way we create that value in the short, medium, long term."[79] Elsewhere, Faber spoke about the need to "balance Danone's dual economic and social project." Pursuing social justice would lead in turn to "the resilience of this business."[80]

Despite significant efforts, Faber couldn't strike the right balance between social impact and economic performance. Danone's share price plummeted by 25 percent in 2020 and the company saw a decline in sales for the first time in decades.[81] Since 2014, Danone's share prices declined in value relative to those of competitors Nestlé and Unilever, and the company also missed profit forecasts on three occasions.[82] As a representative of Blue Bell Capital, an activist investor that had called for Faber's ouster, explained, their complaint wasn't with Faber's pursuit of purpose and a social logic. Rather, it was what they saw as Faber's failure to address the firm's inadequate financial performance: "Faber was trying to use sustainability as part of his defence. But we never called into question Danone's ESG investments, and we care a lot about these topics. . . . Their competitors like Nestlé and Unilever also make ESG a priority, yet have better financial results. Our issue with Faber was not ideological but operational."[83] Blue Bell's cofounder noted that social benefit "can't come at the expense of shareholder returns. The first duty of a public company is to remunerate shareholders."[84]

Faber's downfall doesn't imply that purpose-driven capitalism can't work, as some have wondered. Rather, it suggests the importance of managing shareholder expectations adroitly. Set performance expectations too high, and you'll pay the price when you don't deliver. Faber's downfall also points us to another key derailer that deep purpose leaders must anticipate, what I call the Do-Gooder's Dilemma. Leaders who understand the need to pursue both a social and economic logic might still, in their deep-seated commitment to doing good, fail to deliver sufficient growth and profits. They might presume that success at "doing good" somehow gives them a pass from doing as well as their peers. They might feel so confident that their strategies will yield the greatest good for all stakeholders over the long term that they feel no need to attend to shareholders' short-term needs. Or, as in Faber's case, they might simply run up against bad luck or market challenges that make it difficult or impossible to please investors (Faber contended with a pandemic that led its bottled water sales to collapse, and he was also operating in a highly commoditized dairy space). In each of these situations, leaders seeking to do good struggle to understand how precisely to balance commercial and social logics when pursuing purpose.

As Faber's case suggests, and as research confirms, investors develop even *higher* expectations of leaders who pursue a social logic.[85] The truth is that *nobody* gets a pass on short- and long-term financial performance, whether they've striven to deliver profits for shareholders or not. And certainly, strong, shared-value strategies don't mean leaders can ever take their eyes off the commercial logic. The leaders who go deepest on purpose aren't those who push the social logic at all costs. They're those like Etsy's Josh Silverman or Microsoft's Satya Nadella who attend at all times to both the social *and* commercial logics. Ignoring profits unduly can prove damaging because it might prompt an overreaction that swings the company too far away from its social logic. This is what happened at Boeing during the late 1990s and 2000s, where the drive to reform a company that seemed to neglect the commercial logic led it to place too much emphasis on cost-savings, with disastrous consequences.

Deep purpose companies might make certain decisions that over the short term privilege certain stakeholders and even diminish profits within reasonable bounds. Over the long term, however, they resolve the Do-Gooder's Dilemma and balance commercial and social logics. As they understand, a business always remains precisely that—a business, one that must generate a reasonable return on investment in order to survive. To circumvent the Do-Gooder's Dilemma, they take swift action when they judge that the company has swerved too far from its commercial logic. When the COVID-19 pandemic broke out, Mahindra stepped up to take a number of ambitious socially oriented moves, providing assistance to employees, local communities, and other stakeholders. As the pandemic wore on and an economic crisis unfolded, leaders realized they would have to take painful steps to keep the company on solid ground, including shutting down certain operations and laying off employees. Such decisions were hardly pleasant, but the company went through with them, behaving as compassionately as possible. Mahindra wasn't departing from its purpose but rather positioning itself to survive as an enterprise, continuing its challenging walk along the razor's edge.

Derailer #4: The Purpose-Strategy Split

We've seen that purpose holds directional benefits for companies, serving as a "North Star" for forming cogent growth strategies. Purpose can help channel innovation, focusing leaders so that they can think more holistically and broadly within a narrower area. Conversely, strategy-making devoid of purpose can hamstring leaders, leaving them to respond reactively to market forces and moves by competitors rather than leading markets by pursuing a clear, overriding intent.

Leaders can find it hard to keep strategy aligned with an underlying purpose. They might shunt purpose off into human resources and marketing, regarding it as a "right brain" activity. Regarding strategy as their purview, they might approach that as solely a "left brain" activity involving rigorous analysis of markets. Confronted with pressures from investors, leaders might also feel tempted to choose strategies that yield short-term gains yet fail to advance the company's purpose over the long term. Leaders might lapse into an outward-looking perspective, taking their eye off what makes their company unique and preoccupying themselves with matching competitors blow for blow or with plugging into the latest trends. Leaders might become distanced from customers and the social value that they provide to them. They might simply feel afraid not to pursue some opportunities as they arise, including those that chafe against or contradict the purpose. And the arrival of new leaders who misconstrue or lack commitment to the purpose might also lead to a rift between strategy and the existential intent.

Recognizing how easy it is for strategy and purpose to diverge, deep purpose leaders take steps to keep themselves and other leaders focused on purpose. First, they consider impact goals as part of their strategic planning process and make purpose a starting point when conducting strategic conversations. When Warby Parker developed its new contact lens offering Scout, members of the strategy team and others across the company considered ways to ensure the new offering would be recognizably "Warby" and enable the company to do more good as well as grow its business. Warby Parker's ingrained commitments to its customers and its purpose led team members to keep the price point low, to build an exceptional customer experience, and to prioritize making the new offering's packaging more environmentally friendly than conventional contact lens packaging. And they opted to carry third-party contact lenses in addition to Scout, perceiving that decision as an important step they could take to stay responsive to customer needs.[86]

But deep purpose leaders don't simply attend to the strategy-making process to keep strategy on-purpose. Recognizing how strong the gravitational pull against purpose often is, some of them forge *external* commitments that keep their strategies on the right track over the long term. These commitments vary in their stringency and formality. At one end of the spectrum, some deep purpose companies pledge voluntarily to attain certain goals linked to their purpose and report on their progress. Bühler not only adopted clear goals around sustainability—it repeatedly adopted more aggressive targets during the 2010s. By convening high-profile industry gatherings focused on furthering sustainability, the company further hitched itself reputationally to its existential intent, making it more difficult for its own leaders to depart from the purpose without attracting notice. At many deep purpose companies, integrated reporting and sustainability reports also help external stakeholders hold leaders accountable reputationally for adherence to the purpose.

A stricter way to commit externally to the purpose is to make binding public commitments. Companies can voluntarily bind themselves to external designations such as B Corp, which commits them to externally established ESG standards (a proxy for purpose) and to a third-party certification body. Companies can go even further and transform their legal governance structures. Founded in 2007, Veeva Systems is a rapidly growing provider of cloud-based technology solutions for life sciences companies. Starting with CRM solutions, the company branched out in 2012 to include R&D related solutions, including clinical trials operations. By 2019, Veeva was generating $1 billion in revenues, with a public goal of becoming a $3 billion company by 2025. As cofounder and CEO Peter Gassner told me, he was puzzled by the traditional C Corporation structure while reviewing his company's original articles of incorporation. In a C Corporation, leaders and board members are legally bound to serve as fiduciaries for just one stakeholder: shareholders. "That's a little hollow," he told me in an interview. "You work so hard. You're with customers, you're with employees, it should be about everybody. You can't build a great company if it's just about making money for shareholders."[87] As Gassner thought, it would be much better if Veeva had a governance structure that *obligated* him and other leaders to execute strategies that would deliver value for all.

Despite his misgivings, Gassner signed the articles at the time of Veeva's founding and established it as a traditional C Corporation. Only in 2018, when Veeva was already public and long-term survival seemed assured, did he and cofounder Matt Wallach strongly consider making the firm a public benefit corporation. The latter is a for-profit corporate entity whose leaders bear fiduciary responsibility to act in the best interests of society, employees, community, and the environment in addition to shareholders (by contrast, a B Corporation is merely a designation conferred by an outside body, not a legal status). Becoming a public benefit corporation felt scary; nobody else in their industry had done so. But the founders liked that incorporating as a public benefit entity would publicly bind management long into the future. "This is how we operate the company," Gassner said, "and we've always said it's by vision and values. Now we're writing it down so that everyone can see."[88]

On February 1, 2021, Veeva became the world's first public company to change their articles of incorporation and become a public benefit company, with an impressive 99 percent of voting shareholders in favor of the move. The company's public benefit purpose is "to help make the industries we serve more productive and create high-quality employment opportunities."[89] Gassner is convinced that over the long term becoming a public benefit corporation will keep the company more tightly focused on its strategies, in no small part because of the talent it attracts. "It's going to impact the types of people we get on our board. It's probably going to impact who's the next CEO of Veeva. It fundamentally changes the duty of our board."[90]

Public benefit status could also tie Veeva closer to its customers, many of whom may have resisted buying more software from the company for fear of becoming overly dependent on a single vendor. Public benefit status would signal to customers that Veeva was as deeply committed to them as their shareholders, creating long-term, trusted relationships that can lead to sales growth. The new status would also influence the impact of any future takeover of the company. "It's no longer about maximizing financial return," Gassner said. "It's about doing the right thing for all constituents. The board will be held legally bound to that and they can't be held legally bound to 'Oh, you didn't manage strictly to financial return.'" Finally, public benefit status influences the strategies that leaders might consider. Potential strategies used to come more or less exclusively from the market. "Now I think ideas will come out from the purpose side as well, so it'll be a balancing." Wallach agrees, noting that "some of the ideas will be bigger now. The idea that the FDA could come to Veeva and ask us to do something on their behalf that would help the whole industry—we never imagined that would happen. But now I think it could happen."[91]

To maximize purpose's alignment with strategy, you must inscribe your reason for being in your governance structure. As Emmanuel Faber told me, "I really believe you're incomplete in your search for purpose, unless you've put it as part of your governance. It's a very important part of what makes it possible to pursue purpose efficiently and consistently over time."[92] Faber noted in particular that locking a multi-stakeholder approach into a company's by-laws allows it to survive the departure of any particular leader. Now that he has been forced out at Danone, will strategy and purpose remain aligned there? Because the company is an Entreprise à Mission, it has a fighting chance.

Lessons for Leaders

In early 2020, a trove of Boeing internal communications was released that appeared to confirm the existence of underlying cultural problems at the company. It turns out that several employees had expressed doubt about the 737 Max and spoke disparagingly of regulators and customers. An employee in 2016 used the phrase "dogs watching TV" to refer to regulators. Another that year proclaimed to a colleague that the 737 Max was "a joke" and "ridiculous." Another in 2018 proclaimed that he wouldn't let his own family fly on a 737 Max. Commenting on the messages, a former Boeing employee reflected that "Engineers normally just don't talk that way. It's not the company I knew." One current employee, frustrated with the 737 Max, opined fatalistically that "sometimes you have to let big things fail so that everyone can identify a problem . . . maybe that's what needs to happen rather than continuing to scrape by."[93]

What makes these comments especially damning is that at around this same time Boeing still presented itself as a purpose-driven company with grand ambitions. In 2016, the year of the 737 Max's maiden flight, Boeing's annual report announced that the company's "mission and purpose is to connect, protect, explore and inspire the world through aerospace innovation."[94] The company repeated this mission in its 2017 and 2018 annual reports, adding that it aimed "to be the best in aerospace and an enduring global industrial champion."[95] Boeing appears, in other words, to have become very much a convenient purpose company, its leaders pursuing primarily commercial objectives under the banner of purpose, its underlying culture unsuited to the noble intention of aiding humanity "through aerospace innovation."

As damaging as purpose's erosion is for individual companies, not to mention for customers or innocent bystanders who might be maimed or killed, it also has a systemic impact, setting back the broader cause of reform in capitalism. The pursuit of deep purpose amounts to a fundamental shift in how businesses are organized, led, and operated. It enables leaders and companies to win in every sense of the word, achieving not only better financial performance but unlocking more value for all stakeholders, including employees, communities, and the planet. For capitalism to evolve and make progress in addressing the greatest problems facing humanity, we need leaders and companies everywhere to embrace deep purpose. But every time a superficial purpose company stumbles its way into the media headlines, the promise underlying the pursuit of purpose takes a hit. Leaders and the public at large become cynical about purpose, perceiving it as just another marketing pitch. They greet the claims of deep purpose companies skeptically. And they become all the more reluctant to push purpose more deeply into their own organizations.

I don't mean to fault leaders unduly. While poor decision-making or misplaced priorities often do lead to the demise of deep purpose, many companies that fall prey to the derailers described in this chapter do so *despite* the focus and determination of well-intentioned leaders. The path of deep purpose is immensely difficult—again, a walk on the razor's edge. At any time, one of the derailers might push you off, with potentially disastrous consequences. The deep purpose leader's work doesn't just involve defining, communicating, and embedding the purpose, as challenging as those tasks might be. It also involves remaining vigilant and doing what they can at all times to ensure that the organization's commitment doesn't slip.

Deep purpose leaders don't cave under the burden of endless vigilance. They fervently embrace their responsibilities as guardians of purpose, perceiving this as an essential part of their noble quest. Most leaders aim to execute on a powerful business idea that they believe in. Deep purpose leaders do much more. They aim for an *ideal*, a dream of the future so ambitious that they will in all likelihood never see it fully realized. Theirs is a practical idealism, as we've seen, but idealism nonetheless. And like anyone aiming for an ideal, deep purpose leaders focus foremost on the striving itself, accepting that they'll never fully bring their dreams to fruition (although they hopefully will see meaningful progress). All along, they remain as conscious as possible of their existential intent, staying alert to new opportunities for more fully realizing the purpose and for protecting it from potential derailers.

Consider the derailers we've examined. Do any arouse special concern? What special safeguards might you devise to address them *before* disaster strikes? If no obvious safeguards come to mind, how might you experiment to create novel ways of ensuring that you stay on track? More broadly, ask yourself: Where or in what respects does your organization seem weakest in its pursuit of purpose? And in areas or dimensions in which it might be strong, how might you push even harder and protect the organization even more? Finally, think of specific decisions you face. How might you better balance social and commercial logics to serve *all* stakeholders over the long term and ensure that you remain on-purpose?

Pursuing an ideal is often uncomfortable, even excruciating. But deep purpose leaders and their organizations soldier on, inspired by their existential intent and determined to do their very best. As dedicated members of a moral community, they remain fixated on their ideal with all their hearts and souls, bound to it by an almost religious fervor. Great ideas have their power, but only grand ideals can capture our collective imaginations and harness our energies to the fullest. They empower us to persevere against hardships and over time to change our organizations and the world. I hope your organization pursues such an inspiring ideal, come what may. And for the sake of all of your stakeholders and society at large, I hope you pursue it *deeply*.

GETTING STARTED WITH DEEP PURPOSE

Action Steps to Consider

This book has detailed a new mindset about purpose, one that forces executives to rethink what they do. But rethinking isn't enough. You must move forcefully to put deep purpose into practice if you are to reap its benefits. Here are some further suggestions to help you translate a deep purpose mindset into leadership action.

Chapter I: What Is Purpose *Really?*

Take stock. How fully does your company currently engage with purpose? Are you approaching purpose superficially or conveniently? Are some of your businesses and offerings aligned with your purpose but not all? Do you pursue win-win opportunities but neglect to advance purpose when the commercial viability of these opportunities isn't immediately obvious? Is purpose a clear, tangible part of your operating model? To what degree do your actions and statements reflect the purpose? And think about each of your stakeholders. To what degree do they feel invested in your organization and its purpose?

Challenge your purpose statement. Have your leadership team assess the validity and relevance of your purpose statement as it stands today. If it doesn't pass muster, then restate it. Remember that your purpose must not only convey a goal, but also an elevated aspiration. It should also emphasize both commercial and social logics, articulating the organization's ultimate priorities.

Embrace a new understanding of purpose. Clarify with your leadership team that purpose can help you to become more productive, more engaged with your customers and markets, and more adaptive, with an eye toward building a long-term, durable enterprise. Internalize the idea that purpose, when pursued deeply, can be transformational, a new operating system and the key to high performance.

Chapter 2: Walking on the Razor's Edge

Lean into tradeoffs. Resist the urge to dodge or evade tradeoffs when they arise. Instead, embrace them. Investigate the perspectives of key stakeholders and the likely implications of your decisions. In evaluating potential solutions, explicitly use purpose as your "North Star."

Look beyond win-win. To be a deep purpose leader, you must be willing to invest in ideas that don't necessarily hit the sweet spot of delivering both social and commercial value. When a particular business idea primarily creates social value, aggressively explore options for creating commercial value as well (recognizing that you might want to take the leap before commercial value seems entirely attainable). You will also encounter ideas that primarily drive commercial value. Here, you must have the fortitude to investigate ways to deliver social impact, disengaging when that isn't possible. In legacy businesses where you can't feasibly disengage in the short term, transition by creating a portfolio of businesses, including some that do deliver social impact. Adopt a timeline for disengaging with businesses that lack social impact and building business that aligns better with your purpose.

Communicate your tradeoffs. If you're making hard tradeoffs to balance the interests of stakeholders, communicate the logic of your decisions transparently, as doing so will enhance stakeholders' understanding and demonstrate your commitment to the purpose. Contextualize this logic by referring back to the organization's purpose and the moral vision it contains.

Chapter 3: Four Levers for Superior Performance

Let purpose drive your strategy conversation. When deliberating over specific strategic directions in the short and long term, start with purpose. Make sure that your reason for being informs the strategic choices that you eventually adopt. Muster the discipline and fortitude to decline options that align poorly with your purpose.

Translate purpose into your recruiting and onboarding efforts. Use purpose as a filter when making decisions to hire, onboard, and promote individuals. Break purpose down first into principles and then into specific behaviors. Expect your workforce to internalize these principles and behaviors, using measurement and rewards to make them stick.

Assess your branding: How clearly does your external brand communicate purpose? Is your reason for being an integral part of your identity? Do any opportunities exist to highlight your purpose authentically? Are you taking meaningful public stands in relation to your purpose? Let purpose guide your marketing and branding strategy, including in decisions about whether to take a public stand or stay silent.

Adjust your conversations with stakeholders. Convene customers, suppliers, and others in creative ways around your reason for being. Build greater transparency into your decision-making, using purpose as the basis for communicating specific decisions. Don't hesitate to "fire" or stop pursuing stakeholders that don't align well with the purpose.

Chapter 4: Where Purpose *Really* Comes From: Looking Backward While Looking Forward

Conduct a historical audit of your existing purpose. If you've done some work in this area already, take the opportunity to go deeper, interviewing founders, early employees, early customers, and so forth. If you haven't written a history of your company, you might consider doing that. Consider how you might articulate your purpose to tap more deeply into the "soul" of the company. If you're developing a new purpose statement, start by delving into the past, embarking on a process of discovery that in time will lead to a clearly defined purpose statement.

Hold ongoing "purpose discussions" in which you "stress-test" the purpose. These might take place annually or every few years. Invite senior leaders to discuss the purpose and encourage managers to engage employees as well. Be ready to take action based on these conversations.

Connect the past and the future. In rooting your purpose in the past, avoid letting the past hijack you, preventing you from moving toward the future. You need not adhere slavishly to past practices and priorities. Actively explore future growth opportunities, allowing your purpose to serve as a guide. In the end, aim to arrive at a synthesis of novelty and tradition.

Train people in principled decision-making. Translate purpose into simple, comprehensible principles that others can follow to make purpose-driven decisions autonomously. Give them opportunities to practice applying these principles in real-life situations.

Chapter 5: Are You A Poet, or Just A Plumber?

Define a "Big Story" for your purpose. If you're used to talking narrowly about the impact your offerings have on employees, what kind of grand, sweeping narrative can you frame? Be sure that this narrative speaks authentically to the company's actual intent, and to your own intent as a leader.

Craft your "Big Story" to elicit action. To maximize the story's impact, connect it with your personal story; explicitly convene the organization as a moral community; and frame the "Big Story" in a way that conveys a sense of urgency.

Be vulnerable. Openly explain and dramatize your connection to the purpose, making yourself vulnerable. Explain to your people why *you* feel so driven to convene a moral community at your company. Evoke the process by which you came to discover the purpose and pursue it as your own.

Rethink how you respond during crises. When crises arise, define them in relation to the purpose as moral "choice points." Take the opportunity to cement the purpose even more in people's minds and establish its continued validity.

Live the purpose in everything you do. If some of your leadership behaviors conflict with the purpose, drop them. But then go further and consider steps you might take during your day-to-day work to better embody your organizational purpose and the values that underlie it. These can be small gestures and big policy decisions. Both symbolism and substantive actions matter.

Chapter 6: The "Me" in Purpose

Make work personal. Take a new look at your employees, seeing them as human beings. Show interest in their personal contexts and experiences, asking questions and giving them space to express themselves. Push boldly into areas of difference, looking for the underlying human commonalities while still appreciating individual differences.

Invite employees to probe their own, personal purposes. You might develop a program that allows employees to articulate their personal purposes and share them with others if they so choose. You might consider holding "purpose" meetings across the company during which team members describe their personal purposes. Give people permission to be more vulnerable with one another.

Connect personal and organizational purpose. When people engage with their own purposes, they become more open to seeking ways to connect with the organization's purpose. Foster this connection by explicitly inviting employees to "live" the organization's purpose in their own ways. Celebrate and publicly support employee projects that further both personal and organizational purpose. In your own communications, emphasize how helping the organization pursue its purpose allows *you* to live your own reason for being as well.

Build a culture that preserves individuality. Invest in creating a strong culture that prioritizes individual expression, taking care to also establish a few grounding expectations. Be deliberate in creating norms around hiring, onboarding, developing, and rewarding.

Create clear guidelines for conversations and meetings to ensure that people feel safe and comfortable expressing themselves.

Project caring leadership. Even as you challenge people to perform, you must also demonstrate that you're there to support them in their efforts to achieve those challenging goals. Demonstrate a genuine caring about team members' growth and development as workers and human beings. Do this through your daily interactions as well as your substantive decision-making.

Chapter 7: Escaping the Iron Cage

Break the bureaucratic mindset. Examine and challenge your current organizational design, especially around the two key pillars of autonomy and collaboration. Is bureaucracy stemming from inadequate autonomy and collaboration hobbling your organization, preventing purpose from taking root as fully as it might? In particular, does your organizational structure reflect trust in employees, an element essential for embedding purpose? Reimagine your organization as bound together by a nexus of relationships and commitments, not merely a nexus of contracts.

Explore opportunities to grant more autonomy, within certain bounds. Catalogue your processes and make a list of specific adjustments to allow for more autonomy in pursuit of the purpose. Do more to invite employees to take risks and show initiative, in particular by celebrating their successes and reframing failures as opportunities to learn. Make certain to use purpose to establish clear boundaries that both limit and enable autonomy.

Look for opportunities to enhance the first dimension of collaboration, which is coordination. Implement mechanisms or process shifts to allow information to flow better and connect better with decision-making. Consider whether teams have the common knowledge and understanding they need to engage with one another. Consider changes you might make to the reporting structure to enhance coordination across silos, and whether the creation of cross-functional committees or councils might help. Ask yourself if infusing a sense of purpose would enable such coordination systems to work more effectively.

Look for opportunities to enhance the second dimension of collaboration, which is cooperation. Consider whether you have in place the proper intrinsic and extrinsic reinforcement systems to ensure cooperation or the aligning of behavior within and across silos. If not, make those systems a priority. Use purpose as a rallying cry to help people feel as if they're on the same team, a member of a common moral community. Hold informal events to get people across silos together so that they can build trust and *want* to cooperate. Remind them at these meetings of their common commitment to the purpose. Weave purpose, values, and desired behaviors more explicitly into recruiting and onboarding.

Chapter 8: From Ideas to Ideals: Future-Proofing Purpose

Check your organization's commitment to its purpose. Because purpose naturally decays over time, it requires constant care and attention. Has energy around the purpose lapsed? Does purpose shape how your leadership team makes large and small decisions? Do people still understand the organizational purpose and bring it to life in their daily work? Do external stakeholders believe in the purpose and your ability to execute on it? Has your company, despite its best intentions, drifted into "convenient purpose"?

Inject purpose into succession planning. Leadership handoffs are tricky when it comes to purpose. As you prepare your successor, plan out how they might carry the torch of purpose while also making it their own. Working together, map out specific steps your successor can take that articulate the purpose, and steps you might take to link your successor to the company's purpose. If you're an incoming leader, take an inventory of actions and behaviors you can implement to accept the mantle of purpose.

Get to work on purpose-related metrics. You must measure purpose, even if doing so requires some acceptance of subjectivity and imperfection. Measure purpose-related inputs or enablers of purpose, not just results. Consider a range of methods, including perceptual measures (surveys of a range of internal and external stakeholders) and outcome measures. Pay attention to the growing body of work on measuring ESG and connect it with your measures of purpose. Tailor your metrics to your specific purpose and organizational processes as well as to more specific principles and behaviors you might derive from your purpose. Finally, consider how your metrics might connect with the specific ways that you create long-term value.

Find the balance between social and commercial commitments. Make sure you clarify each stakeholder's expectations, negotiating them when necessary on an ongoing basis to avoid surprises and disappointment. Recognize that stakeholders will benchmark you against your peers, in some cases raising expectations for the entire industry. When performance relative to any stakeholder expectation seems to be slipping, take aggressive action.

Make purpose part of the organization's strategy and operating rhythm. At all phases of strategy-making—when crafting high-level strategies, making strategic choices, and allocating resources—run a purpose "gut check" to ensure compatibility with the purpose. Encourage debate so that others can feel a sense of ownership over purpose's interpretation. Consider whether your organization might make public commitments, increase transparency, and engage with external certifying bodies to ensure long-term alignment between purpose and strategy.

Stay inspired. Focus at all times on aligning your personal purpose with the organization's reason for being. Why are you *really* doing what you're doing? What legacy of leadership do you hope to leave? How would you want future leaders and employees to describe your contribution? If you at one time felt personally inspired by your organization's purpose, does that still hold true? And if not, what changes might you make?

As this list of action steps suggests, the practice of deep purpose is transformational, amounting to a fundamental reshaping and reimagining of your business. If that seems overwhelming, rest assured that you need not accomplish it all at once. Approach deep purpose as an ongoing and open-ended project rather than a discrete, one-off initiative. Start with a few of these steps, choosing those that seem both most relevant and actionable given your current position and resources. Unlike typical change-management exercises, deep purpose gets to the heart of why the firm exists. Little by little, it forces a recalibration of the firm's role as well as its relationship with employees, customers, and society at large.

In this respect, deep purpose transcends the caricatures of purpose so prevalent today. Some regard purpose as a smokescreen that businesses can cynically use to mask wrongdoing. For others, purpose seems to serve as a Trojan horse for greater regulation and taxation of business. The deep purpose leaders I studied see it differently. As practical idealists, they mobilize purpose as a lever for transforming their companies. Creating and sustaining a moral community, they innovate more effectively and operate more efficiently, fueling financial performance. In turbulent markets, purpose gives them a reassuring constancy. It sets them apart from the competition in the eyes of stakeholders. It elevates relationships inside and outside the company, transforming them from standard economic contracts to moral covenants that inspire passionate action.

Purpose also improves performance by prompting leaders to take a long-term view of the business. Although "short-termism" often seems unavoidable, it is really a contortion of capitalism. Adam Smith's notion of the market's functioning as an invisible hand rested on an assumption that operators would attend to both short- *and* long-term interests. Common sense leads us to a similar understanding. Is it really possible to build a stable business, much less a stable society, if everyone only thinks about short-term results? Asking and answering the questions of why your business exists opens up a long-term perspective, leading us to imagine lofty ambitions and visions of the future and to enshrine them in what I've called a Big Story. It also leads us to comprehend the multi-dimensionality of our impact on others and to embrace both a commercial and social logic.

At the outset of this book, I noted the obvious, that humanity stands on a precipice. For all the good capitalism has done since the dawn of industrialization, it has also helped fuel many of the problems besetting humanity. We face an impending climate crisis, extreme economic inequality, a global pandemic, and a host of other social, economic, and public health challenges. Trust in business is at an all-time low. But if it is a villain, business also stands as a potential savior, a role advocated by a growing number of enlightened investors, executives, entrepreneurs, academics, and activists who seek to create a more responsive and benevolent capitalism.

As you ponder deep purpose, I hope you'll remember what's at stake here, both for your business and for humanity. Although government can and must serve as a corrective, the global business community must also put its own house in order. Deep purpose provides companies with a delivery system for doing that. By pursuing deep purpose, companies put themselves on a path that allows them to maximize both their commercial success *and* the value they deliver across society. If many more companies committed to actualizing the deep purpose mindset, the impact on our communities and our environment would be profound.

As I write this, the winds of commerce are shifting. Investors are demanding that executives manage in ways that will create long-term value, steering capital away from those organizations that don't. Consumers and employees are doing the same, choosing companies that stand for something greater. If you feel a gnawing sense that the status quo isn't working and something fundamental needs to change, listen to that impulse. Aim higher. Demand that your organization do more. Because as Etsy, Bühler, Microsoft, LEGO, the Seattle Seahawks, Gotham Greens, and the other deep purpose organizations discussed in this book suggest, more *is* possible. We just have to understand this potential, shift our thinking, and take more concerted action to take purpose deeper.

ACKNOWLEDGMENTS

This book originated in two dialogues I've had in recent years. The first began in a heated debate I had several years ago with two friends, Frank Cooper and Matt Breitfelder. We were discussing the purpose of business and why so few companies had articulated and enacted purposes for themselves. Frank and Matt asked me a difficult question: What was I doing about it as a business educator and researcher?

I didn't have a convincing answer, and it bothered me. But this awkward moment prompted me to think harder about purpose than I had been. Today I look back on this debate and the many subsequent conversations I've had with Frank and Matt and feel deeply grateful for the push they gave me.

At about this time, I was also inspired by the example of BlackRock's CEO, Larry Fink. Among the many deep purpose business leaders I have met over the years, Larry stands out not only for having lived this ideal from the time he cofounded BlackRock, but for encouraging others to do the same. Along with my conversations with Frank and Matt, Larry's public letters and my conversations with him convinced me to set aside other projects and write this book. To him as well, I wish to express my profound thanks.

I was fortunate to have a publishing dream team on my side: my agent Richard Pine and editor Hollis Heimbouch. Richard was instrumental in helping me conceptualize the book. His belief in this project from the very start and optimistic view of the world had a deep impact on me. He is the living embodiment of the sort of "practical idealist" whom I discuss in this book. I likewise consider myself to be lucky to have an editor like Hollis who is all-in once she signs up an author. Her thoughtful feedback on the book was incredibly helpful throughout the writing process. Every writer needs an audience they are writing for. She was the audience I visualized as I wrote this book because I knew she would be the first person who would see that draft.

To research this book I had to channel the wisdom of many others who had practiced deep purpose. First and foremost, I am grateful to the over two hundred business leaders who took time out of their busy schedules to give me candid accounts of their experiments with deep purpose. I feel privileged that I had an opportunity to hear first-hand from some incredible individuals ranging from CEOs to frontline workers. Each shared their trials and tribulations with the pursuit of deep purpose. I just hope I have done them justice in telling their inspiring stories.

Research and writing is anything but a solitary process. Conducting over two hundred interviews and then turning some of those interviews into teaching cases as well as materials for this book was a monumental task that I could not have done by myself. I am grateful to a number of individuals who helped me throughout this process. My long list of research partners includes Monte Burke, Patrick Healy, Akiko Kanno, Joseph Mesfin, Eppa Rixey, Amar Scherzer, Malini Sen, Rohan Sheth, Aseem Shukla, Luciana Silvestri, Rachna Tahilyani, Margaret Vo, Franz Wohlgezogen, and Sam Yogi. I am grateful to Jennifer Beauregard and Susan Kahn of Baker Library for their excellent research assistance and support. I am also thankful to Amber Haynes for her help with the figures in this book. I am especially thankful to Seth Schulman and Rachel Gostenhofer for their superb editorial help. Their deep commitment to this project was evident every step of the way.

As I plowed into the huge body of work that had been done on organizational purpose and related topics, I was lucky to have others who pointed me in the right direction. They patiently listened to my stories, offered their own understanding of my accounts, and helped direct me to some of the relevant prior research. I am grateful to Aaron Chatterji,

Francesca Gino, Denny Gioia, Scott Goodson, Rebecca Henderson, Ioannis Ioannou, Sarah Kaplan, Deepak Malhotra, Joel Podolny, Violina Rindova, Majken Schultz, Jim Sebenius, George Serafeim, and Richard Tedlow. It is very likely that I am forgetting to include some people here. My mistake should not diminish my sincere appreciation for you, and I request your forgiveness. I am grateful to the following individuals who inspired me to think more deeply about purpose: Maria Carolina V. Dominguez, Wai Ching Chan, Niren Chaudhary, Betty Lau, Alicia Morales, and Dilhan Pillay. I am thankful to the entire Temasek team who provided invaluable feedback and inspiration throughout my research process.

It can be tedious to read an incomplete and sometimes incoherent draft manuscript and offer feedback that is at once constructive and encouraging. I was lucky to have dear colleagues and friends who stepped up to do this for me: John Campbell, Rakesh Khurana, Mark Mizruchi, and Peter Murmann. Frank Cooper and Nitin Nohria became fellow travelers with me on this book journey, not only reading multiple drafts but also rolling up their sleeves, brainstorming, and helping me to restructure key sections of the book.

Mary Gros is an extraordinary friend who has been there with me since the time I began my intellectual life. She has the unique capacity to both challenge and support my research endeavors, and she did so again at key junctures as I wrote this book.

I could not have written this book were I not at the Harvard Business School, the very embodiment of a deep purpose organization. I am grateful not only for all the financial support I received from our Division of Research for this book, but also for what this institution stands for. When we say that we "educate leaders who make a difference in the world," we really mean it. Purpose permeates this organization, and so once I zeroed in on the power of purpose, it was easy for me to dig deeper without having to look too far. I also came to appreciate how many of my current and former HBS colleagues had done pathbreaking and influential research on related topics long before I arrived on the scene. I am deeply grateful to many of them, including Joe Badaracco, Chris Bartlett, Julie Battilana, Mike Beer, Joe Bower, Amy Edmondson, Bill

George, Rebecca Henderson, Rosabeth Moss Kanter, Joshua Margolis, Lynn Paine, Michael Porter, Kash Rangan, George Serafeim, and Mike Toffel, for paving the way for this book.

One of the greatest privileges for me at the Harvard Business School was to teach and ultimately chair the Advanced Management Program (AMP). Our students are senior leaders from every corner of the globe and each comes with a commitment to advance themselves as leaders during the seven weeks that they are with us on campus. It was through their eyes that I got my first glimpse of the power of deep purpose. I am forever grateful for all that I learned from them.

A few individuals who are no longer with us but whose work and philosophy have had a profound impact on me include Sumantra Ghoshal, Paul Lawrence, and my parents Sushma and Satya Paul Gulati. Sumantra and Paul remain inspiring models, researchers who studied important problems and sought to distill insights that were relevant both to theory and practice. Each talked about the importance of tackling critical problems facing business and the world at large. Their voices were a constant in my head as I conducted this research. I just wish that they were here to read this book. My parents were each special in their own way. My mother was an embodiment of a deep purpose leader, and my father deeply believed that doing good was an essential precursor to doing well and that we must keep the faith when we take the leap and attempt to do something good.

In pursuit of this project, I sought out others whose work I deeply admire and who have successfully bridged the divide between academia and practice. Each of these scholars was remarkably generous with their time in guiding me on how I might envision this book and navigate the publication process. A big thanks to Angela Duckworth, Adam Grant, and Morten Hansen.

Writing a book requires immense project management skills. As someone who is administratively challenged, I would never have been able to complete this book without Evan Terwilliger and his unfailing effort to ensure that everything got done right. He was involved right from the start and did everything from lining up meetings to helping me sift through company background information. He helped me keep all my materials organized and knew where everything was filed. No matter how complex the task, I knew I could rely upon Evan to get it done. His positive can-do spirit helped me keep going even when this project seemed never-ending.

Working through the book writing process requires immense appreciation for deadlines and attention to detail. Wendy Wong played a crucial role in getting this book published on time. I am also lucky to have worked with Barbara Cave Henricks, Jessica Krakoski, and Nina Nocciolino. They provided superb guidance and direction in making sure the message of this book was read by as many people as possible.

I am blessed to have a circle of dear friends, and they have sustained me through the long and ardous process of writing a book. They patiently accepted my incessant excuse that I would not be able to join them due to pressing and self-imposed deadlines on my book. Their continued presence sustained me and helped me to stay connected with my own deep purpose. I hope to make up for all those absences now that this book is done!

I wish to thank my family for tolerating my long disappearances into my home office as well as my lengthy monologues about deep purpose over the dinner table. The COVID-19 pandemic brought our family together under one roof, but it also made it more difficult for me to remain holed up in my office. I am grateful to my children Varoun and Shivani for their love but even more for who they are as human beings. I hope each of them continues to work toward finding their own purpose in life and trying to live by it. And finally, I want to thank my wife, Anuradha. At so many points, she put her own book on hold so that I could move mine along. Her own work on finding personal purpose inspired me to study deep purpose organizations. She remains one of the most purposeful individuals I have ever met and continues to inspire me to find my own purpose in all that I do. I am grateful for all her love and support that make every day magical.

A NOTE ON RESEARCH METHODOLOGY

B etween 2019 and 2021, I conducted extensive fieldwork into a few, select companies that seemed to be going beyond convenience, pursuing a higher purpose more intently and successfully than the vast majority. A number of frameworks and paradigms about how to embed purpose into companies existed, most viewing this as a conventional change management exercise. But it seemed to me that the most successful companies didn't limit themselves to the basics. They went further in discovering, articulating, embedding, and sustaining their purposes, sometimes doing so in idiosyncratic ways.

I wanted to visit the "cutting edge" of purpose and immerse myself in the strategies and mindsets that prevailed there. My goal wasn't to capture every essential strategy and technique leaders should mobilize when pursuing a reason for being. If I could uncover some key pathways for going deep that most leaders had overlooked, I would have contributed something. James O'Toole begins his historical study of well-intentioned capitalists by observing that "it is hard to do good." I wanted to see if I could make it just a bit easier for companies as well as leaders.[1]

My first task was to select which companies to study. I conducted a quantitative search of all major business media and public company annual reports, searching for companies that were most associated with the word "purpose" or related key words. This yielded a list of fifty-nine companies. Comparing this list against companies mentioned by previous books on purpose, sustainability, and related topics, I found significant overlap, which told me I was on the right track. At the same time, I identified several companies that had dedicated themselves impressively to purpose but seldom received media attention for it.

To reduce my list of exemplar companies to a reasonable size, I searched secondary sources, identifying which companies on my list seemed to take the most concrete action in support of their purpose and removing those whose activities seemed less impressive. That left me with thirty-four companies. From there, I cracked open my Rolodex and interviewed executives inside these companies to gauge in a more detailed way what their organizations were doing to support their purposes. From these conversations, I pared my list down to eighteen companies, adding a few select start-ups and private companies that I happened to learn about through my own personal relationships and discovered to be exceptionally dedicated to realizing their organizational purpose.[2]

Some of the firms on my final list, like Pepsi and Microsoft, were well known to global business readers for their unusual focus on purpose and their enlightened operating models. Others, like the agriculture start-up Gotham Greens, the Swiss food technology firm Bühler, or the Indian conglomerate Mahindra—were lesser known but no less impressive. My goal wasn't to study a specific industry or type of firm, but rather to explore new insights, taking the time to linger on these "deep purpose" companies, as I called them, and understand what allowed them to realize their purposes in unusually meaningful, compelling, and sustained ways. Large or small, public or private, the companies I studied were all energetically acting to realize their purposes, in the process doing their part to safeguard the environment and address serious social problems. They were also dramatically improving their performance, winning over customers, employees, investors, and the general public.

I went on to interview leaders, employees, and customers at these firms—anyone who could enhance my understanding of how these companies approached purpose. At some firms, I interviewed only a handful of individuals. At others, as many as thirty. In conducting and processing my interviews, I loosely followed what academic researchers might call an inductive research process. Rather than start with clear hypotheses and try to validate or disprove them, I generated hypotheses by immersing myself in the conversations I was having with companies. Scrutinizing transcripts of my interviews again and again, I uncovered some of the underlying constructs that seemed to shape their actions. Seeking to develop a theory about how these companies went deeper on purpose, I also analyzed my interviews in dialogue with existing research related to purpose, its articulation, and its activation. This approach allowed me to not merely notice patterns in the data, but also to discover gaps in existing understandings of purpose.[3]

NOTES

Preface

1. Joshua Daniel Margolis and James Patrick Walsh, *People and Profits? The Search for a Link Between a Company's Social and Financial Performance* (Mahwah, NJ: Lawrence Erlbaum, 2001), 10.

2. Cathy Carlisi et al., "Purpose with the Power to Transform Your Organization," BCG, May 15, 2017, https://www.bcg.com/publications/2017/transformation -behavior-culture-purpose-power-transform-organization.

3. "The Business Case for Purpose," *Harvard Business Review Analytic Services Report*, October 1, 2015, 4, https://hbr.org/resources/pdfs/comm/ey/19392HBR ReportEY.pdf.

4. "Larry Fink's 2021 letter to CEOs," BlackRock, accessed April 28, 2021, https:// www.blackrock.com/corporate/investor-relations/larry-fink-ceo-letter.

5. Carmine Di Sibio (global chairman and CEO for the EY organization), interview with the author, June 16, 2021.

Chapter I: What Is Purpose *Really*?

1. Constance L. Hays, "Forrest Mars, 95, Creator of the M & M and a Candy Empire," *New York Times*, July 3, 1999, https://www.nytimes.com/1999/07/03/business /forrest-mars-95-creator-of-the-m-m-and-a-candy-empire.html.

2. Stephen M. Badger II, "Editorial," *Brewery Journal*, January 2014, 3. See also Paul Robert Gilbert and Catherine Dolan, "Mutuality Talk in a Family-Owned Multinational: Anthropological Categories & Critical Analyses of Corporate Ethicizing," *Journal of Business Anthropology* 9, no. 1 (Spring 2020): 21–22, https:// rauli.cbs.dk/index.php/jba/article/view/5958.

3. For an analysis that distinguishes between goal- and duty-based definitions of purpose, see Gerard George et al., "Purpose in the For-Profit Firm: A Review

and Framework for Management Research," *Journal of Management* (April 2021), https://doi.org/10.1177/01492063211006450.

4. A great deal of confusion and inconsistency surrounds the concept of purpose. Countless definitions have appeared, some equating it with a big commercial goal, others arguing that purpose statements should specify whom the company is trying to serve, still others defining purpose as a human resources tool that captures what inspires employees to perform. As I've observed, the best definitions of purpose emphasize an ambitious and idealistic quality at once. They not only identify an organizational goal but lay out grand ambitions for achieving good in the world that go beyond the pursuit of profit. One commentator writes: "Purpose is a definitive statement about the difference you are trying to make in the world." Roy Spence, *It's Not What You Sell, It's What You Stand For: Why Every Extraordinary Business Is Driven by Purpose* (New York: Portfolio, 2009), 10. A handbook on purpose defines purpose as "a company's reason for being that simultaneously helps solve a societal problem and creates significant financial value for the company." Georgina Eckert and Bobbi Silten, eds., "Purpose Playbook: Putting Purpose into Practice with Shared Value," Foundation Strategy Group and the Shared Value Initiative, May 2020, 10. The British Academy writes that "a corporate purpose is the expression of the means by which a business can contribute solutions to societal and environmental problems. Corporate purpose should create value for both shareholders and stakeholders." See the British Academy's white paper entitled "Principles for Purposeful Business," 2019, 16.

5. "The Five Principles," Mars, accessed May 3, 2021, https://www.mars.com/about/five-principles.

6. Joël Glenn Brenner, *The Emperors of Chocolate: Inside the Secret World of Hershey & Mars* (New York: Broadway Books, 2000), 257.

7. "The Five Principles," Mars.

8. Andrew Edgecliffe-Johnson, "Stephen Badger: Balancing Profit with Creating Value for Society," *Financial Times*, November 9, 2019, https://www.ft.com/content/bf039636-007a-11ea-b7bc-f3fa4e77dd47.

9. David Kaplan, "Mars Incorporated: A Pretty Sweet Place to Work," *Fortune*, January 17, 2013, https://fortune.com/2013/01/17/mars-incorporated-a-pretty-sweet-place-to-work/.

10. Edgecliffe-Johnson, "Stephen Badger."

11. Paul Conley, "Mars in Joint Venture to Build Wind Farm in Texas," Food Dive, April 30, 2014, https://www.fooddive.com/news/mars-in-joint-venture-to-build-wind-farm-in-texas/257595/.

12. Alistair Hall and Katie Ellman, "The Next-Generation Sustainability Aims of Mars," GreenBiz, October 6, 2017, https://www.greenbiz.com/article/next-generation-sustainability-aims-mars.

13. Simon Mainwaring, "Purpose at Work: How Mars Is Scaling Sustainability Goals Across Generations," *Forbes*, February 12, 2020, accessed May 3, 2021, https://www.forbes.com/sites/simonmainwaring/2020/02/12/purpose-at-work -how-mars-is-scaling-sustainability-goals-across-generations/.

14. "Economics of Mutuality (EoM)," Mutuality in Business, Briefing Paper 4, Saïd Business School and University of Oxford, June 8, 2015, https://www.sbs.ox.ac .uk/sites/default/files/2018-06/MiB-EoM_Backgrounder_6.6.15.pdf; Mars, "Mars Launches 'Seeds of Change' Accelerator," press release, March 5, 2019, https://www .mars.com/news-and-stories/press-releases/seeds-of-change-accelerator.

15. Quoted in Laura Arrillaga-Andreessen, "Five Visionary Tech Entrepreneurs Who Are Changing the World," *New York Times Style Magazine*, October 12, 2015, https://www.nytimes.com/interactive/2015/10/12/t-magazine/elizabeth-holmes -tech-visionaries-brian-chesky.html?_r=0.

16. "Theranos Trains 100 Global Women Leaders in STEM for State Department's TechWomen Program," *Business Wire*, October 10, 2015, https://www.businesswire .com/news/home/20151010005018/en/Theranos-Trains-100-Global-Women -Leaders-in-STEM-for-State-Department%E2%80%99s-TechWomen-Program.

17. I observed a similar tendency of companies to relegate sustainability goals to the periphery of their businesses in Luciana Silvestri and Ranjay Gulati, "From Periphery to Core: A Process Model for Embracing Sustainability," in ed., Rebecca Henderson, Ranjay Gulati, and Michael Tushman, *Leading Sustainable Change: An Organizational Perspective* (Oxford, NY: Oxford University Press, 2015), 81–110.

18. Most companies that treat purpose (and by implication, social good) as peripheral to the business define their reasons for being narrowly and even vacuously. Instead of adopting an expansive purpose that elevates the company beyond its commercial goals, they take a conventional business mission framed around delivering for customers or dominating a market and treat that as a higher purpose. In effect, they excuse themselves from doing the hard and important work of maximizing value for all stakeholders. Some companies adopt a purpose that seems at first glance to transcend a commercial business mission but that ultimately doesn't lend itself to a multi-stakeholder approach. The industrial conglomerate Danaher, for instance, takes as its purpose "Helping realize life's potential." That sounds altruistic, but it appears to focus the company on serving customers, growing markets, *and then* performing good works for additional stakeholders as part of CSR-type efforts. By this interpretation, Danaher might recognize a social logic, but it distinguishes it from its commercial logic, taking the latter as its core reason for being. It would appear that the company's purpose doesn't compel it to reimagine its core businesses so that they deliver for a wide array of stakeholders.

19. Michael E. Porter and Mark R. Kramer, "Creating Shared Value," *Harvard*

Business Review, January–February 2011, https://hbr.org/2011/01/the-big-idea
-creating-shared-value.

20. Mackey and Sisodia seem to envision a mode of stakeholder capitalism that transcends tradeoffs: "A key difference between a traditional business and a conscious business is that in the former, managers routinely make tradeoffs among stakeholders. A good manager is seen as one who makes tradeoffs that are more advantageous to the investor stakeholders than to others. Conscious businesses understand that if we look for tradeoffs, we *always* will find them. *If we look for synergies across stakeholders, we can usually find those, too.*" The authors also seem to suggest a mode of capitalism beyond tradeoffs in the following passage about conscious organizations: "Since everyone is aligned in the same direction and moving in harmony, friction in the system is minimal. All that creativity and commitment is channeled toward shared ends, generating great value for all stakeholders." John Mackey and Raj Sisodia, *Conscious Capitalism: Liberating the Heroic Spirit of Business* (Boston: Harvard Business Review Press, 2014), 70–71.

21. For an excellent overview of the challenges faced by capitalism, see Rebecca Henderson's book *Reimagining Capitalism in a World on Fire* (New York: Public Affairs, 2020).

22. David Gelles, "C.E.O.s Are Not Here to Save Us," *New York Times*, updated December 2, 2020, https://www.nytimes.com/2019/09/28/business/wework-juul -ebay-ceo.html.

23. "Business Roundtable Redefines the Purpose of a Corporation to Promote 'An Economy That Serves All Americans,'" Business Roundtable, August 19, 2019, https://www.businessroundtable.org/business-roundtable-redefines-the-purpose -of-a-corporation-to-promote-an-economy-that-serves-all-americans.

24. Michael Hiltzik, "Last Year CEOs Pledged to Serve Stakeholders, Not Shareholders. You Were Right Not to Buy It," *Los Angeles Times*, August 19, 2020, https://www.latimes.com/business/story/2020-08-19/big-business-shareholder -value-scam.

25. Hiltzik, "Last Year CEOs Pledged."

26. See, for instance, Anand Giridharadas, *Winners Take All: The Elite Charade of Changing the World* (New York: Alfred A. Knopf, 2018); and Colin Mayer, *Prosperity: Better Business Makes the Greater Good* (Oxford, UK: Oxford University Press, 2018).

27. See, for instance, Paul S. Adler, *The 99 Percent Economy: How Democratic Socialism Can Overcome the Crises of Capitalism* (New York: Oxford University Press, 2019).

28. "Purpose: Shifting from Why to How," *McKinsey Quarterly* (April 2020), 3, https:// www.mckinsey.com/business-functions/organization/our-insights/purpose -shifting-from-why-to-how.

29. See the seminal article by Charles Handy, "What's A Business For?," *Harvard Business Review*, December 2002, https://hbr.org/2002/12/whats-a-business-for.

30. William Damon, *The Path to Purpose: How Young People Find Their Calling in Life* (New York: Free Press, 2008), 33. My emphasis.

31. "Kavvanah," Jewish Virtual Library, accessed May 25, 2021, https://www.jewish virtuallibrary.org/kavvanah.

32. Deepak Chopra, "Are you Living Your True Purpose?," Heal Your Life, June 10, 2013, https://www.healyourlife.com/are-you-living-your-true-purpose.

33. "Reimagining How and Where Fresh Food is Grown," Gotham Greens, accessed May 5, 2021, https://www.gothamgreens.com/our-story/.

34. "High-Tech Hydroponic Farm Transforms Abandoned Bowling Alley," Greenhouse Management, November 3, 2011, https://www.greenhousemag.com/article/gotham-greens-hydroponic-farm-bowling-alley/; Gail Ciampa, "Gotham Greens Opens Its Massive Providence Greenhouse on Thursday. Here's a Look Inside," *Providence Journal*, updated December 4, 2019, https://www.providencejournal.com/news/20191204/gotham-greens-opens-its-massive-providence-greenhouse-on-thursday-heres-look-inside; "Vegetable Growers News," Vegetable Growers, November 13, 2019, https://vegetablegrowersnews.com/news/gotham-greens-opens-largest-urban-agriculture-campus-in-chicago/.

35. PR Newswire, "Gotham Greens Raises $87 Million to Grow Its Indoor Agriculture Footprint, Bringing More Fresh Foods to Shoppers Nationwide," Gotham Greens press release, December 8, 2020, https://www.prnewswire.com/news-releases/gotham-greens-raises-87-million-to-grow-its-indoor-agriculture-footprint-bringing-more-fresh-foods-to-shoppers-nationwide-301187876.html.

36. See the company website, https://www.gothamgreens.com/, accessed May 7, 2021.

37. Viraj Puri (founder of Gotham Greens), interview with the author, September 1, 2020.

38. I owe a debt here to Christopher Bartlett and Sumantra Ghoshal, who argued that purpose precedes strategy and structure. See Christopher A. Bartlett and Sumantra Ghoshal, "Changing the Role of Top Management: Beyond Strategy to Purpose," *Harvard Business Review* 72, no. 6 (November–December 1994): 79 passim. My argument here is informed by my background in sociology, a discipline that focuses on the power of the contexts that surround individuals. Purpose, in the language of Neil Fligstein, can be a new "conception of control" (ideology of economic survival) that can in turn lead to changes in how managers craft their strategy. See Neil Fligstein, *The Transformation of Corporate Control* (Cambridge, MA: Harvard University Press, 1990).

39. Satya Nadella (CEO of Microsoft), interview with the author, June 1, 2020.

40. Michael C. Jensen neatly articulated this economic view of the enterprise: "I

believe it is productive to define an organization as a legal entity that serves as a nexus for a complex set of contracts (written and unwritten) among disparate individuals. The behavior of the organization is like the equilibrium behavior of a market. We do not often characterize the steel market or the wheat market as having preferences and motives or making choices." Michael C. Jensen, *Foundations of Organizational Strategy* (Cambridge, MA: Harvard University Press, 2001), 135, 137.

41. Roland Marchand, *Creating the Corporate Soul: The Rise of Public Relations and Corporate Imagery in American Big Business* (Berkeley: University of California Press, 1998), 7–10.

42. Marchand, *Creating the Corporate Soul*, 87.

43. Philip Selznick, *Leadership in Administration: A Sociological Interpretation,* rev. ed. (Berkeley: University of California Press, 1984), 19.

44. Joel M. Podolny, Rakesh Khurana, and Marya L. Besharov, "Revisiting the Meaning of Leadership," in Nitin Nohria and Rakesh Khurana, eds., *Handbook of Leadership Theory and Practice* (Boston: Harvard Business Press, 2010), 71. Some two decades before Selznick, business executive and management thinker Chester Barnard suggested that meaning and purpose constituted a moral code for people inside an organization to follow, one so intensely felt that it could override their own emotional needs. He gave the example of a telephone operator who stayed at her post even as a house containing her bedridden mother burned down, so devoted was she to "the moral necessity of uninterrupted service" to the company and its customers.

45. Mayer, *Prosperity* (Oxford: Oxford University Press, 2018), 11.

46. See Robert E. Quinn and Anjan V. Thakor, *The Economics of Higher Purpose* (Oakland, CA: Berrett-Koehler Publishers, 2019), especially chapter 5.

47. Satya Nadella, *Hit Refresh: The Quest to Rediscover Microsoft's Soul and Imagine a Better Future for Everyone* (New York: HarperCollins, 2017), 78–79.

48. Ranjay Gulati, "The Soul of a Start-Up," *Harvard Business Review*, July–August, 2019, https://hbr.org/2019/07/the-soul-of-a-start-up.

49. See, for instance, Aaron K. Chatterji and Michael W. Toffel, "Divided We Lead," *Harvard Business Review*, March 22, 2018, https://hbr.org/2018/03/divided-we-lead; and Aaron K. Chatterji and Michael W. Toffel, "The Right and Wrong Way to Do 'CEO Activism,'" *Wall Street Journal*, February 22, 2019, https://www.wsj.com/articles/the-right-and-wrong-way-to-do-ceo-activism-11550874530.

50. Aaron K. Chatterji and Michael W. Toffel, "The New CEO Activists," *Harvard Business Review*, January–February 2018, https://hbr.org/2018/01/the-new-ceo-activists.

51. Quoted in Handy, "What's a Business For?" Some have questioned whether Keynes actually made this statement. See, for instance, "Capitalism: The Nas-

tiest of Men for the Nastiest of Motives Will Somehow Work for the Benefit of All," Quote Investigator, accessed May 25, 2021, https://quoteinvestigator .com/2011/02/23/capitalism-motives/.

Chapter 2: Walking on the Razor's Edge

1. Josh Silverman (CEO of Etsy), interview with the author, June 1, 2020. In addition to the published sources noted, I've based my account of Etsy in this chapter on a number of interviews I conducted with Etsy executives. These interviews also formed the basis of a case study that tells a story similar to the one presented here. See Ranjay Gulati, Luciana Silvestri, and Monte Burke, "Etsy: Crafting a Turnaround to Save the Business and Its Soul," Harvard Business School Case Study (forthcoming).

2. Kiron Roy, "Stand for More Than Just Profits," Coworker.org, accessed May 14, 2021, https://www.coworker.org/petitions/recommit-to-etsy-s-values-and-support -the-etsy-community-for-the-long-term.

3. Roy, "Stand for More."

4. David Gelles, "Inside the Revolution at Etsy," *New York Times*, November 25, 2017, https://www.nytimes.com/2017/11/25/business/etsy-josh-silverman.html.

5. Quoted in Thales S. Teixeira, "Airbnb, Etsy, Uber: Expanding from One to Many Millions of Customers," Harvard Business School Case Study 9–519–087, June 5, 2019, 6.

6. Quoted in Teixeira, "Airbnb, Etsy, Uber," 6.

7. Max Chafkin, "Can Rob Kalin Scale Etsy?," Inc., April 2011, https://www.inc .com/magazine/20110401/can-rob-kalin-scale-etsy.html.

8. Chafkin, "Can Rob Kalin Scale Etsy?"; Tugba Sabanoglu, "Annual Gross Merchandise Sales (GMS) of Etsy Inc. from 2005 to 2020," Statista, March 11, 2021, https://www.statista.com/statistics/219412/etsys-total-merchandise-sales-per -year.

9. "Rob Kalin Out as Etsy CEO," Inc., July 21, 2011, accessed May 18, 2021, https:// www.inc.com/articles/201107/rob-kalin-steps-down-as-etsy-ceo.html.

10. Chad Dickerson, "Etsy's Next Chapter: Reimagining Commerce as a Public Company," *Etsy* (blog), April 16, 2015, https://blog.etsy.com/news/2015/etsys-next -chapter-reimagining-commerce-as-a-public-company/; Kruti Patel Goyal (chief product officer at Etsy), email correspondence with the author, April 23, 2021.

11. Michelle Traub, "Etsy Joins the B Corporation Movement," *Etsy* (blog), May 9, 2012, https://blog.etsy.com/news/2012/etsy-joins-the-b-corporation-movement/.

12. Amy Larocca, "Etsy Wants to Crochet Its Cake, and Eat It Too," *The Cut*, April 2016, https://www.thecut.com/2016/04/etsy-capitalism-c-v-r.html (article appeared in the April 4, 2016, issue of *New York Magazine*).

13. Caitlin Huston, "Five Things to Know About Etsy Before Its IPO," Market-

Watch, April 15, 2015, https://www.marketwatch.com/story/five-things-to-know
-about-etsy-before-its-ipo-2015-03-05.

14. Dickerson, "Etsy's Next Chapter."

15. Quoted in Larocca, "Etsy Wants to Crochet Its Cake."

16. Ben Popper, "Etsy Completes Its IPO, Valuing the Craft Marketplace at Over
$3.5 Billion," Verge, April 16, 2015, https://www.theverge.com/2015/4/16/8428
627/etsy-ipo-goes-public.

17. Gelles, "Inside the Revolution at Etsy."

18. Josh Silverman (CEO of Etsy), interview with the author, June 1, 2020.

19. Academic authors have urged on the idealistic pursuit of "win-win." See R. Edward Freeman, Kirsten E. Martin, and Bidhan L. Parmar, *The Power of And:
Responsible Business Without Trade-Offs* (New York: Columbia University Press,
2020).

20. It is not a new position. One scholar in a 1932 law review article observed that
"public opinion" was becoming more hospitable to "a view of the business corporation as an economic institution which has a social service as well as a
profit-making function." E. M. Dodd, "For Whom Are Corporate Managers
Trustees?," *Harvard Law Review* 45, no. 7 (May 1932): 1148. As Rebecca Henderson has noted, "Reimagining capitalism requires embracing the idea that
while firms must be profitable if they are to thrive, their purpose must be not
only to make money but also to build prosperity and freedom in the context of
a livable planet and a healthy society." Henderson, *Reimagining Capitalism in a
World on Fire*.

21. "Completing Capitalism," Economics of Mutuality, accessed May 18, 2021,
https://eom.org/.

22. Porter and Kramer, "Creating Shared Value," 64 passim.

23. Alex Edmans, *Grow the Pie: How Great Companies Deliver Both Purpose and
Profit* (Cambridge, UK: Cambridge University Press, 2020).

24. Michael Beer et al., *Higher Ambition: How Great Leaders Create Economic* and
Social Value (Boston: Harvard Business Review Press, 2011), 53.

25. Mackey and Sisodia, *Conscious Capitalism*, 35–36.

26. Anand Giridharadas devotes an entire chapter (chapter 2) to criticizing the notion of win-win. See his book *Winners Take All*, 38, 51. The economist Colin
Mayer regards as "dangerous" the concept of "doing well by doing good," faulting
it for presuming that "philanthropy is only valuable where it is profitable" and for
converting "charity into profit-generating entities in the way in which we have
transformed utilities and other public services into shareholder-value maximizing
organizations." Mayer, *Prosperity*, 6–7.

27. Brett Ryder, "What Is Stakeholder Capitalism?," *Economist*, September 19, 2020,
https://www.economist.com/business/2020/09/19/what-is-stakeholder-capitalism;

Andrea Ucini, "What Companies Are For," *Economist*, August 22, 2019, https://www.economist.com/leaders/2019/08/22/what-companies-are-for.

28. Rosabeth Moss Kanter, "How Great Companies Think Differently," *Harvard Business Review*, November 2011, https://hbr.org/2011/11/how-great-companies-think-differently.

29. Julie Battilana et al., "The Dual-Purpose Playbook," *Harvard Business Review*, March–April 2019, https://hbr.org/2019/03/the-dual-purpose-playbook.

30. David A. Lax and James K. Sebenius, *3-d Negotiation: Powerful Tools to Change the Game in Your Most Important Deals* (Boston: Harvard Business School Press, 2008); Barry Schwartz, *The Paradox of Choice: Why More Is Less* (New York: HarperCollins, 2004), 131–32.

31. In these situations, companies implicitly or explicitly identify internal "exchange rates" between social and commercial logics, valuing the impact of a short-term sacrifice by one or more stakeholders against the value of the long-term gains. In determining these exchange rates, companies consider the *minimum thresholds* that individual stakeholders might regard as acceptable in any decision. What are the lowest returns the company can deliver while still placating shareholders? Or conversely, what are the maximum sacrifices they can ask employees to make without alienating them? Julie Battilana et al., "Beyond Shareholder Value Maximization: Accounting for Financial/Social Tradeoffs in Dual-Purpose Companies," *Academy of Management Review* (forthcoming). It's important as well in managing tradeoffs to take into account individual stakeholders and their varying significance for the firm. See Paul Strebel, Didier Cossin, and Mahwesh Khan, "How to Reconcile Your Shareholders with Other Stakeholders," *MIT Sloan Management Review*, July 13, 2020. Alex Edmans also tackles the problem of tradeoffs in his book *Grow the Pie*.

32. "Q4 2018 Financial Results," Etsy, February 25, 2019, https://s22.q4cdn.com/941741262/files/doc_financials/quarterly/2018/q4/Etsy-4Q-2018-Earnings-Presentation.pdf; "Q4/FY 2019 Financial Results," Etsy, February 26, 2020, https://s22.q4cdn.com/941741262/files/doc_financials/2019/q4/Etsy-4Q-2019-Earnings-Presentation_FOR-IR-WEBSITE-FINAL.pdf; "Q2 2020 Financial Results," Etsy, August 5, 2020, https://s22.q4cdn.com/941741262/files/doc_financials/2020/q2/ETSY-2Q-2020-Earnings-Presentation_Final-Version_8.4.20.pdf.

33. Tugba Sabanoglu, "Number of Active Etsy Sellers from 2012 to 2020," Statista, March 11, 2021, https://www.statista.com/statistics/409374/etsy-active-sellers/; "Annual Gross Merchandise Sales (GMS) of Etsy Inc. from 2005 to 2020," Statista, March 11, 2021, https://www.statista.com/statistics/219412/etsys-total-merchandise-sales-per-year/.

34. Anuradha Garg, "Is Etsy Stock a Buy Even After Tripling in 2020?," Market

Realist, August 19, 2020, https://marketrealist.com/p/is-etsy-stock-a-buy/; company data.

35. "Impact Report," Etsy, 2019, https://investors.etsy.com/impact-reporting/default .aspx.

36. Mary Mazzoni, "Etsy Shows Leadership on Diversity in Tech," Triple Pundit, January 22, 2019, https://www.triplepundit.com/story/2019/etsy-shows-leader ship-diversity-tech/81936.

37. Margolis and Patrick Walsh, *People and Profits?*

38. I am indebted for the term to James O'Toole, *The Enlightened Capitalists: Cautionary Tales of Business Pioneers Who Tried to Do Well by Doing Good* (New York: Harper Business, 2019).

39. In negotiating tradeoffs, leaders often aren't simply trying to reconcile the interests of shareholders versus "society," but the conflicting interests of stakeholders who fall in either the "social logic" or "commercial logic" categories. I develop social logic here as a category of analysis for the sake of simplicity. Depending on the company or industry involved, the term can encompass a range of distinct stakeholders with sometimes competing interests, including local communities, the environment, and employees. The number of potential stakeholders further complicates the leader's task of optimizing value creation and distributing the gains.

40. As Sarah Kaplan points out, leaders often evaluate potential projects by asking for a business case, opting not to proceed if the economics don't work. Sarah Kaplan, "Why Social Responsibility Produces More Resilient Organizations," *MIT Sloan Management Review*, August 20, 2020, https://sloanreview.mit.edu/article /why-social-responsibility-produces-more-resilient-organizations/.

41. This account of Recruit draws heavily on Sandra J. Sucher and Shalene Gupta, "Globalizing Japan's Dream Machine: Recruit Holdings Co., Ltd.," Harvard Business School Case Study 9–318–130, April 25, 2018. I also draw on a second case that I wrote with Akiko Kanno: "Freedom Within a Framework at Recruit," Harvard Business School Case Study Number N1–421–042, November 13, 2020.

42. Shogo Ikeuchi (former senior managing corporate executive officer, CHRO and board director, Recruit), interview with the author, May 21, 2020.

43. Sucher and Gupta, "Globalizing Japan's Dream Machine," 19.

44. Sucher and Gupta, "Globalizing Japan's Dream Machine," 19.

45. "59 Bet on Passion," Recruit, accessed May 19, 2021, https://60th.recruit-hold ings.com/stories/no59/.

46. Gulati and Kanno, "Freedom Within a Framework at Recruit," 16.

47. "Recruit Group to Increase Fee for Their Educational Video Contents by Two Times," *Nikkei Newspaper* (morning edition), February 18, 2020, 14.

48. Viraj Puri, interview with the author, September 1, 2020.

49. Kaplan, "Why Social Responsibility Produces More Resilient Organizations."

50. "Carbon-Offset Shipping and Packaging: Delivering a World of Good," Etsy, accessed July 13, 2021, https://www.etsy.com/impact.

51. Chelsea Mozen, "Expanding Our Sustainability Efforts," *Etsy* (blog), April 20, 2020, https://blog.etsy.com/news/2020/expanding-our-sustainability-efforts/.

52. Adele Peters, "Etsy Offsets the Entire Carbon Footprint of Its Shipping—and It Wants Other Retailers to Do the Same," *Fast Company*, April 28, 2020, https://www.fastcompany.com/90483317/etsy-offsets-the-entire-carbon-footprint-of-its-shipping-and-it-wants-other-retailers-to-do-the-same.

53. "Etsy," Great Place To Work, accessed May 19, 2021, https://www.greatplacetowork.com/certified-company/1204864.

54. Paul Strebel, Didier Cossin, and Mahwesh Khan, "How to Reconcile Your Shareholders with Other Stakeholders," *MIT Sloan Management Review*, July 13, 2020, https://sloanreview.mit.edu/article/how-to-reconcile-your-shareholders-with-other-stakeholders/; Edmans, *Grow the Pie*.

55. David M. Cote, *Winning Now, Winning Later: How Companies Can Succeed in the Short Term While Investing for the Long Term* (Nashville, TN: HarperCollins Leadership, 2020), 7–8.

56. Charles Dickens, *A Tale of Two Cities* (London: James Nisbet & Co., 1902), 292.

Chapter 3: Four Levers for Superior Performance

1. Mark Zuckerberg, "Bringing the World Closer Together," Facebook, accessed May 20, 2021, https://www.facebook.com/notes/mark-zuckerberg/bringing-the-world-closer-together/10154944663901634/. The company calls this its "mission," not its purpose.

2. Kathleen Chaykowski, "Mark Zuckerberg Gives Facebook a New Mission," *Forbes*, June 22, 2017, https://www.forbes.com/sites/kathleenchaykowski/2017/06/22/mark-zuckerberg-gives-facebook-a-new-mission/#6f130dd31343.

3. Casey Newton, "The Verge Tech Survey 2020," Verge, March 2, 2020, https://www.theverge.com/2020/3/2/21144680/verge-tech-survey-2020-trust-privacy-security-facebook-amazon-google-apple.

4. For a compendium of negative news media reports about Facebook, see "'Where the Worst of Humanity Has Manifested'—Updating the Facebook Timeline of Scandal and Strife," Creative Future, updated December 9, 2020, https://creativefuture.org/facebook-scandal-timeline/. In crafting my discussion of Facebook in this chapter, I drew heavily on this site in addition to my own research.

5. "WhatsApp Offers $50,000 for Ideas to Stop Fake News Spread as India Orders It to Take Action Over Lynchings," *Telegraph*, July 4, 2018, https://www.telegraph.co.uk/news/2018/07/04/india-calls-whatsapp-help-end-spate-lynchings-sparked-rumours/.

6. Alex Warofka, "An Independent Assessment of the Human Rights Impact of Facebook in Myanmar," Facebook, November 5, 2018, https://about.fb.com/news /2018/11/myanmar-hria/.

7. Gretchen Peters and Amr Al-Azm, "Time to Clean Up Facebook's Dark Side," Morning Consult, June 25, 2019, https://morningconsult.com/opinions/time -to-clean-up-facebooks-dark-side/; Owen Pinnell and Jess Kelly, "Slave Markets Found on Instagram and Other Apps," BBC, October 31, 2019, https://www.bbc .com/news/technology-50228549.

8. "White Supremacist Groups Are Thriving on Facebook," Tech Transparency Project, May 21, 2020, https://www.techtransparencyproject.org/articles/white -supremacist-groups-are-thriving-on-facebook.

9. Shirin Ghaffary, "Mark Zuckerberg on Leaked Audio: Trump's Looting and Shooting Reference 'Has No History of Being Read as a Dog Whistle,'" Vox, June 2, 2020, https://www.vox.com/recode/2020/6/2/21278405/facebook-mark -zuckerberg-internal-employee-q-a-defend-moderate-trump-looting-shooting -post; Shannon Bond, "Critics Slam Facebook but Zuckerberg Resists Blocking Trump's Posts," NPR, June 11, 2020, https://www.npr.org/2020/06/11/874424898 /critics-slam-facebook-but-zuckerberg-resists-blocking-trumps-posts; Brian Fung, "The Hard Truth About the Facebook Ad Boycott: Nothing Matters but Zucker-berg," CNN, updated June 26, 2020, https://www.cnn.com/2020/06/26/tech /facebook-boycott/index.html.

10. Billy Perrigo, "Facebook Has Finally Banned Holocaust Denial. Critics Ask What Took Them So Long," Time, October 12, 2020, https://time.com/5899201 /facebook-holocaust-denial/.

11. Andrew Marantz, "Why Facebook Can't Fix Itself," New Yorker, October 12, 2020, https://www.newyorker.com/magazine/2020/10/19/why-facebook-cant-fix -itself.

12. David Gilbert, "An Outside Oversight Group Is Forcing Facebook to Get Its Shit Together for the Election," Vice, October 1, 2020, https://www.vice.com/en /article/z3epva/an-outside-oversight-group-is-forcing-facebook-to-get-its-shit -together-for-the-election.

13. Giulia Segreti, "Facebook CEO Says Group Will Not Become a Media Com-pany," Reuters, August 29, 2016, https://www.reuters.com/article/us-facebook -zuckerberg/facebook-ceo-says-group-will-not-become-a-media-company -idUSKCN1141WN.

14. Marantz, "Why Facebook Can't Fix Itself"; Fung, "The Hard Truth About the Facebook Ad Boycott: Nothing Matters but Zuckerberg."

15. Roger McNamee, "If Mark Zuckerberg Wants Forgiveness, He's Going to Need to Come Clean First," USA Today, updated October 10, 2017, https:// www.usatoday.com/story/opinion/2017/10/10/if-facebooks-mark-zuckerberg

-wants-forgiveness-hes-going-need-come-clean-first-roger-ncmanee-column/74
4520001/.

16. Roger McNamee, "I Mentored Mark Zuckerberg. I Loved Facebook. But I Can't Stay Silent About What's Happening," *Time*, January 17, 2019, https://time.com /5505441/mark-zuckerberg-mentor-facebook-downfall/.

17. Perrigo, "Facebook Has Finally Banned Holocaust Denial"; Joseph Guzman, "Facebook Finally Bans Holocaust Denial Content, but Critics Say It's Ignoring Larger Problem," *Hill*, October 13, 2020, https://thehill.com/changing-america /respect/equality/520812-facebook-finally-bans-holocaust-denial-content-but -critics.

18. Raj Sisodia, David B. Wolfe, and Jag Sheth, *Firms of Endearment: How World-Class Companies Profit from Passion and Purpose*, 2nd ed. (Upper Saddle River, NJ: Pearson Education, 2014), 7, 14. The authors call these companies "firms of endearment," defining such companies as those that "[endear themselves] to stakeholders by bringing the interests of all stakeholder groups into strategic alignment."

19. "The Business Case for Purpose," *Harvard Business Review Analytic Services Report*, 5.

20. Claudine Madras Gartenberg, Andrea Prat, and George Serafeim, "Corporate Purpose and Financial Performance," Columbia Business School Research Paper no. 16–69 (2016): abstract. A BCG analysis of twenty-five public companies found that virtually all companies that scored high on a measure of purpose delivered returns over a decade that exceeded median returns among the S&P 500. Research has also suggested that companies that serve stakeholders other than shareholders perform better. Analyzing companies that treated employees well, Alex Edmans found that they delivered cumulative stock returns over nearly three decades that were between 89 and 184 percent higher than peer companies. Jim Hemerling et al., "For Corporate Purpose to Matter, You've Got to Measure It," BCG, August 16, 2018, https://www.bcg.com/en-us/publications/2018 /corporate-purpose-to-matter-measure-it; Edmans, *Grow the Pie*, 83.

21. "Profit & Purpose," BlackRock, 2019, https://www.blackrock.com/americas-off shore/2019-larry-fink-ceo-letter.

22. Henderson, *Reimagining Capitalism*, 118.

23. Edmans, *Grow the Pie*, 91–96.

24. My account of Bühler Holding AG draws heavily on a Harvard Business School case study I prepared on the company, N9–822–001 (forthcoming).

25. "The Future Is Now," 2020 Bühler corporate presentation [internal company document], 10, 87.

26. Annual Report, Bühler, 2011, 52.

27. Annual Report, Bühler, 2012, 76.

28. Annual Report, Bühler, 2016, 21, 91.

29. Ian Roberts, "A Challenge Shared," *Diagram*, December 2019, 8.

30. In this respect, Bühler follows the advice presented in Christopher A. Bartlett and Sumantra Ghoshal's classic article "Changing the Role of Top Management: Beyond Strategy to Purpose," *Harvard Business Review* 72, no. 6 (November–December 1994): 79–88.

31. Spence, *It's Not What You Sell*, 13.

32. "The Business Case for Purpose," *Harvard Business Review Analytic Services Report*, 5. See also "The State of the Debate on Purpose in Business," *EY Beacon Institute* (report), 2016, 20–24.

33. Edouard Dubois and Ali Saribas, "Making Corporate Purpose Tangible—A Survey of Investors," *Harvard Law School Forum on Corporate Governance*, June 19, 2020.

34. This point also appears in "The State of the Debate on Purpose in Business," 20–24.

35. "Purpose-Driven Leadership for the 21st Century: How Corporate Purpose Is Fundamental to Reimagining Capitalism," *Horvath and Partners* (report), 2019, 17, 36.

36. Susan Reidy, "Protix Opens Insect Protein Production Plant," World Grain, June 20, 2019, https://www.world-grain.com/articles/12229-protix-opens-insect-protein-production-plant.

37. "New Horizons," Bühler, accessed July 13, 2021, https://www.buhlergroup.com/content/buhlergroup/global/fr/key-topics/Nutrition/Insects.html.

38. Andrew Donlan, "Best Buy Floats Lofty In-Home Health Care Goals in 5-Year Plan," *Home Health Care News*, December 4, 2019, https://homehealthcarenews.com/2019/12/best-buy-floats-lofty-in-home-health-care-goals-in-5-year-plan/.

39. Mark R. Kramer and Sarah Mehta, "Becton Dickinson: Global Health Strategy," Harvard Business School Case Study 718–406, September 2017 (revised February 2018), 12.

40. Thomas W. Malnight, Ivy Buche, and Charles Dhanaraj, "Put Purpose at the Core of Your Strategy," *Harvard Business Review*, September–October 2019, https://hbr.org/2019/09/put-purpose-at-the-core-of-your-strategy.

41. Stefan Scheiber (CEO of Bühler), interview with the author, May 21, 2020.

42. "Meeting with Technology Experts: 'Bühler Networking Days 2016,'" *Miller Magazine*, accessed May 25, 2021, https://millermagazine.com/english/meeting-with-technology-experts-buhler-networking-days-2016/.

43. Ian Roberts (chief technology officer at Bühler), interview with the author, May 21, 2020.

44. Annual Report, Bühler, 2019, 31.

45. See chapter 7 in Sisodia, Wolfe, and Sheth, *Firms of Endearment*.

46. Rebecca Henderson, "Innovation in the 21st Century: Architectural Change,

Purpose, and the Challenges of Our Time," *Management Science* (pre-published online, October 30, 2020), https://doi.org/10.1287/mnsc.2020.3746

47. George Serafeim et al., "The Value of Corporate Purpose: A Guide for CEOs and Entrepreneurs," KKS Advisors, accessed May 25, 2021, 5–10.

48. Queenie Wong, "Facebook Ad Boycott: Why Big Brands 'Hit Pause on Hate,'" CNET, July 30, 2020, https://www.cnet.com/news/facebook-ad-boycott-how-big -businesses-hit-pause-on-hate/.

49. Megan Graham, "Zuckerberg Was Right: Ad Boycotts Won't Hurt Facebook That Much," CNBC, August 4, 2020, https://www.cnbc.com/2020/08/04/some -major-companies-will-keep-pausing-facebook-ads-as-boycott-ends.html.

50. Scott Rosenberg, "Facebook's Reputation Is Sinking Fast," Axios, March 6, 2019, https://www.axios.com/facebook-reputation-drops-axios-harris-poll-0d6c406a -4c2e-463a-af98-1748d3e0ab9a.html.

51. For a guide to a number of recent research studies on the relationship between purpose and reputation, see Afdhel Aziz, "The Power of Purpose: The Business Case for Purpose (All The Data You Were Looking For Pt 1)," *Forbes*, March 7, 2020, https://www.forbes.com/sites/afdhelaziz/2020/03/07/the-power-of-purpose -the-business-case-for-purpose-all-the-data-you-were-looking-for-pt-1/#16bdc7 2230ba.

52. Annual Report, Bühler, 2019, 48–53.

53. Dan Dye (CEO of Ardent Mills), interview with the author, May 21, 2020.

54. Andy Sharpe (president and CEO of Bühler North America), interview with the author, May 21, 2020.

55. Andy Sharpe, interview with the author, May 21, 2020.

56. Stefan Dobrev (former global head of innovation portfolio management at Nestlé), interview with the author, September 17, 2020.

57. Stefan Scheiber (CEO of Bühler), interview with the author, September 17, 2020.

58. See chapter 4 of Beer et al., *Higher Ambition*.

59. Stefan Dobrev (former global head of innovation portfolio management at Nestlé), interview with the author, September 17, 2020.

60. For one of the first studies on how consumers and employees perceive CSR efforts by firms, see C. B. Bhattacharya, Sankara Sen, and Daniel Korschun, *Leveraging Corporate Social Responsibility: The Stakeholder Route to Maximizing Business and Social Value*, (Cambridge, UK: Cambridge University Press, 2011).

61. Nellie Bowles, "'I Don't Really Want to Work for Facebook.' So Say Some Computer Science Students," *New York Times*, November 15, 2018, https://www.ny times.com/2018/11/15/technology/jobs-facebook-computer-science-students .html. Silicon Valley in general has taken a hit in terms of their desirability as employers—what commentators have called a "techlash"—due to perceptions that they are causing harm to society. See Emma Goldberg, "'Techlash' Hits College

Campuses," *New York Times*, updated January 15, 2020, https://www.nytimes
.com/2020/01/11/style/college-tech-recruiting.html.

62. Ghaffary, "Mark Zuckerberg on Leaked Audio"; Charlie Warzel and Ryan Mac,
"Mark Zuckerberg's Biggest Problem: Internal Tensions at Facebook Are Boil-
ing Over," Buzzfeed News, December 5, 2018, https://www.buzzfeednews.com
/article/charliewarzel/facebooks-tensions-zuckerberg-sandberg.

63. Chris Hughes, "It's Time to Break Up Facebook," *New York Times*, May 9, 2019,
https://www.nytimes.com/2019/05/09/opinion/sunday/chris-hughes-facebook
-zuckerberg.html.

64. Sally Blount and Paul Leinwand, "Why Are We Here?," *Harvard Business Review*, November–December 2019, https://hbr.org/2019/11/why-are-we-here.

65. Christopher A. Bartlett and Sumantra Ghoshal, "Changing the Role of Top
Management: Beyond Strategy to Purpose," *Harvard Business Review*, November 1, 1994.

66. Steven J. Heine, Travis Proulx, and Kathleen D. Vohs, "The Meaning Maintenance Model: On the Coherence of Social Motivations," *Personality and Social
Psychology Review* 10, no. 2 (2006): 88–110, https://www2.psych.ubc.ca/~heine
/docs/MMM.PDF.

67. For more on the self-consistency theory in psychology, see Prescott Lecky, *Self-
Consistency: A Theory of Personality* (Fort Myers Beach, FL: The Island Press
Publishers, 1994).

68. Neal Chalofsky, "An Emerging Construct for Meaningful Work," *Human Resource Development International* 6, no. 1 (2003): 78.

69. Henderson, "Innovation in the 21st Century," 4.

70. See, for instance, "Connecting People and Purpose: 7 Ways High-Trust Organizations Retain Talent," 2016 Great Place to Work, 2016, 3.

71. Quinn and Thakor, *The Economics of Higher Purpose*, 48–51.

72. "Purpose: A Practical Guide," LinkedIn, accessed May 25, 2021. Considerable
research bears out the impacts that devotion to a purpose has on an array of human resources metrics, including employee loyalty, engagement, and willingness
to promote their organizations to others. See, for instance, "The Business Case for
Purpose," *Harvard Business Review Analytic Services Report* 9.

73. Vineet Nayar, "A Shared Purpose Drives Collaboration," *Harvard Business Review*, April 2, 2014; Quinn and Thakor, *The Economics of Higher Purpose*, 23.

74. "Gartner Identifies Three Dimensions That Define the New Employer-Employee
Relationship," Street Insider, October 13, 2020, https://www.streetinsider.com
/Business+Wire/Gartner+Identifies+Three+Dimensions+That+Define+The+New
+Employer-Employee+Relationship/17463086.html.

75. Glen Tullman, (founder and executive chairman of Livongo), interview with the
author, March 9, 2021.

76. Raghu Krishnamoorthy (former senior vice president of global human resources at General Electric), interview with the author, September 17, 2020.

77. Irene Mark-Eisenring (chief human resources officer at Bühler), interview with the author, September 17, 2020.

78. Company data.

79. Edward B. Reeves, "Moral Community," *Encyclopedia of Religion and Society*, accessed May 25, 2021, http://hirr.hartsem.edu/ency/MoralC.htm.

Chapter 4: Where Purpose *Really* Comes From:
Looking Backward While Looking Forward

1. "The Power of Sankofa: Know History," *Berea College*, May 29, 2021, https://www.berea.edu/cgwc/the-power-of-sankofa/.

2. I derive my basic account of LEGO in this chapter from my interviews with Jørgen Knudstorp as well as from David C. Robertson, *Brick by Brick: How LEGO Rewrote the Rules of Innovation and Conquered the Global Toy Industry* (New York: Crown Business, 2013); Jan W. Rivkin, Stefan H. Thomke, and Daniela Beyersdorfer, "LEGO," Harvard Business School Case Study 613–004, July 2012; Stefan H. Thomke, "Jørgen Vig Knudstorp: Reflections on LEGO's Transformation," Harvard Business School Background Note 620–133, May 2020; Majken Schultz and Tor Hernes, "A Temporal Perspective on Organizational Identity," *Organization Science* 24, no. 1 (February 2013): 1–21. I draw biographical information about Knudstorp from Sherman Hollar, "Jørgen Vig Knudstorp," Britannica, November 17, 2020, https://www.britannica.com/biography/Jorgen-Vig-Knudstorp.

3. Robertson, *Brick by Brick*, 67–8. See chapter 3 for a detailed account of LEGO's struggles.

4. Quoted in Robertson, *Brick by Brick*, 91.

5. Robertson, *Brick by Brick*, 148.

6. Rivkin, Thomke, and Beyersdorfer, "LEGO."

7. Rivkin, Thomke, and Beyersdorfer, "LEGO."

8. Quoted in Stefan Thomke, "Jørgen Vig Knudstorp: Reflections on LEGO's Transformation," Harvard Business School Note 620–133, May 2020. Emphasis mine.

9. Quoted in Rivkin, Thomke, and Beyersdorfer, "LEGO."

10. Jørgen Vig Knudstorp (former CEO of LEGO), interview with the author, June 26, 2020.

11. Jørgen Vig Knudstorp, interview with the author, June 26, 2020.

12. Schultz and Hernes, "A Temporal Perspective on Organizational Identity," 1–21.

13. Jørgen Vig Knudstorp, interview with the author, June 26, 2020.

14. Robertson, *Brick by Brick*, 16–17.

15. Stefan Thomke, "Jørgen Vig Knudstorp"; and Jørgen Vig Knudstorp, interview with the author, November 23, 2020.

16. Rivkin, Thomke, and Beyersdorfer, "LEGO."

17. Schultz and Hernes, "A Temporal Perspective on Organizational Identity," 1–21.

18. Jørgen Vig Knudstorp, interview with the author, June 26, 2020.

19. Quoted in Schultz and Hernes, "A Temporal Perspective on Organizational Identity," 1–21.; Jørgen Vig Knudstorp, interview with the author, June 26, 2020.

20. Jørgen Vig Knudstorp, interview with the author, June 26, 2020.

21. Others have argued that purpose should flow organically and inductively from inside and outside the company, reflecting the meanings stakeholders—most notably, employees and customers—themselves attribute to it. See, for instance, chapter 8 of Quinn and Thakor, *The Economics of Higher Purpose*, and chapter 2 of Spence, *It's Not What You Sell*.

22. In his book *It's Not What You Sell, It's What You Stand For*, consultant Roy Spence urges readers to "use the founding charter of your organization. Find the original business plan. Keep in mind that what you're looking for is the fundamental motivation that set the organization in motion" (Spence, *It's Not What You Sell*, 36). But most consultants and academic experts pay only a passing nod to history when discussing how to define a purpose.

23. "Moral Community," Oxford Reference, accessed May 25, 2021, https://www .oxfordreference.com/view/10.1093/oi/authority.20110803100208740#:~:text =The%20moral%20community%20is%20characterized,be%20termed%20a%20 moral%20community.

24. Lucia D. Wocial, "In Search of a Moral Community," *Online Journal of Issues in Nursing* 23, no. 1 (January 2018), abstract, DOI: 10.3912/OJIN.Vol23No01 Man02.

25. Émile Durkheim quoted in Reeves, "Moral Community." According to one scholar, values "provide the foundation by which collectives become communities— both within and outside organizational boundaries." Violina P. Rindova and Luis L. Martins, "From Values to Value: Value Rationality and the Creation of Great Strategies," *Strategy Science* 3, no. 1 (March 2018): 323–34.

26. Wocial, "In Search of a Moral Community."

27. Some scholars have identified moral narratives as accounts that might encompass or reference broader external challenges. See Roland Bénabou, Armin Falk, and Jean Tirole, "Narratives, Imperatives, and Moral Reasoning," working paper 24798, *National Bureau of Economic Research* (July 2018): 2. As they write, "The most important narratives, however, pertain to actions with moral or social implications, namely those involving externalities/internalities and (self-) reputational concerns."

28. The Old Testament actually contains two types of "foundation stories," one in which an ancestor settles a new land and "his descendants populate the land and

become its local inhabitants," as in the biblical account of Abraham; and another in which they conquer a population, as in the Exodus story. Both stories contribute to the larger notion of the Hebrews as a "chosen people" anointed by the divine—an especially significant notion that carries implications for group identity and moral community in the present. Guy Darshan, "The Origins of the Foundation Stories Genre in the Hebrew Bible and Ancient Eastern Mediterranean," *Journal of Biblical Literature* 133, no. 4 (Winter 2014): 689–709. See also Bruce Cauthen, "Covenant and Continuity: Ethno-Symbolism and the Myth of Divine Election," *Nations and Nationalism* 10, nos. 1–2 (January 2004): 19–33.

29. Anthony D. Smith, "Chosen Peoples: Why Ethnic Groups Survive," *Ethnic and Racial Studies* 15, no. 3 (September 2010): 436–56, as quoted in Cauthen, "Covenant and Continuity," 22.

30. Anthony D. Smith, "Ethnic Election and National Destiny: Some Religious Origins of Nationalist Ideals," *Nations and Nationalism* 5, no. 3 (1999): 331–55, as quoted in Cauthen, "Covenant and Continuity," 25. For more on mythmaking and nationalism, see, for instance, Veronika Bajt, "Myths of Nationhood: Slovenians, Caranthania and the Venetic Theory," *Annales Series Historia et Sociologia* 21, no. 2 (2011).

31. Eric Hobsbawm and Terence Ranger, eds., *The Invention of Tradition* (Cambridge, UK: Cambridge University Press, 1983).

32. John T. Seaman Jr. and George David Smith, "Your Company's History as a Leadership Tool," *Harvard Business Review,* December 1, 2012.

33. Mary Jo Hatch and Majken Schultz, "Toward a Theory of Using History Authentically: Historicizing in the Carlsberg Group," *Administrative Science Quarterly* 62, vol. 4 (2017): 657–97. My account of Carlsberg in this and the following paragraphs draws heavily from this article. All quotations originally appeared there.

34. Quoted in Hatch and Schultz, "Toward a Theory of Using History Authentically," 672.

35. Quoted in Hatch and Schultz, "Toward a Theory of Using History Authentically," 681.

36. Quoted in Hatch and Schultz, "Toward a Theory of Using History Authentically," 682.

37. Some scholars have referred to values as "identity markers." Rindova and Martins, "From Values to Value."

38. A rich body of research has looked at organizational identity. In the words of one scholar, identity is "those features of an organization that in the eyes of its members are central to the organization's character or 'self image,' make the organization distinctive from other similar organizations, and are viewed as having continuity over time." Dennis A. Gioia et al., "Organizational Identity Formation

and Change," *Academy of Management Annals* 7, no. 1 (June 2013), https://doi.org /10.5465/19416520.2013.762225.

39. The concept of authenticity has sparked much discussion among scholars in various fields. For authenticity in leadership, see Herminia Ibarra, "The Authenticity Paradox," *Harvard Business Review Magazine*, January–February 2015, https://hbr.org/2015/01/the-authenticity-paradox; Bill George, Peter Sims, Andrew N. McLean and Diana Mayer, "Discovering Your Authentic Leadership," *Harvard Business Review*, February 2007, https://hbr.org/2007/02/discovering-your -authentic-leadership. Drawing on the work of other scholars in their analysis of Carlsberg, Mary Jo Hatch and Majken Schultz reference a distinction between "craft" and "moral" authenticity. The former entails remaining true to the original craft practices present in a business, the latter to remaining true to the moral ideals of a business's founders. See Hatch and Schultz, "Toward a Theory of Using History Authentically."

40. Denise M. Rousseau, "Psychological and Implied Contracts in Organizations," *Employee Responsibilities and Rights Journal* 2 (January 1989): 121–39, DOI: 10.1 007/BF01384942.

41. Jane E. Dutton and Amy Wrzesniewski, "What Job Crafting Looks Like," *Harvard Business Review*, March 12, 2020, https://hbr.org/2020/03/what-job-craft ing-looks-like.

42. Jørgen Vig Knudstorp, interview with the author, August 6, 2020.

43. "Responsibility Report," LEGO Group, 2015, https://www.lego.com/cdn/cs /aboutus/assets/blt8630ef4d3066bc76/Responsibility-Report-2015.pdf; "Sustain ability Progress," LEGO Group, 2019, https://s3-us-west-2.amazonaws.com/ungc -production/attachments/cop_2020/483723/original/The_LEGO_Group _2019_Sustainability_progress.pdf?1583318316.

44. Jørgen Vig Knudstorp, interview with the author, August 6, 2020.

45. Sierk Ybema, "Talk of Change: Temporal Contrasts and Collective Identities," *Organization Studies* 31 (2010), DOI: 10.1177/0170840610372205.

46. Nadella, *Hit Refresh*, 64–71.

47. Kathleen Hogan (chief people officer at Microsoft), interview with the author, May 12, 2020.

48. Adam Lashinsky, "The Cook Doctrine at Apple," *Fortune*, January 22, 2009, https://fortune.com/2009/01/22/the-cook-doctrine-at-apple/.

49. Steve Jobs, "Steve Jobs: Apple Brand Purpose," unveiling "Think Different" Apple ad campaign, September 23, 1997, YouTube video, uploaded by @markgoconnor, 6:54, May 23, 2011, https://www.youtube.com/watch?v=ugqcXqTEVMA.

50. Quoted in Killian Bell, "Steve Jobs Legacy Will Live On in the Apple University," Cult of Mac, October 7, 2011, https://www.cultofmac.com/121798/steve -jobs-legacy-will-live-on-in-the-apple-university/.

51. Timothy B. Lee, "How Apple Became the World's Most Valuable Company," Vox, updated September 9, 2015, https://www.vox.com/2014/11/17/18076360/apple.

52. Brian X. Chen, "Simplifying the Bull: How Picasso Helps to Teach Apple's Style," *New York Times*, August 10, 2014, https://www.nytimes.com/2014/08/11/technology/-inside-apples-internal-training-program-.html.

53. For more on Apple University, see Brian X. Chen, "Inside the Secretive Apple University," *Sydney Morning Herald*, updated August 12, 2014, https://www.smh.com.au/business/inside-the-secretive-apple-university-20140812-102yzz.html.

54. Thomas R. Piper, "Johnson & Johnson's Corporate Credo," Harvard Business School Case 304–084, January 2004 (revised May 2008).

55. For the most recent version of the credo as of this writing, see "Code of Business Conduct," Johnson & Johnson, 2020, https://www.jnj.com/sites/default/files/pdf/code-of-business-conduct-english-us.pdf.

56. "Our Credo," Johnson & Johnson, accessed May 26, 2021, https://www.jnj.com/sites/default/files/pdf/our-credo.pdf.

57. "The Power of Our Credo: Johnson & Johnson Chairman and CEO Alex Gorsky Reflects on the Legacy of the Company's Historic Mission Statement," Johnson & Johnson, December 13, 2018, https://www.jnj.com/latest-news/johnson-johnson-ceo-alex-gorsky-reflects-on-the-power-of-the-companys-credo.

58. "Leadership Challenges at Johnson & Johnson," Wharton, January 9, 2014, https://knowledge.wharton.upenn.edu/article/alex-gorsky-leadership-moments-jj/; Erika Janes, "8 Fun Facts about Our Credo—Johnson & Johnson's Mission Statement," Johnson & Johnson, February 5, 2018, https://www.jnj.com/our-heritage/8-fun-facts-about-the-johnson-johnson-credo.

59. Companion video for a Johnson & Johnson case study (Harvard Business School classroom).

60. "The Power of Our Credo."

61. Alex Gorsky, "The Past, Present and Future of Our Credo: A Conversation with Wharton's Adam Grant," LinkedIn, December 13, 2018, https://www.linkedin.com/pulse/past-present-future-our-credo-conversation-whartons-adam-alex-gorsky/.

62. Judith Rehak, "Tylenol Made A Hero of Johnson & Johnson: The Recall That Started Them All," *New York Times*, March 23, 2002, https://www.nytimes.com/2002/03/23/your-money/IHT-tylenol-made-a-hero-of-johnson-johnson-the-recall-that-started.html.

63. Quoted in "Case Study: The Johnson & Johnson Tylenol Crisis," *Department of Defense*, May 26, 2021, https://www.ou.edu/deptcomm/dodjcc/groups/02C2/Johnson%20&%20Johnson.htm.

64. Natasha Singer, "In Recall, a Role Model Stumbles," *New York Times*, January 17, 2010, https://www.nytimes.com/2010/01/18/business/18drug.html.

65. "Patients Versus Profits at Johnson & Johnson: Has the Company Lost Its Way?," Wharton, February 15, 2012, https://knowledge.wharton.upenn.edu/article /patients-versus-profits-at-johnson-johnson-has-the-company-lost-its-way/.

66. Johnson & Johnson's Recall of Children's Tylenol and Other Children's Medicines and the Phantom Recall of Motrin (PART 2): Hearing Before the Committee on Oversight and Government Reform, 111th Congress, September 30, 2010; Clayton S. Rose et. al., "On Weldon's Watch: Recalls at Johnson & Johnson from 2009 to 2010," Harvard Business School Case Study 9–311–029, August 5, 2016.

67. Quoted in "Patients Versus Profits."

68. "Leadership Challenges at Johnson & Johnson."

69. Annual Report, Johnson & Johnson, 2018, 11, https://www.investor.jnj.com /annual-meeting-materials/2018-annual-report.

70. Quoted in Gorsky, "The Past, Present and Future."

71. Annual Report, Johnson & Johnson, 2019, 2, https://www.investor.jnj.com /annual-meeting-materials/2019-annual-report.

72. Line Højgaard (corporate historian at LEGO), interview with the author, December 4, 2020.

73. "Responsibility Report," LEGO, 2015.

74. Jørgen Vig Knudstorp, interview with the author, June 26, 2020.

75. Emma Bedford, "Revenue of the LEGO Group from 2003 to 2020 (in Billion Euros)," Statista, March 10, 2021, https://www.statista.com/statistics/282870/lego -group-revenue/.

76. Emma Bedford, "Net Profit of the LEGO Group Worldwide from 2009 to 2020 (in Million Euros)," Statista, March 10, 2021, https://www.statista.com/statistics /292305/lego-group-net-profit/.

77. Lucy Handley, "LEGO Is the World's Most Reputable Company as Tech Giants Lag, Survey Says," CNBC, March 3, 2020, https://www.cnbc.com/2020/03/03 /lego-is-the-worlds-most-reputable-company-disney-follows.html.

Chapter 5: Are You a Poet, or Just a Plumber?

1. H. Porter Abbott, *The Cambridge Introduction to Narrative* (Cambridge, UK: Cambridge University Press, 2002), 12. Abbott defines narrative as "the representation of an event or a series of events." As he notes, scholars quibble over the finer points of such definitions, but this one suffices for my purposes here. In everyday life, we tend to equate "narrative" and "story." Abbott distinguishes between the two on fairly esoteric technical grounds. For simplicity's sake, I will use these terms interchangeably. For a similar definition of narrative as a "representation of a series of events meaningfully connected in a temporal and causal way," I consulted

Violina P. Rindova and Luis L. Martins, "Futurescapes: Imagination and Temporal Reorganization in the Design of Strategic Narratives," unpublished paper provided to the author. Observers have noted the motivational power of stories. In a *Harvard Business Review* interview, screenwriting coach Robert McKee argued that "a big part of a CEO's job is to motivate people to reach certain goals. To do that, he or she must engage their emotions, and the key to their hearts is story." Bronwyn Fryer, "Storytelling That Moves People: A Conversation with Screenwriting Coach Robert McKee," *Harvard Business Review,* June 2003, https://hbr .org/2003/06/storytelling-that-moves-people; Chip and Dan Heath, authors of the bestseller *Made to Stick,* present storytelling as a key rhetorical principle that makes ideas "sticky," noting the ability of stories to inspire action as well as provide audiences with concrete information about how to act. In a separate chapter of their book, the Heaths describe emotion as a distinct "stickiness" factor, although the inspirational nature of stories would seem to suggest that storytelling also functions by evoking emotion. Chip Heath and Dan Heath, *Made to Stick: Why Some Ideas Survive and Others Die* (New York: Random House, 2008), chapters 5 and 6, especially 206.

2. Experts across a range of disciplines have laid out principles for strong storytelling, including the presence of a riveting tension, introducing a "hero," incorporating sufficient detail, keeping the story concise and simple, and so on. In a business context, see, for example, Dan Schawbel, "How to Use Storytelling as a Leadership Tool," *Forbes,* August 13, 2012, https://www.forbes.com/sites /danschawbel/2012/08/13/how-to-use-storytelling-as-a-leadership-tool/?sh =4c8e94695e8e; Carolyn O'Hara, "How to Tell a Great Story," *Harvard Business Review,* July 30, 2014, https://hbr.org/2014/07/how-to-tell-a-great-story; Fryer, "Storytelling That Moves People"; Dianna Booher, "7 Tips for Great Storytelling as a Leader," *Fast Company,* January 12, 2015, https://www.fastcompany.com /3040709/7tips-for-great-storytelling-as-a-leader.

3. Leaders often use grand, strategic narratives to help people make sense of events, bring strategies alive, and encourage the workforce to buy into transformational change. Some of these narratives comprise what scholars have called "futurescapes," accounts that "articulate a firm's preferred future and the firm's role in creating it" (Rindova and Martins, "Futurescapes," 4). I argue that deep purpose leaders create narratives to support and communicate the organizational purpose, not just a given strategy. Elena Dalpiaz and Giada Di Stefano, "A Universe of Stories: Mobilizing Narrative Practices During Transformative Change," *Strategic Management Journal* 39, no. 3 (March 2018): 664–96; Scott Sonenshein, "We're Changing—Or Are We? Untangling the Role of Progressive, Regressive, and Stability Narratives during Strategic Implementation," *Academy of Management Journal* 53, no. 3 (November 30, 2017), https://doi.org/10.5465/amj.2010.51467

638; Sarah Kaplan and Wanda Orlikowski, "Beyond Forecasting: Creating New Strategic Narratives," *MIT Sloan Management Review*, September 16, 2014, https://sloanreview.mit.edu/article/beyond-forecasting-creating-new-strategic-narratives/.

4. One group of scholars defines moral potency as "the capacity to generate responsibility and motivation to take moral action in the face of adversity and persevere through challenges." See Sean T. Hannah, Bruce J. Avolio, and Douglas R. May, "Moral Maturation and Moral Conation: A Capacity Approach to Explaining Moral Thought and Action," *Academy of Management* 36, no. 4 (October 2011), https://doi.org/10.5465/amr.2010.0128; Neil Morelli, "The Makings of Morality: The Factors Behind Ethical Behavior (IO Psychology)," *Academy of Management Review*, January 9, 2012, http://www.ioatwork.com/the-makings-of-morality-the-factors-behind-ethical-behavior/.

5. Quoted in "Indra K. Nooyi Biography," *Encyclopedia of World Biography*, accessed May 26, 2021, https://www.notablebiographies.com/news/Li-Ou/Nooyi-Indra-K.html#ixzz6iVTnrVhz.

6. "Get Married or Say No to Yale: Indra Nooyi's Knotty Affair," *Economic Times*, updated August 7, 2018, https://economictimes.indiatimes.com/magazines/panache/get-married-or-say-no-to-yale-indra-nooyis-knotty-affair/articleshow/65285868.cms.

7. "Indra Nooyi—a 'Mentor + Inspiration,'" *Indian Express*, January 16, 2019, https://indianexpress.com/article/world/indra-nooyi-a-mentor-inspiration-5540979/.

8. Sherman Hollar, "Indra Nooyi," *Britannica*, accessed May 26, 2021, https://www.britannica.com/biography/Indra-Nooyi; Fiona Walsh, "Indian-Born Nooyi Takes Over at PepsiCo," *Guardian*, August 14, 2006, https://www.theguardian.com/business/2006/aug/15/genderissues.uknews.

9. "PepsiCo Chairman and CEO Reinemund to Retire," Reliable Plant, May 26, 2021, https://www.reliableplant.com/Read/2314/pepsico-chairman-ceo-reinemund-to-retire; "Market Capitalization of PepsiCo (PEP)," Companies MarketCap, accessed May 26, 2021, https://companiesmarketcap.com/pepsico/marketcap/.

10. Joseph L. Badaracco and Matthew Preble, "PepsiCo, Profits, and Food: The Belt Tightens," Harvard Business School Case Study 9–314–055, December 21, 2015, 6.

11. Michael I. Norton and Jill Avery, "The Pepsi Refresh Project: A Thirst for Change," Harvard Business School Case Study 512–018, revised August 2013, 3.

12. In the company's 2006 annual report, Nooyi and Reinemund (who had stayed on for a year as chairman) seem to position Performance with Purpose as an extension or distillation of the company's existing activities: "We believe this is a company with a heart, and recognize the role leading companies like ours play in society. It inspires us to focus on delivering Performance with Purpose—

something we intend to continue doing." Annual Report, PepsiCo, 2006, 3. Else-where, Nooyi and the company described Performance with Purpose as more revolutionary, casting it as a "bold agenda," a "decision to redefine the way we do business," and even "a new strategic mission to try to capture the heart and soul of PepsiCo." See, for instance, Roy Manuell, "PepsiCo Talks Sugar, Sustainability and a Responsible Approach to Development," *New Food Magazine*, November 1, 2016, https://www.newfoodmagazine.com/article/27576/pepsico-sugar-health -development/; Annual Report, PepsiCo, 2008, 4, https://www.pepsico.com/docs /album/annual-reports/2008-annual-english.pdf?sfvrsn=2fe2d333_4.

13. Indra K. Nooyi and Vijay Govindarajan, "Becoming a Better Corporate Citizen," *Harvard Business Review Magazine*, March–April 2020, https://hbr.org/2020/03 /becoming-a-better-corporate-citizen; Rosabeth Moss Kanter et al., "PepsiCo, Performance with Purpose, Achieving the Right Global Balance," Harvard Business School Case 412–079, October 2011 (revised January 2012), 7–9. Else-where, the company presents Performance with Purpose as a three-part struc-ture, omitting the financial sustainability plank, which was perhaps inferred.

14. Katie Kuehner-Hebert, "PepsiCo's CEO and Chair Indra Nooyi Is Leading the Company to New Heights," Chief Executive, April 30, 2018, https://chiefex-ecutive.net/pepsicos-ceo-chair-indra-nooyi-leading-company-new-heights/. Pepsi had categorized its products in this way since the mid-1990s. See "Nan-dan Nilekani Chats up with Indra Nooyi," *Economic Times*, February 7, 2007, https://economictimes.indiatimes.com/news/company/corporate-trends/nandan -nilekani-chats-up-with-indra-nooyi/articleshow/1569097.cms?from=mdr.

15. Badaracco and Preble, "PepsiCo, Profits, and Food," 5.

16. "Indra K. Nooyi on Performance with Purpose," BCG, January 14, 2010, https:// www.bcg.com/publications/2010/indra-nooyi-performance-purpose.

17. Frank Cooper III (former Pepsi chief marketing officer), interview with the au-thor, September 1, 2020.

18. Quoted in Badaracco and Preble, "PepsiCo, Profits, and Food."

19. Michele Simon, "A Leopard Like PepsiCo Cannot Change Its Spots," *Guard-ian*, March 21, 2012, https://www.theguardian.com/sustainable-business/blog /pepsico-corporate-social-responsibility-public-health.

20. Nooyi and Govindarajan, "Becoming a Better Corporate Citizen."

21. John Seabrook, "Snacks for a Fat Planet," *New Yorker*, May 9, 2011, https://www .newyorker.com/magazine/2011/05/16/snacks-for-a-fat-planet.

22. Frank Cooper III, interview with the author, September 1, 2020.

23. I arrive at this general synopsis by drawing on a number of sources, including Nooyi's discussion of Performance with Purpose in a 2019 appearance at NYU's Stern School of Business, "In Conversation with Lord Mervyn King" Series Presents Indra Nooyi, NYU Stern, YouTube video, 1:04:13, November 1, 2019,

https://www.youtube.com/watch?v=MvQf7XStV-Q&feature=youtube; my interview with Frank Cooper cited above; and Nooyi and Govindarajan, "Becoming a
Better Corporate Citizen."

24. "In Conversation with Lord Mervyn King"; "'Performance with Purpose' vs.
Corporate Social Responsibility" Aspen Institute, 2014 Aspen Ideas Festival Af-
ternoon of Conversation with Indra Nooyi and David Bradley, YouTube video,
2:28. July 1, 2014, https://www.youtube.com/watch?v=3ePlLrdusLQ.

25. "Nandan Nilekani Chats Up with Indra Nooyi," *Economic Times*, February 7,
2007, https://economictimes.indiatimes.com/news/company/corporate-trends
/nandan-nilekani-chats-up-with-indra-nooyi/articleshow/1569097.cms?from
=mdr.

26. "Nandan Nilekani Chats Up."

27. "Nandan Nilekani Chats Up."

28. "Emmanuel Faber Speech at Consumer Goods Forum," Danone, YouTube video,
23:12, June 22, 2017, https://www.youtube.com/watch?v=PhuEtyH6SK4&feature
=emb_rel_pause.

29. "Emmanuel Faber Speech at Consumer Goods Forum."

30. Andrew M. Carton, Chad Murphy, and Jonathan R. Clark, "A (Blurry) Vision
of the Future: How Leader Rhetoric about Ultimate Goals Influences Performance," *Academy of Management Journal* 57, no. 4 (June 2014): 1544–70.

31. I am not the first to apply Ganz's model to the subject of purpose. See John Cole-
man, "Use Storytelling to Explain Your Company's Purpose," *Harvard Business Review*, November 24, 2015, https://hbr.org/2015/11/use-storytelling-to
-explain-your-companys-purpose.

32. Marshall Ganz, "Public Narrative, Collective Action, and Power," in *Accountability Through Public Opinion: From Inertia to Public Action*, ed. Sina Odugbemi and
Taeku Lee (Washington, DC: World Bank, 2011), 273.

33. Ganz, "Public Narrative," 273–74.

34. Ganz, "Public Narrative," 283–85.

35. Emmanuel Faber, "Without Social Justice, There Is No Future for the Economy," commencement address published on Medium, June 29, 2016, https://
medium.com/@dominiquebel/without-social-justice-there-is-no-future-for-the
-economy-b87537166e89.

36. "Indra Nooyi: Performance with Purpose," *Fortune*, YouTube video, 3:07, November 9, 2011, https://www.youtube.com/watch?v=BDTVdX-enr4. I've adapted
this quote as best I can from Nooyi's live, conversational diction.

37. Quoted in Indra Nooyi, "Leading with Purpose: Changing the Way We Make
Money to Change the World," LinkedIn, July 11, 2018, https://www.linkedin
.com/pulse/leading-purpose-changing-way-we-make-money-change-world
-indra-nooyi/.

38. Quoted in Gary Burnison, *No Fear of Failure: Real Stories of How Leaders Deal with Risk and Change* (Hoboken, NJ: Jossey-Bass, 2011), 34.

39. Ganz, "Public Narrative," 285–86.

40. Annual Report, PepsiCo, 2008, 4–7.

41. Ganz, "Public Narrative," 286–88.

42. Emmanuel Faber, "Food Is a Human Right, Not a Commodity," LinkedIn, June 22, 2017, https://www.linkedin.com/pulse/food-human-right-commodity-emmanuel -faber/.

43. Sohini Mitter, "PepsiCo CEO Indra Nooyi Reveals Why She Writes Letters to Parents of Her Senior Executives," Mashable, February 2, 2017, https://mash able.com/2017/02/02/pepsico-ceo-indra-nooyi-letters-parents-senior-executives /?utm_cid=mash-prod-nav-sub-st#_G8ocF9WESq3.

44. Marguerite Ward, "Why PepsiCo CEO Indra Nooyi Writes Letters to Her Employees' Parents," CNBC, updated February 1, 2017, https://www.cnbccom /2017/02/01/why-pepsico-ceo-indra-nooyi-writes-letters-to-her-employees -parents.html.

45. Ward, "Why PepsiCo CEO Indra Nooyi Writes Letters."

46. Annual Report, PepsiCo, 2006, https://www.pepsico.com/docs/album/annual -reports/2006-Annual-English.pdf.

47. Leadership scholars have described three levels of leadership mastery: knowing, doing, and being. As the editors of a widely read leadership handbook explain, "To be successful, there are certain things leaders must know (knowledge), certain things they must be able to do (skills), and certain ways they must be (character, identity, worldview)." Scott Snook, Nitin Nohria, and Rakesh Khurana, eds., *The Handbook for Teaching Leadership: Knowing, Doing, and Being* (Los Angeles: SAGE Publications, 2012), xv.

48. Bill George et al., "Discovering Your Authentic Leadership," *Harvard Business Review,* February 2007; Quinn and Thakor, *The Economics of Higher Purpose,* 101–9.

49. Emmanuel Faber (CEO of Danone), interview with the author, December 8, 2020.

50. Quoted in David Gelles, "Indra Nooyi: 'I'm Not Here to Tell You What to Eat,'" *New York Times,* March 21, 2019, https://www.nytimes.com/2019/03/21 /business/indra-nooyi-corner-office-pepsi.html.

51. Burnison, *No Fear of Failure,* 33–35.

52. Indra K. Nooyi and Vijay Govindarajan, "Becoming a Better Corporate Citizen," *Harvard Business Review,* March–April 2020, https://hbr.org/2020/03/becoming -a-better-corporate-citizen.

53. Scott Snook, "Be, Know, Do: Forming Character the West Point Way," *Compass* 1, no. 2 (Spring 2004): 16–19.

54. David De Cremer, "Affective and Motivational Consequences of Leader Self-Sacrifice: The Moderating Effect of Autocratic Leadership," *Leadership Quarterly* 17 (2006): 79–93.

55. "Good for You, Not for Shareholders," *Economist*, March 17, 2012, https://www.economist.com/business/2012/03/17/good-for-you-not-for-shareholders.

56. M. L. Besharov and R. Khurana, "Leading Amidst Competing Technical and Institutional Demands: Revisiting Selznick's Conception of Leadership," in *Institutions and Ideals: Philip Selznick's Legacy for Organizational Studies*, Research in the Sociology of Organization 44 (Bingley, UK: Emerald Group Publishing Limited, 2015), 53–88.

57. Besharov and Khurana, "Leading Amidst Competing Technical and Institutional Demands," 19.

58. The organizational theorist Philip Selznick saw leaders as weavers of grand myths that imbue organizations with meaning and purpose. This wasn't simply a "best practice" in his view, but rather a core responsibility of leadership. Further, leaders had an obligation to *internalize* the purpose and bring it forth from within via their own behaviors. Stakeholders look to leaders to embody otherwise abstract values and purpose to them. If leaders fail at that, the best mythmaking in the world amounts to little. When leaders do manage to embody the purpose, they create an organizational context in which employees do their work passionately and exuberantly. Employees perceive that they are engaging in a moral quest for a better future, one that is palpable and real, and they throw everything they have into it.

59. Andrew M. Carton, "'I'm Not Mopping the Floors, I'm Putting a Man on the Moon': How NASA Leaders Enhanced the Meaningfulness of Work by Changing the Meaning of Work," *Administrative Science Quarterly* 63, no. 2 (2018): 325, https://doi.org/10.1177/0001839217713748.

60. Quoted in Kanter et al., "PepsiCo, Performance with Purpose," 7–9.

61. Jade Scipioni, "Pepsi CEO Indra Nooyi's Last Day: A Look at Her Legacy," FOX Business, October 2, 2018, https://www.foxbusiness.com/features/pepsi-ceo-indra-nooyis-last-day-a-look-at-her-legacy; Nooyi and Govindarajan, "Becoming a Better Corporate Citizen."

62. Indra K. Nooyi and Vijay Govindarajan, "Becoming a Better Corporate Citizen."

63. "In Conversation with Lord Mervyn King Series Presents Indra Nooyi."

64. Nooyi and Govindarajan, "Becoming a Better Corporate Citizen"; "Sustainability Report," PepsiCo, 2017.

65. Julie Creswell, "Indra Nooyi, PepsiCo C.E.O. Who Pushed for Healthier Products, to Step Down," *New York Times*, August 6, 2018, https://www.nytimes.com/2018/08/06/business/indra-nooyi-pepsi.html; John D. Stoll, "How Should Pepsi's Indra Nooyi Be Graded?," *Wall Street Journal*, August 9, 2018, https://www.wsj.com/articles/how-should-pepsis-indra-nooyi-be-graded-1533819601.

Chapter 6: The "Me" in Purpose

1. Hemal Jhaveri, "A Brief History of Super Bowl Media Day in Photos," *USA Today*, January 27, 2019, https://ftw.usatoday.com/gallery/super-bowl-media-day-history.

2. Jeff Legwold, "Lynch: 'I'm Here So I Won't Get Fined,'" ESPN, January 27, 2015, https://www.espn.com/nfl/playoffs/2014/story/_/id/12237417/marshawn-lynch-seattle-seahawks-uses-same-answer-repetition-super-bowl-media-day-here-get-fined.

3. Coby McDonald, "'Bout That Action: How Marshawn Lynch Threw the Sports Media for a Loop," Berkeley (alumni), Fall 2015, https://alumni.berkeley.edu/california-magazine/fall-2015-questions-race/bout-action-how-marshawn-lynch-threw-sports-media-loop.

4. I base my stylized account on a video of Lynch's appearance available at the Daily Motion website (https://www.dailymotion.com/video/x2ftewu). Also see Legwold, "Lynch: 'I'm Here.'"

5. As of 2019, he had over ten thousand rushing yards, five Pro Bowl appearances, and a Super Bowl victory to his credit over the course of his thirteen-year career. Madilyn Zeegers, "NFL: Is Marshawn Lynch a Hall of Fame Running Back?," Sportscasting, June 14, 2019, https://www.sportscasting.com/marshawn-lynch-hall-of-fame-running-back/.

6. Patrick Olde Loohuis, "NFL Ranks Marshawn Lynch's 'Beast Quake' the Greatest Run in History," Seahawks Wire, November 2, 2019, https://seahawkswire.usatoday.com/2019/11/02/nfl-ranks-marshawn-lynchs-beast-quake-the-greatest-run-in-history/.

7. Brandon K., "Marshawn Lynch Continues to Taint Image, Charged with Gun-Related Misdemeanors," Bleacher Report, February 20, 2009, https://bleacherreport.com/articles/127160-marshawn-lynch-continues-to-taint-image-charged-with-gun-related-misdemeanors; "Lynch Gets Probation for Guilty Plea," ESPN, March 5, 2009, https://www.espn.com/nfl/news/story?id=3955441; Terry Blount, "Marshawn Lynch Resolving DUI Case," ESPN, February 20, 2014, https://www.espn.com/nfl/story/_/id/10490851/marshawn-lynch-seattle-seahawks-pleads-guilty-reckless-driving.

8. Kent Babb, "Super Bowl 2014: Seahawks Running Back Marshawn Lynch Gives People Reason to Talk," *Washington Post*, January 30, 2014, https://www.washingtonpost.com/sports/redskins/super-bowl-2014-seahawks-running-back-marshawn-lynch-gives-people-reason-to-talk/2014/01/30/b874cc6a-89ff-11e3-833c-33098f9e5267_story.html; McDonald, "'Bout That Action."

9. Others saw it more positively as a "power move for Black athletes." Jenée Desmond-Harris, "Marshawn Lynch's Selective Silence Is a Power Move for Black Athletes," Vox, January 31, 2015, https://www.vox.com/2015/1/31/7956685/marshawn

-lynch-media-race. Lynch seems to have regarded the media as phony, intrusive, and distracting, perceiving that journalists were trying to shine a spotlight on him, neglecting the role played by his teammates. "Marshawn Lynch Talks About Why He Doesn't Talk to the Media," *USA Today*, updated January 29, 2015, https://www.usatoday.com/story/sports/nfl/2015/01/29/marshawn-lynch-talks -about-why-he-doesnt-talk-to-the-media/22533561/; Sam Laird, "It's About the Team: Why Marshawn Lynch Doesn't Talk to Media," Mashable, January 28, 2015, https://mashable.com/2015/01/28/marshawn-lynch-media/.

10. Ed Sherman, "Jerk Mode: Marshawn Lynch and Why Athletes Need to Talk to Media," Sherman Report, November 25, 2014, http://www.shermanreport.com /jerk-mode-marshawn-lynch-and-why-athletes-need-to-talk-to-media/.

11. Katie Sharp, "Super Bowl 2015: Why Does Marshawn Lynch Grab His Crotch When He Scores a Touchdown?," SB Nation, January 30, 2015, https://www .sbnation.com/2015/1/30/7945155/super-bowl-2015-why-marshawn-lynch-grab -his-crotch-touchdown.

12. McDonald, "'Bout That Action."

13. Quoted in Parker Molloy, "Super Bowl XLIX Media Day—as It Happened," *Guardian*, updated March 29, 2018, https://www.theguardian.com/sport/live /2015/jan/27/super-bowl-xlix-media-day-live.

14. Pete Carroll (head coach and executive vice president of the Seattle Seahawks), interviews with the author, April 6 and 10, 2020.

15. Michael Bennett (former Seattle Seahawks defensive lineman), interview with the author, May 7, 2020.

16. Pete Carroll, interviews with the author, April 6 and 10, 2020.

17. Pete Carroll, interviews with the author, April 6 and 10, 2020.

18. During the middle of the twentieth century, scholars depicted culture as a form of "non-coercive persuasion" and chronicled the making of "organization men" inside business enterprises. See William H. Whyte, *The Organization Man* (Philadelphia: University of Pennsylvania Press, 2002); Edgar H. Schein, Inge Schneier, and Curtis H. Barker, *Coercive Persuasion: A Socio-Psychological Analysis of the "Brainwashing" of American Civilian Prisoners by the Chinese Communists* (New York: W.W. Norton, 1971).

19. As the thinking goes, people can't just "do their own thing" inside organizations. If they did, organizations would devolve into chaos, or at the very least, underperform. But organizations also can't easily monitor people and their behavior. Formal systems for tracking behavior can prove costly, and they can flounder either because the managers implementing them haven't bought in or because behaviors and their outcomes defy easy measurement. Charles O'Reilly, "Corporations, Culture, and Commitment: Motivation and Social Control in Organizations," *California Management Review* (Summer 1989).

20. O'Reilly, "Corporations, Culture, and Commitment," 12.

21. Looking back on his time as CEO of IBM during the 1990s, Lou Gerstner reflected, "The thing I have learned at IBM is that culture is everything." "Gerstner: Changing Culture at IBM—Lou Gerstner Discusses Changing the Culture at IBM," *Harvard Business School* (Working Knowledge), December 9, 2002, https://hbswk.hbs.edu/archive/gerstner-changing-culture-at-ibm-lou-gerstner -discusses-changing-the-culture-at-ibm.

22. Strong cultures can become oppressive forces. See for example, John Van Maanen, "The Asshole," in Peter K. Manning and John van Maanen, eds., *Policing: A View from the Streets* (Santa Monia, CA: Goodyear, 1978), 221–38; Philip Selznick, *The Organizational Weapon: A Study of Bolshevik Strategy and Tactics* (New Orleans, LA: Quid Pro Books, 2015); and Rosabeth Moss Kanter, "Commitment and Social Organization: A Study of Commitment Mechanisms in Utopian Communities," *American Sociological Review* 35 (August 1968): 499–517.

23. Donald Sull, Stefano Turconi, and Charles Sull, "When It Comes to Culture, Does Your Company Walk the Talk?," *MIT Sloan Management Review*, July 21, 2020, https://sloanreview.mit.edu/article/when-it-comes-to-culture-does-your -company-walk-the-talk/.

24. Internal Ovia documents.

25. Internal Ovia documents present the company's vision as: "Every woman, parent and child deserves to have equal care, longitudinal support, life-saving interventions, and a healthy, happy family." Wallace also elaborated on the company's purpose during an interview I conducted with him: Paris Wallace (CEO of Ovia Health), interview with the author, February 11, 2021.

26. Emphasis mine. Internal Ovia document.

27. Paris Wallace, interview with the author, February 11, 2021.

28. Paris Wallace, interview with the author, December 17, 2020.

29. Molly Howard (Chief Operating Officer of Ovia), interview with the author, January 6, 2021.

30. Bruce N. Pfau, "How an Accounting Firm Convinced Its Employees They Could Change the World," *Harvard Business Review*, October 6, 2015, https://hbr .org/2015/10/how-an-accounting-firm-convinced-its-employees-they-could -change-the-world.

31. Pfau, "How an Accounting Firm."

32. Bruce Pfau (former vice chair of human resources and communications at KPMG), interview with the author, January 13, 2021.

33. Kathleen Hogan, interview with the author, May 12, 2020.

34. In depicting this episode, I draw on Nadella's book as well as interviews I conducted with several members of his team. See Nadella, *Hit Refresh*, 1–11.

35. Quoted in Francesca Gino, Allison Ciechanover, and Jeff Huizinga, "Culture

Transformation at Microsoft: From 'Know it All' to 'Learn it All,' Harvard Business School Case Study 9–921–004, revised November 2020, 5.

36. Doug J. Chung, "Commercial Sales Transformation at Microsoft," Harvard Business School Case Study 519–054, January 2019 (revised October 2019), 4.

37. Satya Nadella, interview with the author, June 1, 2020.

38. Nadella, *Hit Refresh*, 11.

39. Research has shown that people who view their work as a calling "have a stronger and more rewarding relationship to their work, which is associated with spending more time at work, and gaining more enjoyment and satisfaction from it." Amy Wrzesniewski, "Finding Positive Meaning at Work," in K. S. Cameron, J. E. Dutton, and R. E. Quinn, eds., *Positive Organizational Scholarship: Foundations of a New Discipline* (San Francisco: Berrett-Koehler, 2003), 302. For a concise overview of job crafting, see Patrick F. Bruning and Michael A. Campion, "Exploring Job Crafting: Diagnosing and Responding to the Ways Employees Adjust Their Jobs," *Business Horizons* 65, no. 5 (September–October 2019): 625–35. For insight into the many ways that employees can shape or craft their jobs, see Dorien T. A. M. Kooij et al., "Job Crafting Towards Strengths and Interests: The Effects of a Job Crafting Intervention on Person–Job Fit and the Role of Age," *Journal of Applied Psychology* 102, no. 6 (June 2017): 971–81.

40. Eric Garton and Michael Mankins, "Engaging Your Employees Is Good, but Don't Stop There," *Harvard Business Review*, December 9, 2015, https://hbr.org /2015/12/engaging-your-employees-is-good-but-dont-stop-there.

41. Matt Breitfelder (global head of human capital and senior partner at Apollo Global Management), interview with the author, January 15, 2021.

42. Kathleen Hogan, "The 5Ps of Employee Fulfillment," LinkedIn, December 11, 2018, https://www.linkedin.com/pulse/5ps-employee-fulfillment-kathleen-hogan/.

43. Ron Carucci, "Balancing the Company's Needs and Employee Satisfaction," *Harvard Business Review*, November 1, 2019, https://hbr.org/2019/11/balancing-the -companys-needs-and-employee-satisfaction.

44. Suzanne Choney, "For the Love of Aaron, and All Children Who May Be Susceptible to SIDS," Microsoft, June 7, 2017, https://news.microsoft.com/features /love-aaron-children-may-susceptible-sids/; Erin Dietsche, "This Microsoft Team Volunteered Their Time to Develop a SIDS Research Tool," Med City News, June 12, 2017, https://medcitynews.com/2017/06/microsoft-sids-research -tool/; "A Child's Sudden Death Leads Data Scientists on a Quest for Answers," Bloomberg, August 31, 2017, https://www.techatbloomberg.com/blog/childs -sudden-death-leads-data-scientists-quest-answers/.

45. Others have remarked on multiple kinds of personal purpose. See, for instance, Dan Pontefract, *The Purpose Effect: Building Meaning in Yourself, Your Role, and Your Organization* (Boise, ID: Elevate, 2016).

46. Note that this purpose embodies a strictly commercial logic rather than the deeper purpose described in chapter 2, which fuses the commercial and the intent to perform some higher social good.

47. For press coverage, see Selena Ross and Kelly Greig, "Laurent Duvernay-Tardif Opts Out of NFL Season, Saying He Won't Risk Spreading COVID-19," CTV News Montreal, updated July 25, 2020, https://montreal.ctvnews.ca/laurent -duvernay-tardif-opts-out-of-nfl-season-saying-he-won-t-risk-spreading-covid-19 -1.5038706; Adam Kilgore, "His Team Is Going to the Super Bowl. He's Staying on the Coronavirus Front Lines," *Washington Post*, February 1, 2021, https://www .washingtonpost.com/sports/2021/02/01/laurent-duvernay-tardif-coronavirus -super-bowl/.

48. Joshua Brisco, "Andy Reid Proud, Not Surprised by Laurent Duvernay-Tardif's Choice to Stay on COVID-19 Front Lines," *Sports Illustrated*, updated July 26, 2020, https://www.si.com/nfl/chiefs/news/andy-reid-laurent-duvernay-tardif-opt -out-covid-19.

49. Pete Carroll, interview with the author, April 6 and 10, 2020.

50. Kathleen Hogan, interview with the author, May 12, 2020.

51. Hogan, "The 5Ps."

52. Satya Nadella, interview with the author, June 1, 2020.

53. Scott Barry Kaufman, *Transcend: The New Science of Self-Actualization* (New York: TarcherPerigree, 2020), xxxv, 155.

54. Kaufman, *Transcend*, xv.

55. Kaufman, *Transcend*, 218. Also see the preface and chapter 1. I am grateful to Angela Duckworth as well for cueing me into Maslow's concept of transcendence.

56. Ranjay Gulati, Matthew Breitfelder, and Monte Burke, "Pete Carroll: Building a Winning Organization Through Purpose, Caring, and Inclusion," Harvard Business School Case Study 421–020, March 2021, 17.

57. Gino, Ciechanover, and Huizinga, "Culture Transformation at Microsoft," 13.

58. Austin Carr and Dina Bass, "The Most Valuable Company (for Now) Is Having a Nadellaissance," Bloomberg, May 2, 2019, https://www.bloomberg.com/news /features/2019-05-02/satya-nadella-remade-microsoft-as-world-s-most-valuable -company.

59. Joe Whittinghill, corporate vice president of talent, learning and insights, quoted in Gino, Ciechanover, and Huizinga, "Culture Transformation at Microsoft," 6.

60. "Pete Carroll," Statscrew, accessed May 27, 2021, https://www.statscrew.com /football/stats/c-carropet001; "Is Seahawks' Pete Carroll a Hall of Fame Coach?," Herald Net, January 24, 2020, https://www.heraldnet.com/sports/is-seahawks -pete-carroll-a-hall-of-fame-coach/; Bryan DeArdo, "10 Current NFL Coaches with a Shot at Hall of Fame, Ranked by Tiers with Two Absolute Locks at the Top," CBS Sports, February 3, 2020, https://www.cbssports.com/nfl/news/10

-current-nfl-coaches-with-a-shot-at-hall-of-fame-ranked-by-tiers-with-two-absolute-locks-at-the-top/. These results are as of 2020. Carroll's record also reflects his earlier years with the New York Jets and New England Patriots.

61. Joel M. Podolny, "Discussion of 'How to' Session," Conference on Organizations with Purpose, September 16–17, 2016.

62. Kaufman, *Transcend*, 151–53, 217–27.

63. Pete Carroll, interviews with the author, April 6 and 10, 2020.

Chapter 7: Escaping the Iron Cage

1. Christopher Jensen, "In General Motors Recalls, Inaction and Trail of Fatal Crashes," *New York Times*, March 2, 2014, https://www.nytimes.com/2014/03/03/business/in-general-motors-recalls-inaction-and-trail-of-fatal-crashes.html.

2. Quoted in Scott Neuman, "Mother of Victim: More Killed by GM Ignition Switch Defect," Iowa Public Radio, April 1, 2014, https://www.iowapublicradio.org/2014-04-01/mother-of-victim-more-killed-by-gm-ignition-switch-defect; Jonathan Abel, "In One Week, Six Traffic Deaths on Tri-County Roads," *Washington Post*, July 31, 2005, https://www.washingtonpost.com/wp-dyn/content/article/2005/07/30/AR2005073000044.html.

3. In accessory mode, a car's engine and certain safety features like the airbags are off but the windows and other accessories still work.

4. I base these sentences on the description in a GM press release issued shortly after the company recalled its 2005–2010 Chevy Cobalts. See "GM to Replace Lock Cylinder During Ignition Switch Recall," GM (corporate newsroom), April 10, 2014, https://media.gm.com/media/us/en/gm/news.detail.html/content/Pages/news/us/en/2014/Apr/0410-ignition.html.

5. Michelle Murillo, "After Md. Teen's Death, Family Fights for General Motors Accountability," WTOP News, February 28, 2014, https://wtop.com/news/2014/02/after-md-teens-death-family-fights-for-general-motors-accountability/; "NHTSA GM Ignition Switch Chronology," Center for Auto Safety, accessed May 27, 2021, https://www.autosafety.org/wp-content/uploads/import/NHTSA%20Cobalt%20Chronology_1.pdf.

6. Brad Plumer, "The GM Recall Scandal of 2014," Vox, updated May 11, 2015, https://www.vox.com/2014/10/3/18073458/gm-car-recall; Clifford Atiyeh, "GM Expands Recall to Every Car Built With Faulty Ignition Switch, Will Fix 2.2 Million Cars in U.S.," *Car and Driver*, March 28, 2014, https://www.caranddriver.com/news/a15365392/gm-recalls-every-car-built-with-faulty-ignition-switch-will-fix-2-2-million-cars-in-u-s/; Clifford Atiyeh, "GM Ignition-Switch Review Complete: 124 Fatalities, 274 Injuries," *Car and Driver*, August 3, 2015, https://www.caranddriver.com/news/a15353429/gm-ignition-switch-review-complete-124-fatalities-274-injuries/.

7. Danielle Ivory and Bill Vlasic, "$900 Million Penalty for G.M.'s Deadly Defect Leaves Many Cold," *New York Times*, September 17, 2015, https://www.nytimes.com/2015/09/18/business/gm-to-pay-us-900-million-over-ignition-switch-flaw.html.

8. Clifford Atiyeh, "GM, After Six-Year Battle, Settles Another Ignition-Switch Lawsuit for $120 Million," *Car and Driver*, March 28, 2020, https://www.caranddriver.com/news/a31965015/gm-settles-lawsuit-ignition-switch-car-values/. The company also apparently "resolved or dismissed" some three thousand other cases.

9. Michelle Arrouas, "Congress Pulls GM Over for Failing to Fix Defect," *Time*, March 31, 2014, https://time.com/43318/congress-pulls-gm-over-for-failing-to-fix-defect/.

10. For a detailed chronology of GM's handling of its ignition switch problems, see Randall W. Harris and W. Scott Sherman, "General Motors and the Chevy Cobalt Ignition Switch Crisis," *Case Research Journal* 37, no. 4 (Fall 2017). My recounting of the Chevy Cobalt ignition switch story is especially indebted to this case study. See also Clifford Atiyeh, "GM Internal Audit: One Ugly Mess," *Car and Driver*, June 11, 2014, https://www.caranddriver.com/news/a15363168/gm-internal-audit-one-ugly-mess/; Plumer, "The GM Recall Scandal of 2014"; Joseph B. White, "A Recall Bares GM's Love of Red Tape," *Wall Street Journal*, March 7, 2014, https://www.wsj.com/articles/SB100014240527023047328045794253813097641144; Tanya Basu, "Timeline: A History Of GM's Ignition Switch Defect," NPR, March 31, 2014, https://www.npr.org/2014/03/31/297158876/timeline-a-history-of-gms-ignition-switch-defect; Todd Spangler, "Delphi Told GM Ignition Switch Didn't Meet Specs," *USA Today*, updated March 30, 2014, https://www.usatoday.com/story/money/cars/2014/03/30/gm-ignition-switches-recall-congressional-report/7085919/; "NHTSA GM Ignition Switch Chronology," Center for Auto Safety, accessed May 27, 2021, https://www.autosafety.org/wp-content/uploads/import/NHTSA%20Cobalt%20Chronology_1.pdf.

11. Michael A. Fletcher and Steven Mufson, "Why Did GM Take So Long to Respond to Deadly Defect? Corporate Culture May Hold Answer," *Washington Post*, March 30, 2014, https://www.washingtonpost.com/business/economy/why-did-gm-take-so-long-to-respond-to-deadly-defect-corporate-culture-may-hold-answer/2014/03/30/5c366f6c-b691-11e3-b84e-897d3d12b816_story.html.

12. "Max Weber on Bureaucratization in 1909," *RSU.edu*, accessed May 27, 2021, https://www.faculty.rsu.edu/users/f/felwell/www/Theorists/Weber/Whome3.htm.

13. Paul J. DiMaggio and Walter W. Powell, "The Iron Cage Revisited: Institutional Isomorphism and Collective Rationality in Organizational Fields," *American Sociological Review* 48 (April 1983): 147–60.

14. Ranjay Gulati, *Reorganize for Resilience: Putting Customers at the Center of Your Business* (Boston: Harvard Business Review Press, 2010).

15. Gary Hamel and Michele Zanini, *Humanocracy: Creating Organizations as Amazing as the People Inside Them* (Boston: Harvard Business Review Press, 2020), 58.

16. "CEO Mary Barra's Written Congressional Testimony Now Available," GM (corporate newsroom), March 31, 2014, https://media.gm.com/media/us/en/gm/news.detail.html/content/Pages/news/us/en/2014/mar/0331-barra-written-testimony.html.

17. Patrick George, "GM's Scathing Internal Inquiry Is a Tale of Bureaucratic Incompetence," Jalopnik, June 5, 2014, https://jalopnik.com/gms-scathing-internal-inquiry-is-a-tale-of-bureaucratic-1586756793. See, for example, "Highlights from General Motors Investigation," Motley Fool, June 5, 2014, https://www.fool.com/investing/general/2014/06/05/highlights-from-general-motors-investigation.aspx. For the original report, see Anton R. Valukas, "Report to Board of Directors of General Motors Company Regarding Ignition Switch Recalls," G.M. Internal Investigation Report (redacted), May 29, 2014.

18. Valukas, "Report to Board of Directors," 265.

19. Valukas, "Report to Board of Directors," 266.

20. Valukas, "Report to Board of Directors," 256–8 et passim.

21. Quoted in "After Bankruptcy, G.M. Struggles to Shed a Legendary Bureaucracy," CNBC, November 13, 2009, https://www.cnbc.com/2009/11/13/after-bankruptcy-gm-struggles-to-shed-a-legendary-bureaucracy.html.

22. Valukas, "Report to Board of Directors," 266.

23. Harris and Sherman, "General Motors and the Chevy Cobalt," 11.

24. Ben Heineman, "GC and CEO Responsibility for GM's Dysfunctional Culture," Harvard Kennedy School Belfer Center, June 6, 2014, https://www.belfercenter.org/publication/gc-and-ceo-responsibility-gms-dysfunctional-culture.

25. Atiyeh, "GM Internal Audit."

26. At one time, the company had a dress code enshrined in a ten-page document. As head of HR, Barra shelved that, allowing managers to determine appropriate dress for their teams. She also eliminated layers of bureaucracy in the company's product development arm. Richard Feloni, "GM CEO Mary Barra Said the Recall Crisis of 2014 Forever Changed Her Leadership Style," Business Insider, November 14, 2018, https://www.businessinsider.com/gm-mary-barra-recall-crisis-leadership-style-2018-11; Amy C. Edmondson, "Mary Barra Brings Teaming to General Motors," *Harvard Business Review*, January 14, 2014, https://hbr.org/2014/01/mary-barra-brings-teaming-to-general-motors.

27. Jamie L. LaReau, "GM: We Encourage Employees, Dealers to Tattle after Ignition Switch Crisis," *Detroit Free Press*, updated September 6, 2019, https://www

.freep.com/story/money/cars/general-motors/2019/09/06/gm-ignition-switch
-nhtsa-recalls-safety-defects/2099289001/.

28. "Transforming a Business Starts with Employees," General Motors Green, June 29, 2017, https://www.generalmotors.green/product/public/us/en/GMGreen/social _impact.detail.html/content/Pages/news/us/en/gm_green/2017/0629-trans forming-a-business.html.

29. Quoted in Bill Snyder, "Mary Barra: Simplify Bureaucracy, and Don't Be Afraid to Job Hop," Stanford Business, June 5, 2017, https://www.gsb.stanford.edu /insights/mary-barra-simplify-bureaucracy-dont-be-afraid-job-hop.

30. For GM's mission circa 2008, see "General Motors Mission, Vision, and Values," UK Essays, December 5, 2017, https://www.ukessays.com/essays/business/general -motors-values.php.

31. "General Motors," Business Roundtable, accessed May 27, 2021, https://www .businessroundtable.org/policy-perspectives/energy-environment/sustainability /general-motors.

32. Jessica James, "General Motors Named One of the 2020 World's Most Ethical Companies by the Ethisphere Institute," GM (corporate newsroom), February 25, 2020, https://media.gm.com/media/us/en/gm/home.detail.html/content/Pages /news/us/en/2020/feb/0225-ethical.html.

33. "Business Roundtable Redefines the Purpose of a Corporation to Promote 'An Economy That Serves All Americans,'" Business Roundtable, August 19, 2019, https://www.businessroundtable.org/business-roundtable-redefines-the-purpose -of-a-corporation-to-promote-an-economy-that-serves-all-americans; David Gelles and David Yaffe-Bellany, "Shareholder Value Is No Longer Everything, Top C.E.O.s Say," New York Times, August 19, 2019, https://www.nytimes.com/2019 /08/19/business/business-roundtable-ceos-corporations.html; James, "General Motors Named One of the 2020 World's Most Ethical Companies."

34. General Motors Company Schedule 14A, Proxy Statement Pursuant to Section 14(a) of the Securities Exchange Act of 1934, United States Securities and Exchange Commission, https://www.sec.gov/Archives/edgar/data/1467858/0001 19312519110751/d613802ddef14a.htm.

35. "General Motors, the Largest U.S. Automaker, Plans to Be Carbon Neutral by 2040," GM (corporate newsroom), January 28, 2021, https://media.gm.com /media/us/en/gm/home.detail.html/content/Pages/news/us/en/2021/jan/01 28-carbon.html.

36. Shipra Kumari, interview by Rachna Tahilyani (senior associate director of Harvard Business School's India Research Center), July 20, 2020.

37. "Mahindra & Mahindra Today," Mahindra, accessed May 28, 2021, https:// www.mahindrafarmequipment.com/home/evolutions/evolution.

38. Shipra Kumari, interview by Rachna Tahilyani (senior associate director of the India Research Center), July 20, 2020.

39. Lokesh Lakhchoura (Mahindra & Mahindra, regional manager at Uttar Pradesh & Uttarakhand), interview with author, July 20, 2020.

40. Rajesh Jejurikar (president of Mahindra's Farm Equipment Sector and member of the Group Executive Board), interview with the author, August 30, 2019.

41. Ranjay Gulati and Rachna Tahilyani, "The Mahindra Group: Leading with Purpose," Harvard Business School Case Study 421–091, April 10, 2021, 6. My account of Mahindra in this chapter draws heavily on this case study. Unless otherwise indicated, all quotes presented here from Mahindra executives originally appear there.

42. Anand Mahindra (chairman of Mahindra & Mahindra), interview with the author, May 7, 2019.

43. Ramesh Iyer (Managing Director of Mahindra and Mahindra Financial Services), interview with the author, January 10, 2019.

44. Sherna Sheldon (HR business partner at Mahindra Electric), interview with the author, February 14, 2020.

45. See, for instance Marylène Gagne and Devasheesh P. Bhave, "Autonomy in the Workplace: An Essential Ingredient to Employee Engagement and Well-Being in Every Culture," in V. Chirkov, R. Ryan, K. Sheldon, (eds.) *Human Autonomy in Cross-Cultural Context Perspectives on the Psychology of Agency, Freedom, and Well-Being* (Dordrecht, Netherlands: Springer, 2011).

46. A great deal of work has appeared on the importance of intrinsic motivators and their impact, including the human need for autonomy. See, for instance, Dan Pink, *Drive: The Surprising Truth about What Motivates Us* (New York: Penguin, 2009); and Paul R. Lawrence and Nitin Nohria, *Driven: How Human Nature Shapes Our Choices* (San Francisco: Jossey-Bass, 2002). J. R. Hackman and G. R. Oldham's well-known job characteristics model also includes autonomy among five key characteristics of a fulfilling job.

47. See, for instance, Richard M. Ryan and Edward L. Deci, *Self-Determination Theory: Basic Psychological Needs in Motivation, Development, and Wellness* (New York: Guilford, 2017).

48. "History," Warby Parker, accessed May 28, 2021, https://www.warbyparker.com/history.

49. "Buy a Pair, Give a Pair," Warby Parker, accessed May 28, 2021, https://www.warbyparker.com/buy-a-pair-give-a-pair.

50. "Buy a Pair."

51. Ranjay Gulati and Sam Yogi, "Warby Parker: Scaling a Startup," Harvard Business School Case Study 419–042, November 14, 2018, 2. My account of Warby Parker draws heavily on this case study.

52. Warby Parker eventually dropped its B Corp affiliation, possibly in preparation for an IPO: Dennis R. Shaughnessy, "The Public Capital Markets and Etsy and Warby Parker," *Northeastern*, October 20, 2018, accessed May 28, 2021, https://www.northeastern.edu/sei/2018/10/the-public-capital-markets-and-etsy-and-warby-parker/.

53. "Impact Report," Warby Parker, 2019, 42.

54. Gulati and Yogi, "Warby Parker," 2.

55. Gulati and Yogi, "Warby Parker," 4.

56. As of this writing, it appears that Warby Parker has phased out its Warbles initiative.

57. Neil Blumenthal (cofounder and co-CEO of Warby Parker), interview with the author, March 5, 2021.

58. The company's precise language was: "Presume positive intent: trust but verify."

59. "Impact Report," Warby Parker.

60. Dave Gilboa, "Here's What Happens When Employees Don't Trust Their Managers," *Fortune*, October 7, 2015, https://fortune.com/2015/10/07/employees-dont-trust-managers/.

61. Henderson, "Innovation in the 21st Century," 4–6.

62. Henderson, "Innovation in the 21st Century," 4–6. Others have spoken of the creation of covenantal relationships, solemn promises of mutual assistance that often carry overtones of the sacred. See Quinn and Thakor, *The Economics of Higher Purpose*. See also Cam Caldwell and Zack Hasan, "Covenantal Leadership and the Psychological Contract: Moral Insights for the Modern Leader," *Journal of Management Development* 35, no. 10 (November 2016): 1302–12.

63. "Sadly, trust is often a scarce commodity in large companies. In a 2016 Ernst & Young global survey, fewer than half of the ten thousand employees surveyed said they had a 'great deal of trust' in their colleagues or the company overall." Hamel and Zanini, *Humanocracy*, 78.

64. Jesse Sneath (director of social innovation at Warby Parker), interview with the author, February 16, 2021.

65. George Serafeim and his coauthors bring authenticity into the mix, observing a "nexus of purpose, authenticity, trust and value." They argue that companies can "signal" the authenticity of organizational purpose by taking steps such as becoming a B Corp, adopting integrated reporting, and aligning compensation with the company's transcendent vision. Serafeim, "The Value of Corporate Purpose," 6 et passim.

66. Ranjay Gulati, "Structure That's Not Stifling," *Harvard Business Review*, May–June 2018.

67. Research suggests that self-management yields more stress and burnout while proving less practicable in conflict and crisis situations. Michael Y. Lee and Amy

C. Edmondson, "Self-Managing Organizations: Exploring the Limits of Less Hierarchical Organizing," *Research in Organizational Behavior* 37 (2017): 51.

68. Others have provided different formulas for exerting control inside organizations, although they don't tend to emphasize the liberating quality of these controls themselves. Simons, for instance, identifies four "levers of control": belief systems (including purpose), diagnostic control systems (output goals and metrics), boundary systems ("thou shalt not" rules), and "interactive control systems" (real-time performance metrics). See Robert Simons, *Control in an Age of Empowerment*, as well as Robert Simons, *Levers of Control: How Managers Use Innovative Control Systems to Drive Strategic Renewal* (Boston: Harvard Business School Press, 1994). For another model, see Tatiana Sandino's discussion of "structured empowerment" in "Control or Flexibility? Structured Empowerment Offers Both—Lessons from Retail & Service Chains," Harvard Business School Technical Note 118–082, March 2018 (revised March 1, 2019).

69. I draw this account from a presentation Mueller gave to my class at Harvard Business School on September 30, 2015.

70. Quoted in Morten T. Hansen, "Preventing the Terrorist Attack: Massive Failure in Collaboration," *Harvard Business Review*, December 31, 2009, https://hbr .org/2009/12/the-terrorist-attack-massive-f.

71. In offering this account of the FBI's transformation under Mueller, I draw heavily on Jan V. Rivkin, Michael Roberto, and Ranjay Gulati, "Federal Bureau of Investigation, 2007," Harvard Business School Case Study 710–451, March 9, 2010; Jan V. Rivkin, Michael Roberto, and Ranjay Gulati, "Federal Bureau of Investigation, 2009," Harvard Business School Case Study 9–710–052, March 2010 (revised May 2010); and Ryan Raffaelli et al., "Strategic Framing in the Wake of a Crisis: Outcome and Process Frames at the Federal Bureau of Investigation," unpublished paper (October 28, 2020), 2, 14–20.

72. I'm heavily indebted on this point to my late adviser Paul R. Lawrence and my colleague Jay Lorsch. Their seminal work, *Organization and Environment*, described how organizations must manage so-called differentiation (the creation of modular units) and "integration" (the forging of connection between these units). Paul R. Lawrence and Jay W. Lorsch, *Organization and Environment* (Boston: Harvard Business Review Press, 1968).

73. Donald Sull, Rebecca Homkes, and Charles Sull, "Why Strategy Execution Unravels—and What to Do About It," *Harvard Business Review Magazine*, March 2015, https://hbr.org/2015/03/why-strategy-execution-unravelsand-what -to-do-about-it.

74. See my article "Silo Busting: How to Execute on the Promise of Customer Focus," *Harvard Business Review Magazine*, May 2007, https://hbr.org/2007/05/silo -busting-how-to-execute-on-the-promise-of-customer-focus; and Ranjay Gulati,

Franz Wohlgezogen, and Pavel Zhelyazkov, "The Two Facets of Collaboration: Cooperation and Coordination in Strategic Alliances," *Academy of Management Annals* 6 (2012): 531–83.

75. "John Ashcroft and FBI Director Robert Mueller on the FBI Reorganization," PBS, May 29, 2002, https://www.pbs.org/newshour/show/john-ashcroft-and -fbi-director-robert-mueller-on-the-fbi-reorganization.

76. Rivkin, Roberto, and Gulati, "Federal Bureau of Investigation, 2009," Harvard Business School supplement, March 18, 2010 (revised May 18, 2010), 3.

77. "John Ashcroft and FBI Director Robert Mueller."

78. "Statement of Robert S. Mueller III Director Federal Bureau of Investigation," Committee on Homeland Security and Government Affairs United States Senate, September 13, 2011, https://www.hsgac.senate.gov/imo/media/doc/Testimony Mueller20110913.pdf.

79. Rivkin, Roberto, and Gulati, "Federal Bureau of Investigation, 2009," 4.

80. "Statement of Robert S. Mueller III."

81. "John Ashcroft and FBI Director Robert Mueller"; "Transcript: Robert S. Mueller III: The Director (Part 2)," NBC News, February 3, 2021, https://www.nbc news.com/podcast/the-oath/transcript-robert-s-mueller-iii-director-part-2 -n1256675.

82. Robert S. Mueller, "Testimony," FBI, accessed May 28, 2021, https://archives .fbi.gov/archives/news/testimony/the-fbi-transformation-since-2001. This collaboration would prove vital during the Boston Marathon bombing. Local police provided videos of the bombing scene, while the FBI had technology required to analyze these videos quickly and identify the suspects. The FBI also developed collaborations with other federal agencies, such as the Drug Enforcement Administration (DEA).

83. As Rebecca Henderson notes, employees who believe in a company's purpose tend to be "temperamentally inclined to trust others and to enjoy working with them." Teams comprising such "pro-social" individuals have an easier time establishing atmospheres where it seems psychologically "safe" to work together and communicate. Henderson, *Reimagining Capitalism*, 92–93. See also "Purpose-Driven Leadership for the 21st Century: How Corporate Purpose Is Fundamental to Reimagining Capitalism," *Leaders on Purpose* (research report) (2019), 26.

84. "Impact Report," Warby Parker, 2019, 52.

85. Netflix is well known for offering employees an unusual degree of autonomy in their daily job tasks and for instilling a collaborative culture, apparently without orienting itself around a deep purpose. Although the company does have something resembling a mission (to "entertain the world"), the company's famous Culture Deck enshrining its operating philosophy makes only passing mention of it. As successful as Netflix's operating model has been at unleashing innovation and

agility, we might argue that its neglect of a social purpose represents an untapped opportunity. See Ranjay Gulati, Allison Ciechanover, and Jeff Huizinga, "Netflix: A Creative Approach to Culture and Agility," Harvard Business School Case Study 420–055, September 23, 2019.

86. Quoted in Gulati and Tahilyani, "The Mahindra Group: Leading with Purpose, 16.

87. Tony Simons, "Taking Aim at False Empowerment: How Leaders Can Build a Culture of Trust," Cornell, April 16, 2018, https://business.cornell.edu/hub/2018/04/16/false-empowerment-leaders-build-trust/.

Chapter 8: From Ideas to Ideals: Future-Proofing Purpose

1. "Boeing Completes First Flight of the 737 Max," Boeing, YouTube video, 3.03, February 1, 2016, https://www.youtube.com/watch?v=k82e08kdKyw.

2. William W. George and Amram Migdal, "What Went Wrong with Boeing's 737 Max?," Harvard Business School Case Study 9–320–104, June 2020 (revised October 2020), 2. My account of the 737 Max debacle draws heavily throughout on this case study. Also see Jacopo Prisco, "Boeing 737: How World's Most Successful Airplane Became Its Most Troubled," CNN, December 25, 2020, https://www.cnn.com/travel/article/boeing-737-story-behind-the-troubled-aircraft/index.html.

3. "Timeline: A Brief History of the Boeing 737 Max," *Seattle Times*, updated June 21, 2019, https://www.seattletimes.com/business/boeing-aerospace/timeline-brief-history-boeing-737-Max/; Dominic Gates, "Boeing Announces Design Changes for 737 MAX," *Seattle Times*, updated November 3, 2011, https://www.seattletimes.com/business/boeing-announces-design-changes-for-737-Max/.

4. "Airbus Offers New Fuel Saving Engine Options for A320 Family," Airbus, December 1, 2010, https://www.airbus.com/newsroom/press-releases/en/2010/12/airbus-offers-new-fuel-saving-engine-options-for-a320-family.html.

5. George and Migdal, "What Went Wrong with Boeing's 737 Max?," 5.

6. "737 Max Completes Successful First Flight," Boeing, February 2, 2016, https://www.boeing.com/company/about-bca/washington/737max-first-flight-success-02-02-16.page/.

7. George and Migdal, "What Went Wrong with Boeing's 737 Max?," 14.

8. "Boeing Sets New Airplane Delivery Records, Expands Order Backlog," Boeing, January 8, 2019, https://www.boeing.com/company/about-bca/washington/2018-deliveries-strong-finish.page.

9. George and Migdal, "What Went Wrong with Boeing's 737 Max?," 7.

10. Jake Hardiman, "Five Years Ago the Boeing 737 Max Made Its Maiden Flight," Simple Flying, January 30, 2021, https://simpleflying.com/737-Max-five-years/.

11. Dominic Gates et al., "Investigators Find New Clues Pointing to Potential Cause

of 737 Max Crashes as FAA details Boeing's Fix," *Seattle Times*, updated March 15, 2019, https://www.seattletimes.com/business/boeing-aerospace/investigators -find-new-clues-to-potential-cause-of-737-Max-crashes-as-faa-details-boeings -fix/.

12. George and Migdal, "What Went Wrong with Boeing's 737 Max?," 9, 15–16.

13. Quoted in Andy Pasztor and Andrew Tangel, "Boeing Withheld Information on 737 Model, According to Safety Experts and Others," *Wall Street Journal*, updated November 13, 2018, https://www.wsj.com/articles/boeing-withheld -information-on-737-model-according-to-safety-experts-and-others-154208 2575.

14. Hannah Beech and Muktita Suhartono, "'Spend the Minimum': After Crash, Lion Air's Safety Record Is Back in Spotlight," *New York Times*, November 22, 2018, https://www.nytimes.com/2018/11/22/world/asia/lion-air-crash-safety-fail ures.html.

15. James Glanz et al., "After a Lion Air 737 Max Crashed in October, Questions About the Plane Arose," *New York Times*, February 3, 2019, https://www.nytimes .com/2019/02/03/world/asia/lion-air-plane-crash-pilots.html.

16. Dominic Gates and Lewis Kamb, "Indonesia's Devastating Final Report Blames Boeing 737 Max Design, Certification in Lion Air Crash," *Seattle Times*, updated October 27, 2019, https://www.seattletimes.com/business/boeing-aerospace/indo nesias-investigation-of-lion-air-737-max-crash-faults-boeing-design-and-faa -certification-as-well-as-airlines-maintenance-and-pilot-errors/.

17. George and Migdal, "What Went Wrong with Boeing's 737 Max?," 5–6.

18. "Q&A: What Led to Boeing's 737 MAX Crisis," *Seattle Times*, November 18, 2020, https://www.seattletimes.com/business/boeing-aerospace/what-led-to-boe ings-737-max-crisis-a-qa/.

19. Gates and Kamb, "Indonesia's Devastating Final Report." These quotes come from a draft of the final report quoted by the *Seattle Times*.

20. George and Migdal, "What Went Wrong with Boeing's 737 Max?," 9–10.

21. John Cassidy, "How Boeing and the F.A.A. Created the 737 Max Catastro phe," *New Yorker*, September 17, 2020, https://www.newyorker.com/news/our -columnists/how-boeing-and-the-faa-created-the-737-max-catastrophe.

22. Chris Isidore, "These Are the Mistakes That Cost Boeing CEO Dennis Muilen burg his job," CNN, December 24, 2019, https://www.cnn.com/2019/12/24 /business/boeing-dennis-muilenburg-mistakes/index.html.

23. Peter Economy, "Boeing CEO Puts Partial Blame on Pilots of Crashed 737 Max Aircraft for Not 'Completely' Following Procedures," Inc., April 30, 2019, accessed May 29, 2021, https://www.inc.com/peter-economy/boeing-ceo -puts-partial-blame-on-pilots-of-crashed-737-max-aircraft-for-not-completely -following-procedures.html; Chris Isidore, "Boeing CEO says 737 Max Was

Designed Properly and Pilots Did Not 'Completely' Follow Procedure," CNN, April 30, 2019, https://www.cnn.com/2019/04/29/investing/boeing-annual-meeting/index.html.

24. Gates et al., "Investigators Find New Clues."

25. Natalie Kitroeff and David Gelles, "At Boeing, C.E.O.'s Stumbles Deepen a Crisis," *New York Times*, updated December 23, 2019, https://www.nytimes.com/2019/12/22/business/boeing-dennis-muilenburg-737-max.html.

26. Isidore, "These Are the Mistakes."

27. David Gelles and Natalie Kitroeff, "Boeing Pilot Complained of 'Egregious' Issue With 737 Max in 2016," *New York Times*, updated October 23, 2019, https://www.nytimes.com/2019/10/18/business/boeing-flight-simulator-text-message.html; David Gelles and Natalie Kitroeff, "Boeing Fires C.E.O. Dennis Muilenburg," *New York Times*, December 23, 2019, https://www.nytimes.com/2019/12/23/business/Boeing-ceo-muilenburg.html. More damning messages were released in the months that followed. David Gelles, "'I Honestly Don't Trust Many People at Boeing': A Broken Culture Exposed," *New York Times*, updated February 10, 2020, https://www.nytimes.com/2020/01/10/business/boeing-737-employees-messages.html.

28. Jon Hemmerdinger, "Boeing Estimates 737 Max Crisis Will Cost $18.6 Billion," Flight Global, January 29, 2020, https://www.flightglobal.com/air-transport/boeing-estimates-737-max-crisis-will-cost-186-billion/136429.article.

29. Gelles and Kitroeff, "Boeing Fires C.E.O. Dennis Muilenburg."

30. Brakkton Booker, "Boeing's 737 Max Cleared to Return to European Skies, Regulator Says," NPR, January 27, 2021, https://www.npr.org/2021/01/27/961110827/boeings-737-Max-cleared-to-return-to-european-skies-regulator-says. The FAA cleared it in November 2020, European regulators the following January.

31. Ben Baldanza, "Boeing Addresses 737 Max Issues but Program May Never Make Up for Damages," *Forbes*, January 7, 2021, https://www.forbes.com/sites/benbaldanza/2021/01/07/boeing-addresses-737max-issues-but-program-may-never-make-up-for-damages/?sh=4d02d461e60f.

32. Paul Spitzer, "Boeing as a Start-Up Company, 1915–1917," *Pacific Northwest Quarterly* 95, no. 3 (Summer 2004): 144.

33. Robert J. Serling, *Legend and Legacy: The Story of Boeing and Its People* (New York: St. Martin's Press, 1992), 26.

34. Annual Report, Boeing, 1965.

35. Jeff Cole, "Boeing's Cultural Revolution—Shaken Giant Surrenders Big Dreams for the Bottom Line," *Seattle Times*, December 13, 1998.

36. Jerry Useem, "The Long-Forgotten Flight That Sent Boeing Off Course," *Atlantic*, November 20, 2019.

37. Leon Grunberg and Sarah Moore, *Emerging from Turbulence: Boeing and Stories of the American Workplace Today* (Lanham, MD: Rowman & Littlefield, 2016), 1–3.
38. Jeff Cole, "Boeing's Cultural Revolution."
39. Useem, "The Long-Forgotten Flight."
40. "Boeing Revenue 2006–2021," Macrotrends, accessed May 29, 2021, https://www.macrotrends.net/stocks/charts/BA/boeing/revenue; Annual Report, Boeing, 2005, https://www.annualreports.com/HostedData/AnnualReportArchive/b/NYSE_BA_2005.pdf.
41. George and Migdal, "What Went Wrong with Boeing's 737 Max?," 5–6.
42. Michael A. Cusumano, "Boeing's 737 Max: A Failure of Management, Not Just Technology," *Communications of the ACM* 64, no. 1 (January 2021): 22–25. See also Natasha Frost, "The 1997 Merger That Paved the Way for the Boeing 737 Max Crisis," Quartz, June 4, 2020.
43. "Starbucks Company Timeline," Starbucks, accessed May 29, 2021, https://www.starbucks.com/about-us/company-information/starbucks-company-timeline; Janet Adamy, "Starbucks Chairman Says Trouble May Be Brewing," *Wall Street Journal*, February 24, 2007, https://www.wsj.com/articles/SB11722524 7561617457.
44. Nancy F. Koehn et al., "Starbucks Coffee Company: Transformation and Renewal," Harvard Business School Case Study 9–314–068, June 2, 2014, 2–3, 8. My account of Starbucks draws heavily on this case study.
45. Howard Schultz, *Onward: How Starbucks Fought for Its Life without Losing Its Soul* (New York: Rodale, 2011), 24.
46. Schultz, *Onward*, 112, 114.
47. Corie Barry (CEO of Best Buy), interview with the author, April 16, 2021.
48. Kevin Johnson (president and chief executive officer of Starbucks), interview with the author, November 23, 2020.
49. Quoted in Mark R. Kramer and Sarah Mehta, "Becton Dickinson: Global Health Strategy," Harvard Business School Case Study, 718–406, September 2017 (revised February 2018), 6. This paragraph draws heavily on pages 4–6 and 10–13 of this case study.
50. Gary Cohen (executive vice president, global health at Becton Dickinson), interview with the author, July 31, 2020.
51. Gary Cohen, interview with the author, July 31, 2020.
52. Vince Forlenza (former chief executive officer of Becton Dickinson), interview with the author, July 31, 2020.
53. Gary Cohen, interview with the author, July 31, 2020.
54. Vince Forlenza, interview with the author, July 31, 2020.
55. Kramer and Mehta, "Becton Dickinson: Global Health Strategy," 8. This paragraph draws heavily from pages 14–15 and 20 of this case study.

56. Gary Cohen, interview with the author, July 31, 2020.

57. Vince Forlenza, interview with the author, July 31, 2020.

58. Robert S. Kaplan and David P. Norton, "Putting the Balanced Scorecard to Work," *Harvard Business Review Magazine*, September–October 1993, https://hbr.org/1993/09/putting-the-balanced-scorecard-to-work; John Doerr, *Measure What Matters* (Portfolio Penguin, 2018).

59. Doerr, *Measure What Matters*.

60. Edouard Dubois and Ali Saribas, "Making Corporate Purpose Tangible—A Survey of Investors," *Harvard Law School Forum on Corporate Governance*, June 19, 2020, https://corpgov.law.harvard.edu/2020/06/19/making-corporate-purpose-tangible-a-survey-of-investors/.

61. "Welcome to the Purpose Power Index," Purpose Power Index, accessed May 29, 2021, https://www.purposepowerindex.com/. Compare this methodology with that used by Just Capital, which queries members of the general public to identify company behaviors related to being a "just company" and then creates metrics and collects results-based data around those behaviors. See the "Full Ranking Methodology," Just Capital, accessed May 30, 2021, https://justcapital.com/full-ranking-methodology/. Other methodologies include the Forbes Just 100 and also the certification process for becoming a B Corporation.

62. "Purpose Strength Model," DPMC, accessed July 15, 2021, https://www.dpmc.us/purpose-strength-model/.

63. Tom A. Elasy and Gary Gaddy, "Measuring Subjective Outcomes," *Journal of General Internal Medicine* 13 (November 1998), doi:10.1046/j.1525-1497.1998.00228.x.

64. Gulati and Tahilyani, "The Mahindra Group," 32.

65. Florian Berg, Julian Koelbel, and Roberto Rigobon, "Aggregate Confusion: The Divergence of ESG Ratings," MIT Sloan School Working Paper 5822–19, August 15, 2019.

66. Robert G. Eccles, "The Purpose of the IBC/WEF Stakeholder Capitalism Metrics Initiative: A Conversation with Brian Moynihan," *Forbes*, December 19, 2020; Billy Nauman and Patrick Temple-West, "BofA Chief Leads New Effort to Tame Unruly ESG Metrics," *Financial Times*, January 14, 2020, https://on.ft.com/3x8EooS.

67. Annual Report, Bühler Group, 2020, 7, https://assetcdn.buhlergroup.com/asset/874601345621/b59a311e2a10445aa4b9ed8d3db002d8. See also "Sustainability: A Stakeholder Perspective," Bühler Group, 2020, https://assetcdn.buhlergroup.com/asset/874601345621/c8931642a0294c438648d091aeed4e05.

68. "Impact Reporting," Etsy, accessed May 29, 2021, https://investors.etsy.com/impact-reporting/default.aspx.

69. Josh Silverman (CEO of Etsy), remarks during an appearance at Harvard Business School, September 16, 2020.

70. One Mighty Mill, "One Mighty Mill Impact Strategy," internal document provided to the author.

71. "Measuring Stakeholder Capitalism: Toward Common Metrics and Consistent Reporting of Sustainable Value Creation," World Economic Forum white paper, September 2020, http://www3.weforum.org/docs/WEF_IBC_Measuring _Stakeholder_Capitalism_Report_2020.pdf; Ernst & Young internal documents.

72. Carmine Di Sibio, (global chairman and CEO for the EY organization), interview with the author, June 16, 2021.

73. Andrew Hill, "The Difficulty in Managing Things That Cannot Easily Be Measured," *Financial Times*, November 25, 2018, https://www.ft.com/content /0e1cc35c-ed88-11e8-89c8-d36339d835c0.

74. "Emmanuel Faber's Ousting Puts Danone on 'Impact Watch,'" Impact Alpha, March 24, 2021, https://impactalpha.com/emmanual-fabers-ousting-puts-danone -on-impact-watch/; Lauren Hirsch, "A Boardroom Shake-up at the Food Giant Danone Sets off Shareholder Infighting," *New York Times*, March 16, 2021, https://www.nytimes.com/2021/03/16/business/Danone-Emmanuel-Faber .html.

75. "Danone Rethinks the Idea of the Firm," *Economist*, August 9, 2018, https:// www.economist.com/business/2018/08/09/danone-rethinks-the-idea-of-the -firm.

76. "Entreprise à Mission," Danone, accessed May 29, 2021, https://www.danone .com/about-danone/sustainable-value-creation/danone-entreprise-a-mission .html; Dean Best, "Danone 'Entreprise à Mission' Status Will Help Drive Shareholder Value, CEO Insists," Just Food, updated July 31, 2020, https://www .just-food.com/news/danone-enterprise-a-mission-status-will-help-drive -shareholder-value-ceo-insists_id144130.aspx.

77. Quoted in Nick Kostov, "Danone's CEO on Going Organic and Why It's Critical to Be Fair," *Wall Street Journal*, December 20, 2016, https://www.wsj.com /articles/danone-ceo-reflects-on-balacing-economic-social-goals-1482247802.

78. At a 2015 investor seminar, he specifically spoke of profitable growth. Emmanuel Faber, "Transcript: Conclusion," Evian, 2015, https://www.danone.com/content /dam/danone-corp/danone-com/investors/en-investor-seminars/2015/day-3-- november-18,-2015/TranscriptEF.pdf; "Danone Rethinks the Idea of the Firm."

79. Quoted in Best, "Danone 'Entreprise à Mission' Status Will Help."

80. Kostov, "Danone's CEO on Going Organic."

81. Corinne Gretler, "Danone Starts Search for New CEO as Faber to Give Up

Role," *Bloomberg*, March 1, 2021, https://www.bloomberg.com/news/articles /2021-03-01/danone-bows-to-investor-pressure-to-split-chairman-ceo-roles.

82. "The Fall from Favour of Danone's Purpose-Driven Chief," *Financial Times*, March 16, 2021, https://www.ft.com/content/2a768b96-69c6-42b7-8617-b3be6 06d6625.

83. "The Fall from Favour."

84. Laurence Fletcher and Leila Abboud, "The Little-Known Activist Fund That Helped Topple Danone's CEO," *Financial Times*, March 23, 2021, https://www .ft.com/content/dd369552-8491-40a2-b83b-9a1b2e32407a.

85. One study found that CEOs of poorly performing firms stand a much greater chance of being fired if they'd previously invested in CSR initiatives. Timothy D. Hubbard, Dane M. Christensen, and Scott D. Graffin, "Higher Highs and Lower Lows: The Role of Corporate Social Responsibility in CEO Dismissal," *Strategic Management Journal* 38 (2017): 2255–65, DOI: 10.1002/smj.2646.

86. Molly Rhodes (vice president of strategy at Warby Parker), interview with the author, March 30, 2021.

87. Peter Gassner (CEO and Cofounder of Veeva), interview with the author, June 26, 2019.

88. Peter Gassner, interview with the author, June 26, 2019.

89. "Veeva: A Public Benefit Corporation," Veeva, accessed May 29, 2021, https:// www.veeva.com/br/pbc/.

90. Peter Gassner, interview with the author, June 26, 2019.

91. Matt Wallach (Cofounder and Board Member of Veeva Systems), interview with the author, April 25, 2019.

92. Emmanuel Faber (former CEO of Danone), interview with the author, December 8, 2020.

93. Gelles, "'I Honestly Don't Trust Many People at Boeing.'"

94. Annual Report, Boeing, 2016, 1, https://s2.q4cdn.com/661678649/files/doc _financials/annual/2016/2016-Annual-Report.pdf.

95. Annual Report, Boeing, 2018, 1, https://s2.q4cdn.com/661678649/files/doc_finan cials/annual/2019/Boeing-2018AR-Final.pdf; Annual Report, Boeing, 2017, https://s2.q4cdn.com/661678649/files/doc_financials/annual/2017/2017-Annual -Report.pdf.

Appendix: A Note on Research Methodology

1. See the introduction and conclusion of O'Toole, *The Enlightened Capitalists*.

2. Some researchers harbor an aversion to field-research-based insights, especially those that selectively sample firms. Fearing that confirmation bias might skew their conclusions, they opt for large-sample analyses of populations of firms. Wherever possible, I use insights from such research in this book, but the pri-

mary insights here derive from careful field research that encompasses twenty-four firms at which I conducted over two hundred interviews. My "theoretical sampling" of exemplary deep purpose firms helps to build up new theory on the underlying mechanisms and processes underway in these contexts. Given the rarity of deep purpose firms, these extreme cases are "unusually revelatory, extreme exemplars" from which we can learn. Kathleen M. Eisenhardt and Melissa E. Graebner, "Theory Building From Cases: Opportunities and Challenges," *Academy of Management Journal* 50, no. 1 (February 2007): 27, https://doi.org/10.5465/amj.2007.24160888. Theoretical sampling, a common qualitative method used to develop new theory, refers to the selection of cases based on a theoretical commonality including a common track record of success. See Deborah Dougherty and Cynthia Hardy, "Sustained Product Innovation in Large, Mature Organizations: Overcoming Innovation-to-Organization Problems," *Academy of Management Journal* 39, no. 5 (October 1996): 1120–53. By allowing for a comparison of the processes underlying the basis of similarity, it is viewed by some as "more important than statistical sampling in an exploratory qualitative study." Kathy E. Kram, "Phases of the Mentor Relationship," *Academy of Management Journal* 26, no. 4 (December 1983): 611.

3. I conducted my research as an inductive analysis to uncover constructs that my respondents identified as critical in becoming a purpose-driven organization. In alignment with the principles of grounded research I began with no a priori theory or hypothesis. Kathy Charmaz, *Constructing Grounded Theory* (London: Sage, 2014); J. Corbin and A. Strauss, *Basics of Qualitative Research* 3rd ed. (Los Angeles: Sage, 2008). Following longstanding traditions in field research, my goal here was "to identify within and across our(my) interviews the patterns, processes, and relationships that appeared connected" to the phenomenon of interest to me. Cheng Gao et al., "Overcoming Institutional Voids: A Reputation-Based View of Long-Run Survival," *Strategic Management Journal* 38, no. 11 (February 2017): 2147–67, DOI:10.1002/smj.2649. I subsequently iterated between my data and existing theory to uncover the key constructs and mechanisms described in this book.

INDEX

ABOUT THE AUTHOR

Ranjay Gulati is the Paul R. Lawrence MBA Class of 1942 Professor at the Harvard Business School. He is the former chair of the Advanced Management Program, the school's flagship senior leader executive program. Ranked as one of the top ten most cited scholars in economics and business, Gulati studies how resilient organizations—those that prosper in both good times and bad—drive growth and profitability. He advises corporations large and small around the globe and has served on the advisory boards of several entrepreneurial ventures. Gulati holds degrees from Harvard, Massachusetts Institute of Technology's Sloan School of Management, Washington State University, and St. Stephen's College, New Delhi. He lives in Newton, Massachusetts.